A Wealth of History

150 Years with Phoenix

1851-2001

A Wealth of History

150 Years with Phoenix

Marian Calabro

GREENWICH PUBLISHING GROUP, INC.
LYME, CONNECTICUT

Produced and published by
Greenwich Publishing Group, Inc.
Lyme, Connecticut

Design by Clare Cunningham Graphic Design

Library of Congress Card Number: 00-112093

ISBN: 0-944641-46-6

Internal reference number: C01

First Printing: March 2001

Photography Credits:

p. 2:	courtesy, Josephine Melusky
p. 13, top:	courtesy, Robert Chipkin
p. 28, right:	courtesy, Edward A. Richardson
p. 29, left:	courtesy, Frederick W. Sawyer
p. 31, top:	photo by Brown Brothers
p. 36, top:	courtesy, Robert Chipkin
p. 37:	courtesy, Josephine Melusky
p. 41:	estate of Herb Pennock under license authorized by CMG Worldwide, Inc., www.cmg.com
p. 45:	courtesy, Josephine Melusky
p. 49:	courtesy, William Hampton
p. 54:	courtesy, Margaret Murphy
p. 59:	© Thomas Photography
p. 63:	Photograph by Arthur J. Wormsley/*The Hartford Courant*
p. 73:	© Frank White, Inc.
p. 87:	© Pablo Bartholomew / Liaison International
p. 91:	© James Marshall/Corbis
p. 104, right:	courtesy, Dona D. Young
p. 121:	courtesy, Josephine Melusky
p. 128-129:	© Fred Gaylor
p. 130:	© Doug Fishman
p. 131:	illustration by Jay Dollard
p. 133:	© Brennan Beer Gorman / Architects; illustration by James Akers

All other images courtesy of The Phoenix Companies, Inc.

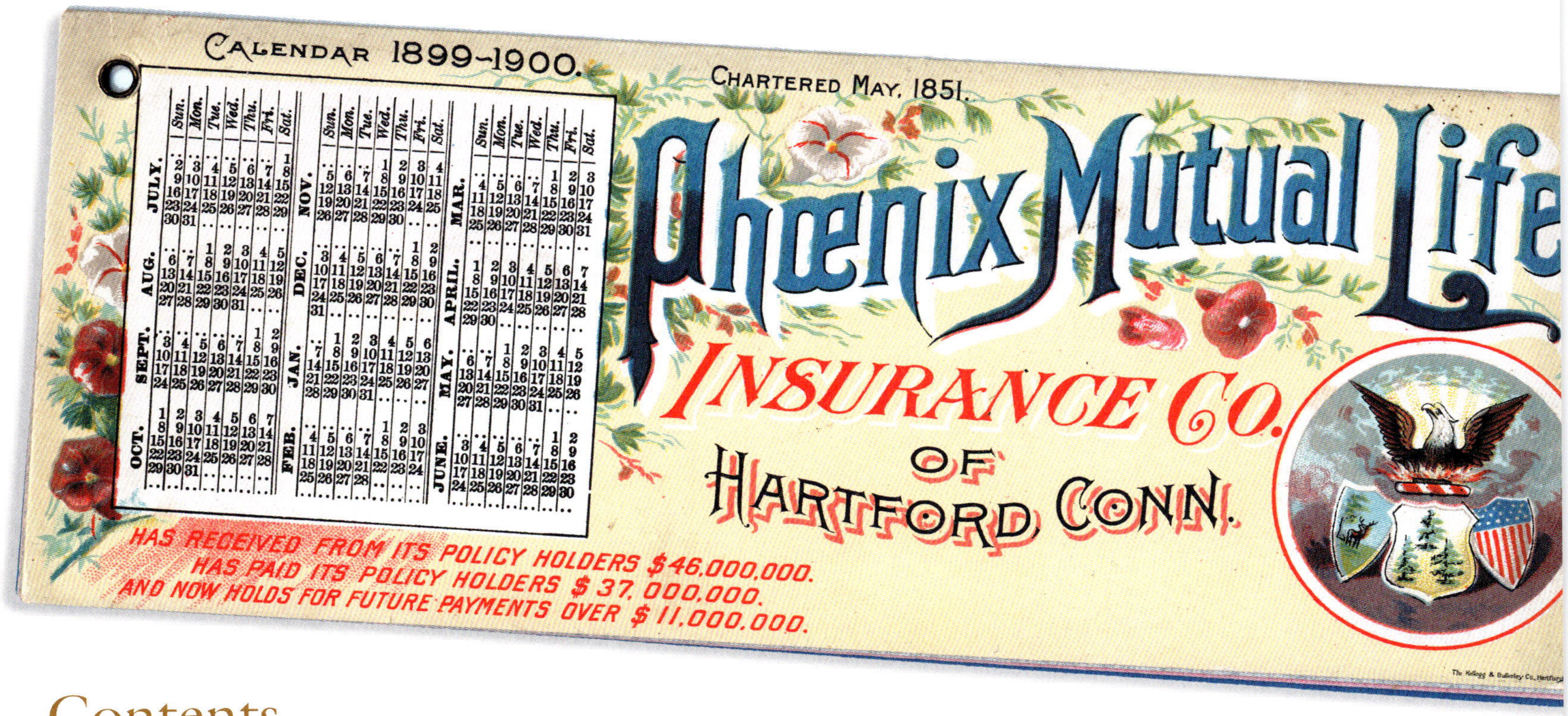
Calendar 1899-1900.
Chartered May, 1851.
Phœnix Mutual Life
Insurance Co.
of
Hartford, Conn.
Has received from its policy holders $46,000,000.
Has paid its policy holders $37,000,000.
And now holds for future payments over $11,000,000.

Contents

Prologue

The story of Phoenix is rich in industry firsts and meaningful events, as you will discover in this book. Propitiously, our 150th anniversary comes at the most exciting time in our lineage.

We are tightly focused as a premier wealth management enterprise and we have just completed our demutualization. The timing couldn't be better. It brings us back to our roots.

The founders of Phoenix and Home Life, including Francis Gillette and W. S. Griffith, were driven by noble purposes as well as a keen business sense. Both companies were built on policyholder value and shareholder value. Both were stock or part-stock companies that eventually changed structure in response to changing business conditions.

They did so for one reason, and it's one of the same reasons we decided to pursue demutualization: in order to continue to best deliver value to our policyholders.

Our 11th president, Bob Jackson, liked to quote his father, Henry H. Jackson, who was also at one time the chief actuary of National Life of Vermont. "A life insurance company can be run for the benefit of its managers, its agents or its policyholders," Jackson would say. "We're here for the policyholders."

I believe that commitment has never changed and will never change, even as new shareholders join policyholders in the ownership of Phoenix. To remain as a mutual might have been more comfortable for managers and producers, but it would not have been to the ultimate benefit of policyholders.

I read the events of our past as a story of adaptation. No company can survive for 150 years without being willing to adapt, innovate and partner with others. What has helped us reach this landmark anniversary is an inclusive and open culture. As you'll see in these pages, there is no "Phoenix type." The diversity of our people, and our mix of longtime employees and new blood, keeps us young.

The story that follows is a glimpse of 150 years in the lives of two companies that became one. It's a time capsule. To paint the entire picture, to share all the extraordinary tales, would have required a thousand pages. Everyone who reads *A Wealth of History* could have written it differently. But I believe it will give you a true feeling for who we are and where we are headed.

Robert W. Fiondella

Robert W. Fiondella
Chairman and CEO

FIRST ANNUAL FIELD DAY • PHOENIX MUTUAL LIFE INS. CO.
LAKE COMPOUNCE JUNE 30TH 1915

CHAPTER ONE

1851-1889

Foundations Deep and Strong

The directors of this company are determined to lay its foundation deep and strong, that, with the blessing of Heaven it may stand for ages as the shield and protection of the Widow and the Orphan.

— From an early annual report of Home Life Insurance Company

BARTLETT
C.M.HOOKER
DENTIST
PHOTO
MUTUAL
LIFE

In a sense, this is the history of three companies: Phoenix Mutual, Home Life and the entity created by their historic merger in 1992. Published on Phoenix's sesquicentennial anniversary, this book actually commemorates and celebrates 300 overlapping years of history: the 150 years since the founding of Phoenix, the 141 years since the founding of Home Life and the nine years since their merger, which in many ways have been as eventful as the century-plus preceding.

The story begins with Phoenix's predecessor, the American Temperance Life Insurance Company, founded in 1851 in Hartford, Connecticut. Although Hartford was already America's insurance city, the new American Temperance had only one in-town rival in life insurance, the five-year-old firm of Connecticut Mutual. The rest of the city's numerous insurers, including The Hartford and Aetna, were then chartered to sell solely marine and fire policies. The United States — all 31 of them — had scores of fire insurance companies but barely a dozen life insurers.

Technically, however, American Temperance had no competitors. It was the first and only American insurer built on the principle of temperance, an anti-alcohol movement almost equal in public fervor to the cause of abolishing slavery. Until American Temperance transformed itself into Phoenix Mutual, 10 years after its founding, only nondrinkers could become policyholders.

When Home Life Insurance Company was founded in 1860 in Brooklyn, New York, the life insurance industry had expanded fivefold to 62 companies. Yet Home Life was one of the first life insurers in the state of New York. Indeed, that state's insurance department was just a few months old itself when it issued Home Life's charter.

POLICYHOLDERS FIRST

Phoenix and Home Life would develop along similar but far from identical lines until their pioneering alliance in 1992, the first merger of two major mutual insurers. Phoenix tended to be a reserved company, modest about its achievements and innovations — quintessentially New England, one might say — while Home Life was more outwardly confident, more "New York." But they were alike where the essentials were concerned. As Home Life's first president, Walter S. Griffith, summarized: "This company is to be conducted solely with reference to the interests of its policyholders."

In human terms, Phoenix had something of a premature birth and shaky childhood. Its founders were as devoted to temperance and to their own principal businesses as to their new venture. The creation of Home Life was more like a full-term birth to wealthy and well-prepared parents. It was healthy and kicking from day one.

America itself, in that era, could be compared to an adolescent. The country was full of energy and ambition, troubled with growing pains and inventing itself as it went along. Despite the discovery of gold in California in 1849, the West was mostly unsettled. The East was the center of banking, education and international trade, although farming was the main occupation. The states were united by a federal government but little else — and would soon be further divided, North against South, by the Civil War. The railroads and telegraph system that eventually would link the sprawling nation were still new and local. Most people rarely traveled beyond their hometown, much less their state borders.

PHOENIX'S FORERUNNER

Hartford was already an economic power when American Temperance received its charter to operate in May 1851. River trade had thrived since the 1700s, and the city bustled with the manufacture and export of shoes, hats, buttons, paper, bricks and fabric. The newspaper founded as the *Connecticut Courant* — now the *Hartford Courant,* America's oldest continuously published newspaper — had been publishing for 87 years already. Samuel Colt's firearms factory, founded in 1847, was a notable employer, as were banks and fire insurers. For culture, people visited the Wadsworth Atheneum — now recognized as America's oldest public museum — to view exhibits and hear the lecturers and singers of the day.

Many of the city's leading citizens were crusaders for temperance. They often gathered for informal meetings held either at B&W Hudson, a dry goods and furniture store at 360 Main Street, or at the offices of the *Fountain,* a temperance newspaper. (Ironically, the latter was said to be located above a saloon.) Together, the crusaders hatched the idea of a company that would "insure none but temperance men." It made good sense. A similar life insurer in England, where temperance was also popular, had discovered that policyholders who abstained from alcohol were excellent risks. Crude studies of mortality in America concurred, indicating that nondrinkers lived about 10 years longer than those who imbibed.

American Temperance Life Insurance

Company promised to be a triple win. The company would profit its stockholders (including the founders), advance the "holy cause" of temperance and reward policyholders for their abstinence with rates 25 percent lower than those offered by any other U.S. life insurer.

Hartford had been known as the "Insurance City" since the early 1800s. This etching, depicting Main Street in 1860, appeared on the policies of the American Temperance Life Insurance Company, Phoenix's forerunner. The photo on page 9 shows Main Street in Hartford, including Phoenix's first home office at the corner of Pearl Street (center).

STOCK SELLS OUT IN 48 HOURS

The company's seven incorporators were a distinguished lot. Barzillai Hudson, proprietor of B&W Hudson and a well-known temperance leader; Benjamin E. Hale, clergyman and editor of the *Fountain*; Edson Fessenden, hotel proprietor and a co-founder of Connecticut Mutual; joined with local businessmen James B. Hosmer, Thomas S. Williams and Francis Parsons. Most famous, from a wider perspective, was incorporator Francis Gillette. Brother-in-law of Harriet Beecher Stowe, whose classic 1852 novel *Uncle Tom's Cabin* aroused national sentiment against slavery, Gillette was a famed abolitionist and temperance man himself.

This leadership mix clearly met with investor approval. Dozens of stockholders committed $50 per share, causing the initial offering of 2,000 shares to sell out in two days.

After collecting 10 percent of the $100,000 starter capital in cash, American Temperance opened for business on July 24, 1851. The founders leased the second floor of "C. W. Johnson's fine brick building" at the southwest corner of Main and Pearl Streets, diagonally opposite the State House and a short walk from Hudson's store. The small office housed few

"Do you take the pledge?"

In the 1800s, with alcoholism sharply on the rise in the United States, untold numbers of Americans took the pledge not to drink. Churches used their widespread power to address the growing problem of "intemperance," as drinking was called; ministers preached that any use of alcohol was evil because it violated God's will. Thus America's temperance movement was born.

With missionary zeal, the American Temperance Society and local organizations spread the cause nationwide. They enlisted the support of prominent ministers, teachers and financiers. By 1851, even the living ex-presidents of the United States had taken the pledge. Only the issue of slavery aroused more public emotion.

Temperance had a devoted following in New England, where most states enacted laws prohibiting the sale and consumption of liquor. Hartford figured prominently in the movement because the *Fountain*, a major temperance newspaper, was published there. It was in the offices of the *Fountain* that Barzillai Hudson and Benjamin Hale, active temperance leaders, raised the idea of creating the American Temperance Life Insurance Company, which would become Phoenix Mutual.

Within 10 years, the original company realized it would have to insure nonabstainers in order to stay in business. However, the temperance movement remained powerful. It flourished on every continent, as did the use of alcohol. In the United States, temperance won its last victory in 1919, when passage of the Eighteenth Amendment to the U.S. Constitution made it a crime to sell liquor or drink in public. Americans openly flouted Prohibition, as it was called, and in 1933, Congress finally enacted the Twenty-first Amendment, repealing Prohibition.

According to the leaders of the temperance movement, abstinence from alcohol was "the great promoter of health, wealth and morality." Cartoons such as "The Drunkard's Progress" depicted the supposed tragedy of an intemperate lifestyle.

employees at first; it was basically a meeting place for the incorporators and officers. The first president was Hudson himself, whose annual salary was the modest sum of $500. The vice president, Hartford financier Tertius Wadsworth, earned $1,200. The discrepancy suggests that Hudson expected to spend little time on the new venture. Basically a token president, chosen for his name value, he stepped down in October 1852.

In addition to its temperance affiliation, the new company was unusual in that it was part mutual, part stock. Most insurers were one or the other. But the founders believed their structure combined the advantages of both: cash dividends for policyholders, cash interest on invested capital for stockholders. Nonetheless, their priorities were clear. Business would be conducted "for the benefit of the holders of life policies and not for stockholders." Also, American Temperance would take cash premiums only. Many other life insurance companies operated on the so-called "half-note" system, which accepted policyholder IOUs as partial payment for premiums.

American Temperance enjoyed a built-in distribution system from the start: "The directors, in employing general agents for the states, will endeavor to secure the services of the best and ablest temperance lecturers." One such general agent was co-founder Hale. Called in from the field to succeed President Hudson in 1852, he lasted just five months at the home office. Hale returned to his beloved Western territory to sell, and Fessenden took the helm in Hartford in the spring of 1853.

RISE AND FALL OF TEMPERANCE

Thanks to its temperance affiliation, American Temperance in a way was selling group insurance. It examined and insured members of temperance lodges *en masse*, rather than assessing individual risk. This approach worked reasonably well early on; in its first two years, the company sold 900 small policies and paid only three death claims. (One was that of the very first policyholder, John A. Hale.)

By 1858, it had only 1,067 policyholders but nearly $1.6 million of insurance in force. The average face value of a policy was a respectable $1,500, equivalent only to about $25,000 today but approximately three times the average yearly income back then. This implies that the company's customers, while probably not rich, were solid citizens. Clearly they believed in this new product called life insurance and in the young company offering it. Mortality experience remained better than average, a strong argument in favor of temperance.

But American Temperance's finances were shaky, as they were for other small insurers. The company held only $97,000 in assets and had an expense ratio of almost 21 percent, meaning that as much as 21 cents out of every premium dollar went toward operating expenses. (By contrast, the much larger Connecticut Mutual had an expense ratio of about 5 percent.) Worse, the company's reserves barely topped $3,500. Massachusetts had enacted a landmark law requiring insurers to set aside certain levels of reserves in proportion to premiums; American Temperance would need to make some changes if it hoped to be ready for the passage of similar legislation in Connecticut.

At the same time, temperance was proving to be a limiting factor rather than a growth factor for business. Competitors invaded the niche, happy to sell to the temperate and nontemperate alike. And the movement, while far from dead, was overshadowed by the bigger social issues of slavery and the impending war. Northern life insurance companies were finding it more difficult to do business in the South, previously a productive area for American Temperance.

By 1861, the directors of American Temperance accepted the reality of these trends. On June 21, two months after the Civil War began, they amended the charter to permit sales to the nontemperate. Most

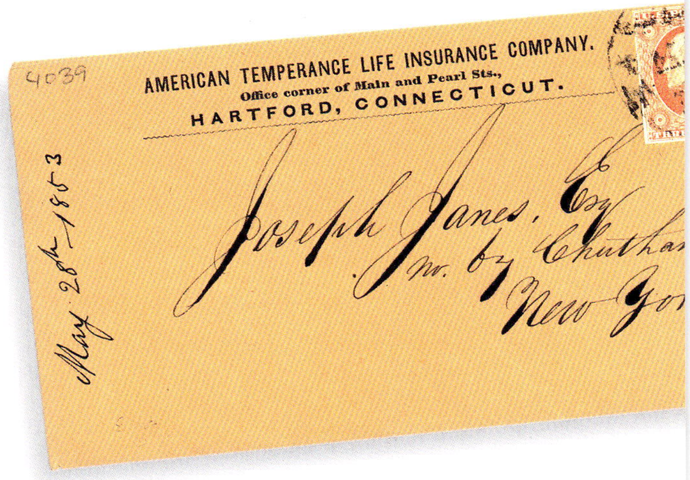

Secretary J. Augustus Wright wrote to shareholder Joseph James communicating the company's plan to expand its operations into New York. Phoenix rented space on Pearl Street, below. In 1897, the company erected a stately, six-story home office on the vacant lot across the street.

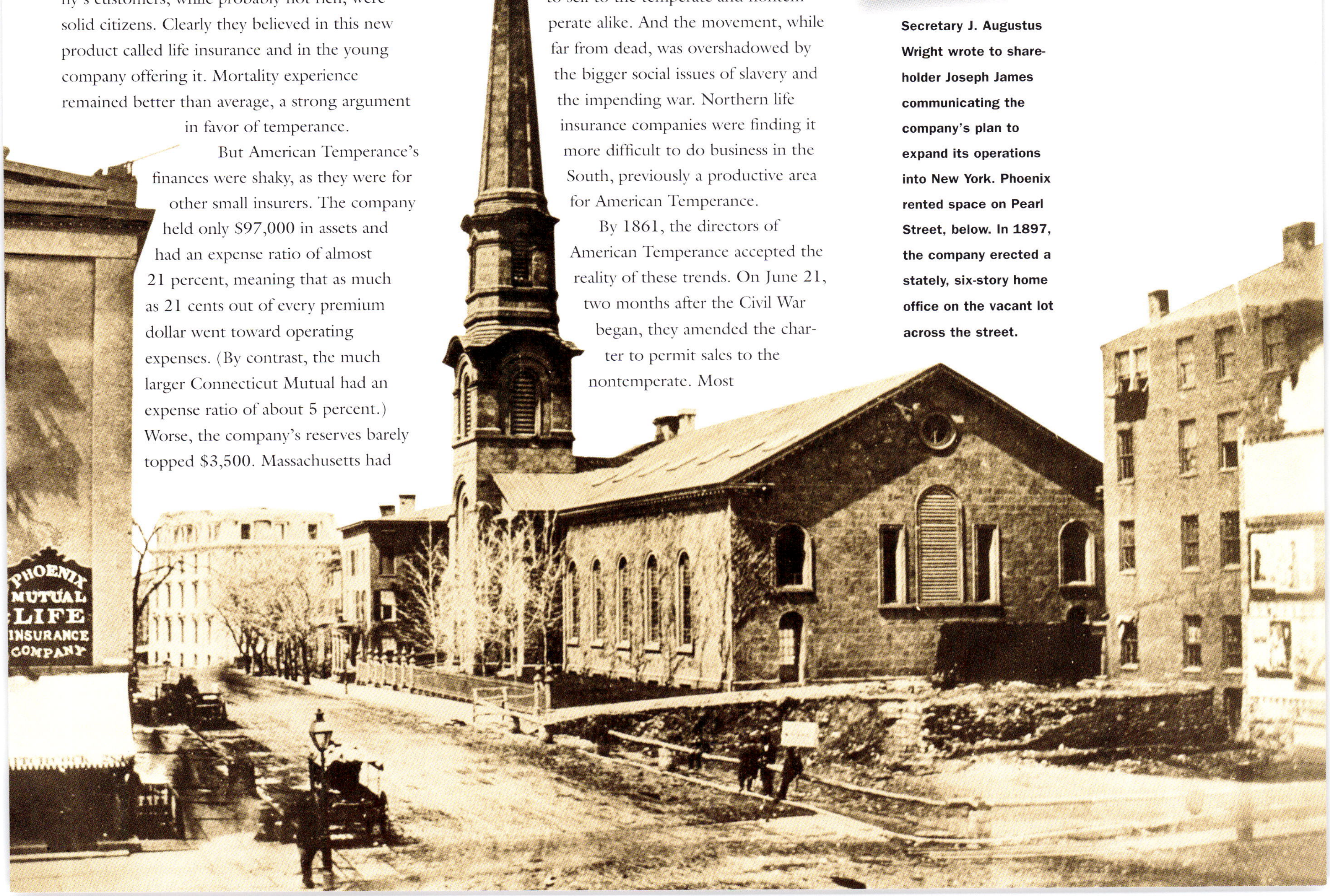

Francis Gillette

One of Phoenix's original seven founders, Francis Gillette worked tirelessly for temperance and against slavery. "He gave up his Bloomfield [Connecticut] estate to establish one on Forest Street in Hartford where he could be in more constant touch with those who were promoting great causes," says the unpublished company history. When a U.S. senator from Connecticut died unexpectedly in 1854, Gillette was chosen to take his place. In his later years, he was also known as the father of William Gillette, a playwright and actor famed for his portrayals of Sherlock Holmes on stage and in early silent film. Artifacts from the Gillette family are on view at William's former estate, now Gillette Castle State Park, in East Haddam, Connecticut.

notably for history, they changed the company's name to Phoenix Mutual Life Insurance Company. (The reasons for the selection are lost to history.)

Competing in an open market for the first time, the company also adopted the half-note system. As future Phoenix president John M. Holcombe later explained:

"The rates of...the half-note plan...were much higher than those heretofore in use, but one-half of each of the first four premiums was to be paid by note [i.e., IOU], the calculation being that the dividend on the fifth and subsequent years would at least equal this proportion of the stipulated premium and that at maturity four unpaid dividends would cancel the outstanding notes, leaving the full amount of the policy to be paid in cash."

At first, the notorious half-note system seemed miraculous. "During the next decade business increased so rapidly," recalled Holcombe, "[that Phoenix] was among the very first in the country in amount of business secured."

FOUNDING OF HOME LIFE

Born under the twin shadows of a receding financial panic and an approaching war, Home Life Insurance Company took form on January 30, 1860. On that bitterly cold day, a dozen prominent citizens gathered at an office of the Nassau Bank in Brooklyn, which was then an independent city, third in size only to neighboring New York City and to Philadelphia. They easily raised capital totaling $125,000, sold in $100 shares, which they invested in government securities. Home Life was an all-stock company, although that would eventually change.

The incorporators were 34 prosperous and entrepreneurial men like Abiel A. Low, an importer who owned a fleet of clipper ships that traded with China, and Walter S. Griffith, a retired wholesale grocer who was on the boards of major banks and fire insurance companies. Griffith became the company's first president, at a salary of $2,500 per year.

Authorized by the state as a business on April 28, Home Life opened its doors on May 1, 1860. It paid $100 per month to rent a three-room office on Court and Joralemon Streets in downtown Brooklyn. The landlord, not coincidentally, was Abiel Low. And although no bridge yet spanned the East River to New York City (the Brooklyn Bridge was built in 1883), the company set up a two-room branch at 16 Wall Street. Even then, an office in the heart of America's financial district was a distinct plus.

It was not an ideal time to launch a business. The threat of war stirred fear in the populace and gyrations in financial markets, which the election of the untested Abraham Lincoln as president did little to quell. It was a particularly precarious time in the life insurance business. Medical knowledge was still slight and life expectancy low, about 40 years. For most families, even a small premium was a sacrifice: only one man in a hundred earned $850 or more per year, of which 75 percent went to food and shelter and the rest to church, clothes and other necessities.

Despite these realities, Home Life prospered, both by expanding ambitiously and by targeting a more affluent clientele. In its first quarter, it set up 12 agencies in the East. President Griffith himself traveled to St. Louis, Chicago and other "Western towns" to help launch additional agencies. In its first year, the company wrote a remarkable $1 million of business. When the country went to war in 1861, the young company was solvent enough to announce: "If any clerk should join the Army, his situation shall be retained for him, and his salary continued during his absence." Many recruits did not return; the Civil War lasted four years and claimed 600,000 lives in battle.

Whether Phoenix Mutual held the jobs of its

First Policyholders

The American Temperance Life Insurance Company (later Phoenix) sold its first policy on September 11, 1851, to John A. Hale of Glastonbury, Connecticut. Hale was 30, married, a father and a clerk at the Hartford Post Office. For an annual premium of $9.20 — plus a $1.00 commission to agent J. Augustus Wright — he insured his life for $500. This modest face value probably represented a year's salary for Hale.

The fledgling company issued seven other policies on the same day as John Hale's. Some were larger than Hale's, because they totaled $8,000 in face value — a more than respectable beginning.

Obviously convinced of the value of life insurance, Phoenix's first policyholder became an agent himself. Hale joined Aetna when that company expanded into life insurance in 1853. (Why he chose not to sell for American Temperance is unknown.) Hale died of typhus fever just a year later. American Temperance promptly paid the claim, and future generations continued to put their trust in Phoenix. Almost 100 years later, policy number 965,134 was issued to Hale's great-great grandson, Newell D. Hale of Northbridge, Massachusetts.

Home Life had a more favorable mortality experience with its first policyholder. Lewis Roberts, a businessman from Brooklyn, was so eager to insure his life that he applied to Home Life two weeks before it officially opened its doors on May 1, 1860. His $10,000 policy was quite a large one for the time; Roberts paid a staggering annual premium of $260, about half of the average man's entire yearly earnings then. Well-off and clearly a staunch believer in the importance of planning for the future, Roberts symbolized what would become the typical Home Life customer.

Records show that Home Life's medical examiner performed a "thorough examination on the heart and chest" of the 34-year-old Roberts, who lived to age 79.

Early policies contained strict limitations that companies would begin removing in the 1860s. Until then, however, policyholders such as John Hale had to obtain written permission from their insurer if they planned to:

- Travel upon the seas
- Visit California or Oregon
- Visit the South between June 1 and November 1 (due to the greater risk of disease in hot climates)
- Enter into military or naval service
- Become a train engineer, fireman or gunpowder manufacturer

Violation carried a high price. If policyholders disobeyed these provisions, or failed to pay premiums, they forfeited the policy and any value it had accumulated.

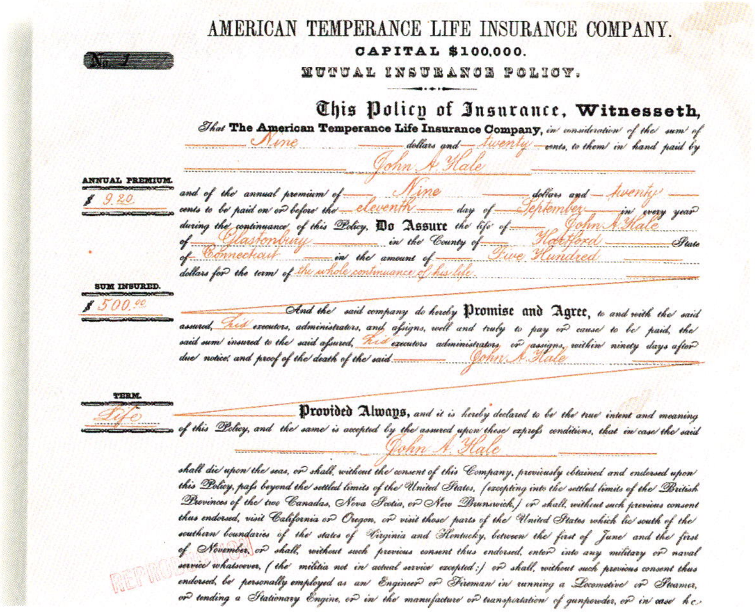
AMERICAN TEMPERANCE LIFE INSURANCE COMPANY.
CAPITAL $100,000.
MUTUAL INSURANCE POLICY.

No. 1

This Policy of Insurance, Witnesseth,
That The American Temperance Life Insurance Company, in consideration of the sum of Nine dollars and twenty cents, to them in hand paid by John A. Hale

ANNUAL PREMIUM. $ 9.20

and of the annual premium of Nine dollars and twenty cents to be paid on or before the eleventh day of September in every year during the continuance of this Policy, Do Assure the life of John A. Hale of Glastonbury in the County of Hartford State of Connecticut in the amount of Five Hundred dollars for the term of the whole continuance of his life.

SUM INSURED. $ 500.00

And the said company do hereby Promise and Agree, to and with the said assured, his executors, administrators, and assigns, well and truly to pay or cause to be paid, the said sum insured to the said assured, his executors administrators or assigns, within ninety days after due notice and proof of the death of the said John A. Hale

TERM. Life

Provided Always, and it is hereby declared to be the true intent and meaning of this Policy, and the same is accepted by the assured upon these express conditions, that in case the said John A. Hale shall die upon the seas, or shall, without the consent of this Company, previously obtained and endorsed upon this Policy, pass beyond the settled limits of the United States, (excepting into the settled limits of the British Provinces of the two Canadas, Nova Scotia, or New Brunswick,) or shall, without such previous consent thus endorsed, visit California or Oregon, or visit those parts of the United States which lie south of the southern boundaries of the states of Virginia and Kentucky, between the first of June and the first of November, or shall, without such previous consent thus endorsed, enter into any military or naval service whatsoever, (the militia not in actual service excepted;) or shall, without such previous consent thus endorsed, be personally employed as an Engineer or Fireman in running a Locomotive or Steamer, or tending a Stationary Engine, or in the manufacture or transportation of gunpowder, or in case he

REPRODUCTION

The first policy issued by American Temperance insured the life of John Hale but warned that coverage would be forfeited if the policyholder died in a duel.

recruits is not known, but the company has its own claim to fame regarding the Civil War era. On January 9, 1865, as the war approached its climax, the board voted that the premiums on policies issued to President Abraham Lincoln, former vice president Hannibal Hamlin and Speaker of the House Schuyler Colfax "be tendered to them as a gratuity." Within three months, the war would be over, and a week later, Lincoln would be assassinated. Two days after his death, with the country shocked and in mourning, Phoenix's directors made an appropriately thoughtful gesture. They issued a policy, "free for one year," to the new president, Andrew Johnson.

In spite of poor business conditions during the long war and its tragic aftermath, Home Life generated the respectable sum of $10,213,000 of life insurance in force in its first five years. In 1866, it became the first insurance company to remove all travel restrictions and made this change retroactive on all policies — one of many industry firsts for Home Life. (At that time, life insurers sharply restricted coverage for travel both within and beyond U.S. borders or charged extra premiums to travelers.) By 1868, Home Life had outgrown Brooklyn and was in a position to buy its first home — a four-story walk-up building on Broadway, opposite New York City Hall — for $140,000. Home Life's famous skyscraper headquarters would later rise around this core.

RECKLESS 1860s

The Civil War marked the start of an expansion in life insurance so rapid and dramatic it nearly destroyed the industry. Many existing companies couldn't keep up with their own growth, while dozens of new companies sprang up with unrealistic expectations of instant riches. Reserve levels were becoming state mandated, but enforcement was spotty and some companies openly flouted the laws. Competition was fierce and often dirty.

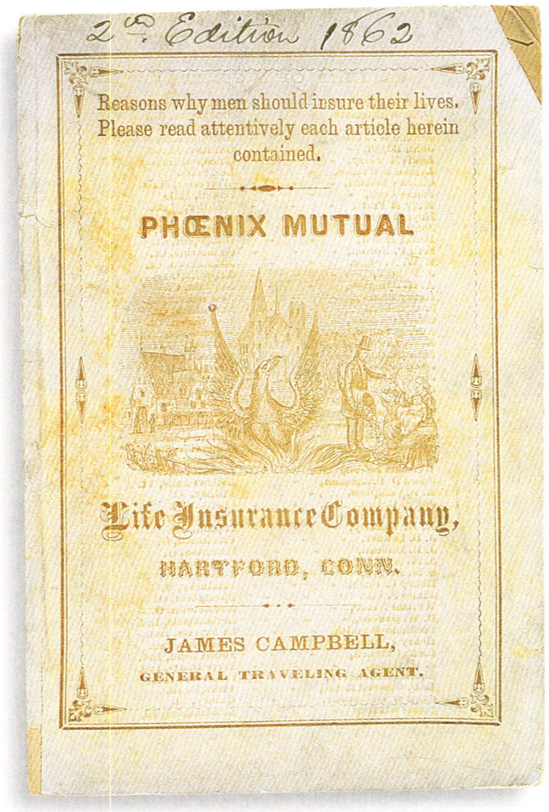

This 1862 rate book, one of the first to feature the Phoenix name, was distributed by James Campbell, a New England agent whose story is told by his grandson on the opposite page. Campbell was one of 54 Phoenix agents, from Maine to Illinois, listed inside. The book also mentions the half-note plan, stating that "the applicant can, if preferred, give his note for one-half the premium, when it amounts to thirty dollars or more."

The public was easy prey because of the frenzy that arose at the war's end. The 1860s might be compared to the 1980s: people were speculating wildly on real estate and stocks, as well as all sorts of get-rich-quick schemes — including life insurance policies on the half-note plan.

Sales at Phoenix had risen from a paltry 426 policies annually, in 1861, to a remarkable 9,000 policies and $20 million in force nine years later. The company was also moving into mortgage lending, first in cities and then in the vast farm country of the Midwest. Phoenix's Central Farm Loan Office, eventually located in Davenport, Iowa, would prove quite important to the company's financial success. It lasted for almost 100 years, financing mortgages for generations of farmers, until its closure in the mid-1980s.

To accommodate this growth, the company expanded its headquarters in 1871 from the second floor to all three floors of offices at the building on the corner of Main and Pearl Streets in Hartford. Records show that the home office had six employees in 1866; though not documented, it is probable that the staff had tripled since that time, although the company would have needed the extra space just to store the additional paperwork.

By the end of the 1860s, Aetna and Connecticut Mutual had abandoned the half-note plan, citing "dangers which were rapidly approaching." Phoenix officers also suspected a worm lurking in the apple: they adopted two rate books, one for half-note policies and one for all-cash premiums. In practice, the half-note system was king.

Home Life was slightly bigger than Phoenix in 1870, with 11,009 policies and about $23 million in force, but notably stronger. The company resisted the half-note temptation, was far stricter than competitors in its underwriting and more rigorous in its annual accounting. At the end of the company's first decade, President Griffith looked back:

Early Sales Methods

Howard Goodwin, a Phoenix vice president, worked in claims and underwriting from 1907 to the 1950s. He had the unique experience of settling death claims on policies sold by his grandfather up to 100 years earlier. As recalled by Goodwin in 1957:

"My grandfather, James Campbell of Manchester, Connecticut, was a Director of the Company and also carried the imposing title of 'General Agent for New England.' He wrote a considerable business for the American Temperance Life [later Phoenix] in the 1850s.... To cover his extensive field, my grandfather would hitch up his horse and buggy and travel for two weeks and longer. He would stop at various towns along the way and, as part of his sales technique, would offer to tend the baby of prospective policyholders who might go out 'of an evening,' or he would help with pitching the hay or washing the dishes. Once in a while, he would take over a church service and preach the sermon for a minister who had to be away. Then, when the parson returned, General Agent Campbell would get his signature on the dotted line."

One of Home Life's first agents was R. A. W. Bruehl, a Methodist minister who joined the company's Cincinnati office in 1861, just as the Civil War began. Bruehl's vast territory spanned Ohio, Indiana, Kentucky, Illinois, Iowa, Wisconsin and Michigan. "He was gone for months at a time on a field sales trip," an early company history says:

"He traveled by slow, uncomfortable train, stage-coach, horse and buggy, saddle — and on foot. On many trips he reported covering 20 miles a day through wilderness and forest.... On one occasion he had to ask 10 men to gather in one village from all directions, traveling many miles themselves, to meet the medical examiner — and then the examiner and himself set out to find the additional 11 applicants who had not come to the central location — keeping at the strenuous job until midnight, when the 21st had been duly examined and the papers were prepared to start on their long journey east."

Four generations of Bruehls went on to sell for Home Life in Cincinnati.

The life insurance industry grew quickly in the 1860s, creating fierce competition, and Phoenix sales aids were designed to catch the eye of potential policyholders.

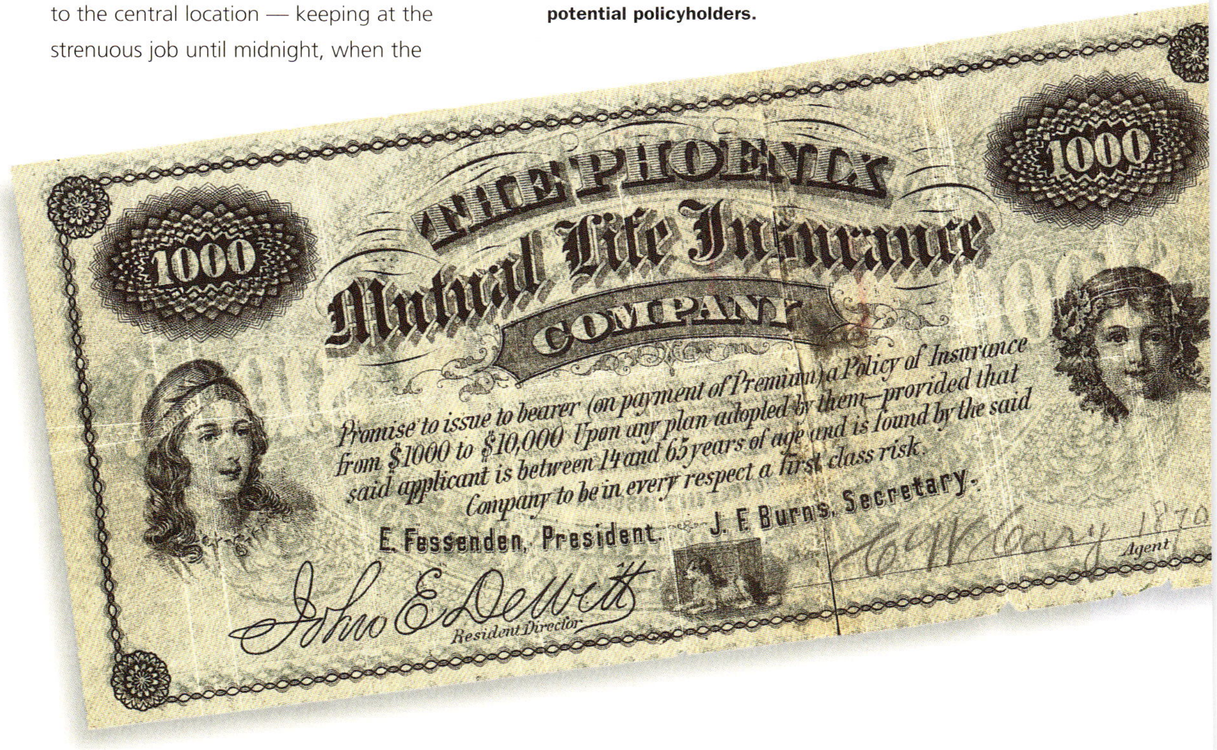

"[Our results show] no 'mushroom' growth but a steady, sound accretion which, year by year, adds to our membership and strength as rapidly as with the present wild and unscrupulous competition, we have found it practicable to do.... This is the Era of 'reckless speculation' in Life Insurance — a business which ought to be far above such a baleful influence. But here as in Europe 'Wild Cat' enterprises in life insurance are to have their day. Meanwhile, sound companies have no choice but to pursue their business with all the industry, energy and prudence they can command."

This was also the philosophy of George C. Ripley, Home Life's secretary since inception, who succeeded Griffith as president in 1872.

PANIC OF 1873

As bad as the 1860s were, the 1870s eclipsed them. The decade opened with major cities reduced to rubble by huge fires: Chicago in 1871; Boston in 1872. (Wooden buildings were the norm, and large-scale fire protection was impossible.) Inflation was rampant. Extensive mining worldwide had sharply boosted silver supplies and severely devalued money, which was pegged to the silver standard. When business barons such as Jay Gould attempted to control gold supplies, financial markets went haywire. Finally, after a major panic in 1873, the U.S. government established the gold standard in an attempt to restore financial order.

Between 1868 and 1877, some 104 life insurance companies went under. Few of them paid their obligations. Where were the regulators and state commissioners of insurance? Barely cutting their teeth. The Phoenix archives contain an incredible letter from John R. Hegeman, an early president of Metropolitan Life, who recounted the day that Orlow Chapman, New York State superintendent of insurance from 1872 to 1876, walked into his office and said: "They have made me Superintendent of Insurance of this state. I know about as much of insurance as a little neck clam. Sit down if you please, Mr. Hegeman, and tell me all you know about it in 15 minutes."

The industry suffered in the public eye, but not Home Life. In fact, its strength made it a target for an unwanted takeover in 1874. Facing an outside effort to buy up the majority of stock, the board took a novel step to persuade shareholders not to sell. It paid them their dividend that year in solid gold.

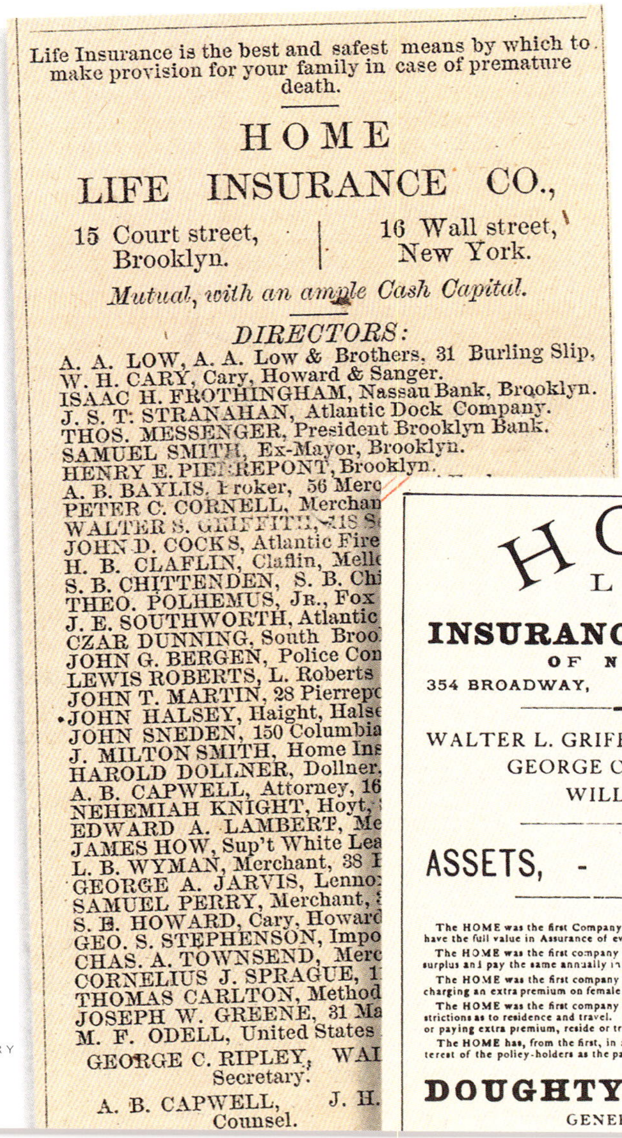

Life Insurance is the best and safest means by which to make provision for your family in case of premature death.

HOME
LIFE INSURANCE CO.,

15 Court street, Brooklyn. | 16 Wall street, New York.

Mutual, with an ample Cash Capital.

DIRECTORS:

A. A. LOW, A. A. Low & Brothers, 31 Burling Slip,
W. H. CARY, Cary, Howard & Sanger.
ISAAC H. FROTHINGHAM, Nassau Bank, Brooklyn.
J. S. T. STRANAHAN, Atlantic Dock Company.
THOS. MESSENGER, President Brooklyn Bank.
SAMUEL SMITH, Ex-Mayor, Brooklyn.
HENRY E. PIERREPONT, Brooklyn.
A. B. BAYLIS, Broker, 56 Merc
PETER C. CORNELL, Merchan
WALTER S. GRIFFITH, 218 S
JOHN D. COCKS, Atlantic Fire
H. B. CLAFLIN, Claflin, Mell
S. B. CHITTENDEN, S. B. Chi
THEO. POLHEMUS, JR., Fox
J. E. SOUTHWORTH, Atlantic
CZAR DUNNING, South Broo
JOHN G. BERGEN, Police Con
LEWIS ROBERTS, L. Roberts
JOHN T. MARTIN, 28 Pierrepo
JOHN HALSEY, Haight, Halse
JOHN SNEDEN, 150 Columbia
J. MILTON SMITH, Home Ins
HAROLD DOLLNER, Dollner,
A. B. CAPWELL, Attorney, 16
NEHEMIAH KNIGHT, Hoyt,
EDWARD A. LAMBERT, Me
JAMES HOW, Sup't White Lea
L. B. WYMAN, Merchant, 38 I
GEORGE A. JARVIS, Lenno
SAMUEL PERRY, Merchant,
S. B. HOWARD, Cary, Howard
GEO. S. STEPHENSON, Impo
CHAS. A. TOWNSEND, Merc
CORNELIUS J. SPRAGUE, 1
THOMAS CARLTON, Method
JOSEPH W. GREENE, 31 Ma
M. F. ODELL, United States

GEORGE C. RIPLEY, Secretary. WAI

A. B. CAPWELL, Counsel. J. H.

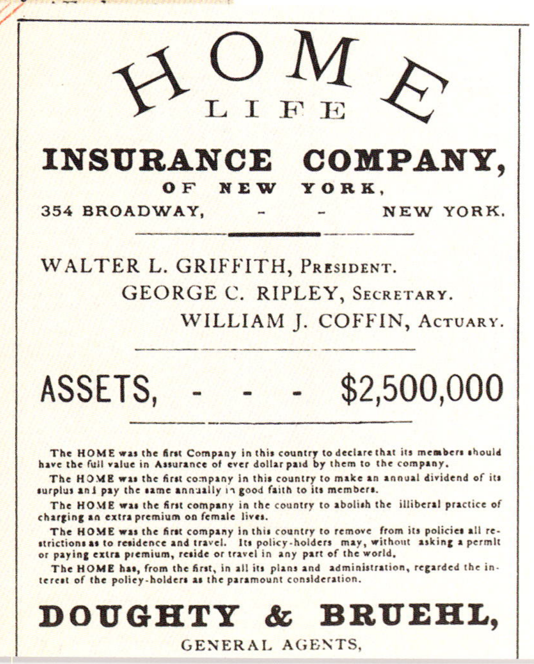

HOME
LIFE
INSURANCE COMPANY,
OF NEW YORK,
354 BROADWAY, - - NEW YORK.

WALTER L. GRIFFITH, PRESIDENT.
GEORGE C. RIPLEY, SECRETARY.
WILLIAM J. COFFIN, ACTUARY.

ASSETS, - - - $2,500,000

The HOME was the first Company in this country to declare that its members should have the full value in Assurance of ever dollar paid by them to the company.

The HOME was the first company in this country to make an annual dividend of its surplus and pay the same annually in good faith to its members.

The HOME was the first company in the country to abolish the illiberal practice of charging an extra premium on female lives.

The HOME was the first company in this country to remove from its policies all restrictions as to residence and travel. Its policy-holders may, without asking a permit or paying extra premium, reside or travel in any part of the world.

The HOME has, from the first, in all its plans and administration, regarded the interest of the policy-holders as the paramount consideration.

DOUGHTY & BRUEHL,
GENERAL AGENTS,

Although this early newspaper advertisement cites the word "mutual," Home Life was founded as a stock company. The ad at right, perhaps because it ran in Cincinnati, contains some discrepancies: Home Life's first president was Walter S. (not L.) Griffith, and its first home was at 254 Broadway, not 354. As the photo opposite indicates, Home Life grew so quickly that it soon ousted neighboring businesses to build its famous headquarters building on this same site, adopting the address of 256 Broadway.

THE REBIRTH OF PHOENIX

In the mid-1870s, Phoenix entered a difficult period. The company splendidly lived up to its name, overcoming formidable challenges and emerging reborn from the ashes of certain misfortunes. By 1889 it would confidently shed its part-stock, part-mutual structure in favor of full mutuality. But the intervening years would test the young company's mettle.

John Holcombe later described the dilemmas that rose to the surface after the chaotic post-Civil War era and the economic Panic of 1873: "The struggle then became one for existence. Dividends to policyholders had been reduced and the chief source of recuperation, the premium income, was rapidly diminishing, while the death rate was showing a marked increase and the agents were defaulting with discouraging frequency."

To trace what happened at Phoenix is like following the plot of a complicated mystery novel. Previous company histories have portrayed Aaron Goodman, a company founder, director and president from 1875 to 1889, as the villain. But the record is much more complex and ambiguous. It helps to step back and review some key facts about the stock structure of the company.

When Phoenix began as American Temperance in 1851, the company launched itself by raising $100,000 in guarantee capital, selling 2,000 shares of capital stock at $50 each. However, investors had to pay only $8 of each $50 share in cash; American Temperance accepted a guarantee, or verbal promise from stockholders, for the remainder.

The gap between paid-in capital and face-value capital eventually plays an important role in this story, as do dividends. Curiously, the original bylaws did not mention any payment of dividends to policyholders. Bylaw amendments in 1854 and 1862, however, specified that the company would be run as a mutual, with all profits after shareholders' dividends going to policyholders. Shareholders' dividends were not to exceed 6 percent of guarantee capital. However, that 6 percent was paid on the full $50 per share price. For each $8 paid in, then, an investor could earn $3.00 — for an effective return of 37.5 percent.

In 1867 and 1868, Phoenix's bylaws were again amended. A notable new provision specified that the 6 percent shareholder dividends would be paid only on the actual paid-in capital — that

The President Asks for a Raise

Negotiating a raise in compensation is always a delicate process. The first president of Home Life, Walter S. Griffith, was a master.

In his seventh year at the helm, 1866, Griffith wrote a letter to the board of directors. After a few gentlemanly salvos — "the labor and anxiety [of the presidency] have taxed me severely, but I have enjoyed it, for I love the work" — Griffith got down to business. He wanted his salary guaranteed at $10,000 per year, tying the raise to Home Life's achievement of reaching $1 million in assets. That $10,000 was a staggering sum then, when the average worker in New York was lucky to earn $700 a year.

"[If] the Board at its next meeting shall see fit to pass a resolution fixing my salary from and after the first of May last at that sum I shall be relieved of pecuniary embarrassments and satisfied to serve the Home to the utmost of my abilities while I live," Griffith said. Cleverly he also let drop that he had responded to "overtures by other companies" by telling them that "the Home can afford to pay me as much as any other institution and I was not in the market at any price."

Griffith got his raise and served to 1871. His name lives on in WS Griffith & Co., the broker/dealer created by Home Life more than a century later and now a wholly owned subsidiary of Phoenix.

is, on the $8 per share paid by investors. Evidence would later show that the dividends continued to be paid on the full $50 per share.

ACTIONS OF A NEW PRESIDENT

Company co-founder Goodman owned 250 of the original Phoenix shares. Although Goodman had moved to New York, where he dealt in paper manufacturing and book selling, he maintained his interest in Phoenix. In fact, starting in 1868, he began amassing Phoenix stock. Goodman bought most of his shares from Phoenix president Edson Fessenden.

By 1875 — at a time when the entire insurance industry, like the rest of the American economy, remained in decline following the Panic of 1873 — Goodman owned 807 shares, or 40 percent of the company. He left his New York business and returned to Hartford to become president of Phoenix, perhaps to protect his substantial investment in the company.

Within months, Goodman ordered a financial review of the company. The findings were alarming. In five years, surplus had been depleted. Overall, Phoenix faced a deficit of $79,100. Goodman took action. In 1876, the company opened a new set of books and replaced its bylaws. The new bylaws, curiously, failed to mention any rights of stockholders or policyholders to earnings.

Most significantly, Goodman called in the guaranteed capital — the $42 difference between the par value of each share of original stock and the $8 some stockholders had paid. This put $84,000 into Phoenix's coffers, including Goodman's own contribution of $40,000. With a slim surplus of $4,900, Phoenix also began a practice known as "withering policies." Phoenix turned some negotiated percentage of the reserve it was holding for a particular policy over to the policyholder in exchange for canceling the policy. The remainder of the reserve was designated as surplus. Obviously these actions reduced the total amount of life insurance in force. But they made it possible for Phoenix not only to avoid insolvency but gradually to rebuild its surplus.

As president, Goodman continued to buy Phoenix stock. By 1882 he owned 51 percent of the shares, thus controlling the company and board. Goodman then set dividends at 12 percent of paid-in capital, rising to 24 percent in future years. Without notice to the Connecticut Insurance Commission, he also set up a stock department with its own set of books. Goodman transferred the company's primary $100,000 in capital, as well as retroactive dividends, into this department.

General business conditions improved for many insurance companies in the 1880s. Home Life, for one, quietly increased its assets by 200 percent in that decade. Phoenix, however, went from having agents in 28 states and Canada — which had admittedly spread it too thin — to six active agents in Connecticut, Maine and upstate New York. Sales by this "stalwart and faithful core," as John Holcombe later called it, along with income from mortgages on Midwestern farms, moved Phoenix forward.

COMPANY PUT UP FOR SALE

On April 9, 1889, the *Hartford Courant* announced the possible sale of Phoenix Mutual:

"Editorial. Most of our readers will be astonished to read this morning that one of our great life insurance companies is reported to be on the eve of a change in control by a negotiation entered into by one director, apparently without the knowledge of any other member of the board or any policyholder. And they will be equally astounded to read that the reported figures of sale are at the rate of $1,000 for each $100 of stock — the round sum of $501,000 for $50,100 of stock. This is not a private business transaction. The reputation of Hartford is involved and the interests of 17,000 persons [i.e., policyholders] are at stake."

This news evidently stunned everyone except Aaron Goodman, who refused public comment. He had made a secret agreement to sell Phoenix, which was revealed when the potential buyer searched openly for capital to close the deal. The next day, the *Courant* revealed that would-be buyer as John J. MacFarlane, a Pennsylvania state senator, the president of American Life Insurance Company and a vice-president of the Bank of America in Philadelphia. (This bank, which later failed, is not related to the current Bank of America.) MacFarlane claimed that his steep bid was necessary because Goodman had turned down other, lower offers.

Within a week, the Phoenix board met to investigate how it could avert takeover by turning management over to the policyholders. The fact remained that the majority of Phoenix stock — thus the company itself — was legally Aaron Goodman's to sell. It was also a fact that the company's condition had improved under Goodman. Total insurance had dropped from $60 million to $25 million, in part due to "withering policies," but surplus had risen from $4,900 to almost $1 million.

Concerned policyholders also responded quickly. At an emergency meeting, they cited earlier bylaws, which had required the company to operate as a mutual and to limit stockholders' dividends to 6 percent. The fact that those bylaws had been repealed was not well-known. The policyholders found an ally in Erasmus Fyler, the Connecticut Insurance Commissioner. As fate would have it, Phoenix was scheduled in 1889 for a routine review by the state. Fyler, whose actions would show him to be a meticulous regulator, accelerated the schedule at the news of the possible sale.

By early May, Goodman and the Phoenix board had reached an agreement. Goodman would sell his shares to a trust composed of board members, called the Hartford Syndicate. Operating as a sort of temporary holding company, this syndicate would gather the stock so policyholders could authorize the company to use its surplus to buy back all shares (including shares owned by the board members). The price was set at $250 per share, much less than MacFarlane's offer but still a hefty price.

On the government front, the state legislature was expected to pass a resolution giving policyholders some control of Phoenix management. Goodman placated the state by publicly agreeing to sell some of his shares locally, so that no one individual could control Phoenix. The sale to the Hartford Syndicate would accomplish this. However, the government effort lagged and Goodman was still trying to extricate himself from his agreement with MacFarlane, who demanded a large premium to cancel the deal. Goodman refused to pay it.

After a plea by Phoenix's board — excluding Goodman and his nephew, who was also a board member — state regulators did intervene. All parties and their lawyers sat down together and agreed on a fair buyout plan to take place in December. The general provisions of the plan allowed that policyholders could authorize the company to purchase back the stock at a maximum $250 per share. Commissioner Fyler would hold said shares, and once all the shares were gathered, the stock would be retired. The details were worked into a formal resolution to be presented to the state legislature.

Through his investigations, Fyler claimed that Phoenix had done business in an "improper and illegal" manner from June 1882 through February 1889 by paying dividends of 24 percent to stockholders. He ordered the company to stop paying all dividends until further notice. Board members retorted that the dividend scale had been implemented in the bylaws seven years earlier, with no dissent from the state. Sensing a rift, MacFarlane opportunistically reminded everyone that his offer still stood.

ELEVENTH-HOUR WORKOUT

Suddenly Phoenix was facing crucial deadlines. Goodman's option to sell his shares was set to expire on June 15 and so the Connecticut state legislature had to pass Phoenix's resolution by then. With only 10 days left in the session, some senators tried to postpone the Phoenix vote. They didn't understand the complexities and wanted more time to study the details. As was the leisurely custom of the times, the legislators would not convene again for two years! Fortunately, the state senate and house did pass the resolution on June 14.

And so Phoenix demanded surrender of Goodman's stock on June 15. As company secretary, John Holcombe personally presented Goodman with certified bank checks for the purchase. According to Holcombe, Goodman "did not deny or question the contract" — yet he refused to turn over his shares. He told Holcombe, in effect, "see my lawyer." There was widespread belief that the sale of Phoenix to MacFarlane still percolated under the surface, and that Goodman was simply waiting for the bill to be killed. Two days later, the Hartford County Sheriff attached the assets of Aaron Goodman to the value of $300,000 and summoned him to Superior Court to answer the complaint of the board for his failure to produce the shares.

An eleventh-hour situation ticked toward midnight. On the very last day of the legislative session, Connecticut Governor Morgan G. Bulkeley vetoed the Phoenix bill. However, the legislature emphatically overturned Bulkeley's veto, crushing any opportunity for Goodman and MacFarlane to consummate their deal.

Phoenix was free to be fully owned by its policyholders. That would in fact happen — although not without years of intrigue.

URGENT LETTER TO STOCKHOLDERS

On July 3, 1889, Goodman publicly surrendered his shares of stock, resigned as president and director, and accepted a $250,000 buyout from the board members who made up the Hartford Syndicate. However, he had transferred 10 shares of stock from his nephew to himself just the day before.

Jonathan Bunce succeeded Goodman as president; John Holcombe became vice president. A wool merchant and Civil War quartermaster general, Bunce had been a long-time director of Phoenix. Insurance Commissioner Fyler later faulted him for his activities during Phoenix's difficult years, but stopped short of demanding Bunce's removal. Bunce disapproved of typewriters, a new invention; during his 14 years as president he would write his own letters and reports with a quill pen. But Bunce allowed a clerk to type a letter urging Phoenix stockholders to join with the syndicate and share the cost of the buyout. The letter, however, generated no response.

Insurance Commissioner Fyler completed and issued his formal report in November. Certain findings vexed him. He noted that the insurance department was only now learning of Phoenix's stock department, which had been set up seven years prior. He noted that half of the 24 percent annual dividends, which he maintained were excessive, were paid from stock department profits. He insisted that the present and future profits of Phoenix belong to the policyholders. John Holcombe replied on behalf of the directors, honorably offering to submit the question of dividend payments to "the proper tribunal" and to refund all payments if a judgment went against Phoenix shareholders.

Mutualization came up for a vote at the annual policyholder meeting in December. Some 200 stockholders and policyholders attended, as did the ever-watchful Fyler. Lively discussions ensued over the events of previous months and years. Fyler had reservations about the maximum $250 per share buyout price, believing that many stockholders had already profited from high dividends, but declined public comment on that issue until after the vote was taken. Appropriately, Fyler did assure policyholders that the $250 price would not impair company reserves.

The outcome of the vote was a foregone conclusion, because management controlled over 4,000 proxies. Still, the voters in attendance approved mutualization by a vigorous three-to-one margin. And so on December 3, 1889, Phoenix Mutual Life Insurance Company voted to become 100 percent mutual.

However, it could not technically do so until Aaron Goodman's 10 shares were purchased and retired! That would not happen until 1893, the result of a settlement that ended years of lawsuits and countersuits between Phoenix and Goodman. In the meantime, the company could be grateful that it averted ownership by John MacFarlane, whose Philadelphia businesses ultimately failed. MacFarlane fled to Brazil to escape arrest, then returned and served four years in prison.

HISTORICAL PERSPECTIVE

Goodman regarded himself as a savior of Phoenix. Responding to one of Phoenix's lawsuits, he claimed that he rescued the company in 1875. Putting his other actions aside, one cannot dispute that Goodman reversed Phoenix's financial deficit — and averted its possible ruin — by calling in the guaranteed capital and rebuilding the surplus at a critical time.

Charles Gross, who represented Phoenix's

directors when they formed the Hartford Syndicate that bought Goodman's shares, saw him as an entrepreneur gone wrong. Gross observed in 1890: "His shrewdness was that of the proverbial inventor of a new saw, who illustrated its workings by sawing off the limb upon which he was sitting."

A contemporary viewpoint is offered by retired Senior Vice President Frederick W. Sawyer III, FSA, MAAA, a diligent student of Phoenix history. "Goodman saved the company from bankruptcy," Sawyer says. "He did it in ways that today would be unacceptable but were legal then. Goodman did have the right to buy up the stock, own a majority of the company and sell it if he so chose. We don't have to like him for the way he went about doing it, but he had every right to want to sell his shares and finally retire from a company he had worked years to save." In Sawyer's view, the company's hybrid structure couldn't help but cause difficulties, because mutual ownership and stock ownership are at cross-purposes: "Part-mutual, part-stock didn't work."

The acknowledged hero of the story is the quiet, steady, effective John Holcombe. Gross wrote to him: "How would it now be with you, my friend, if your integrity had not been proof against their bribes and snares." Commissioner Fyler applauded Holcombe for "saving the company from the perilous position in which it was found to be in 1875, the entire credit of which was due to Mr. Holcombe."

Phoenix emerged stronger for its long agony. Like Home Life, it had forged a foundation deep and strong. Its supporters proved to be resolutely committed to its survival and stronger than the "bribes and snares" that threatened to erode its dedication to policyholders. "The foundations were not disturbed," Holcombe said, "and the principles upon which the institution rests were shown to be sound and lasting."

Logos

The founders of Home Life were family men. They believed in the sanctity of the home and the importance of life insurance as a domestic safeguard, hence the company name. The logo, naturally, was a picture of "a comfortable cottage, symbol of security and good living." Over the decades, the original image adopted in 1860 evolved into a grander and more modern home.

The directors of American Temperance left no explanation of why they chose Phoenix as the new name for their company in 1861. Probably the symbolic connotation of renewal appealed to them as they left temperance behind. According to Egyptian mythology, the phoenix is a bird that will never die. It consumes itself by fire every 500 years and rises reborn from its own ashes. The word was also well-known and respected in local financial circles. Phoenix Bank — never affiliated with Phoenix Mutual — had been a solid Hartford institution since 1814.

This early rendering of Home Life's logo was used prior to 1871, while Walter Griffith remained company president.

CHAPTER TWO

1890-1929

Coming of Age

If you are to be successful, you will have self-confidence and enthusiasm. If you would be self-confident, as you throw your whole self into the work, it is essential that you know the whys and wherefores of the policy; and to know them you inquire into the fundamental principles of life insurance.

— From Lesson III of Phoenix's Agent Training Course,
the first such course in the industry, introduced in 1906

Change seems to accelerate at the turn of each century. As the twentieth century arrived, Phoenix and Home Life were well-established, financially solid and poised to achieve significant firsts. Both managements began to adopt bolder sales methods, because the times demanded them. The era can be compared to the Internet age 100 years later: the economy was changing in ways no one could predict. Developments such as railroads, electricity and telephones were altering the human experience of distance and time. Business was beginning to benefit from these new technologies. Cars, for example, would make a big difference to field sales once someone figured out how to make the new contraptions affordable. That would happen in 1909, when Henry Ford invented the assembly line. Almost 50 years later, Phoenix would proudly invest a record $5 million to help finance the expansion of the Ford Motor Company.

NEW BLOOD

Under the stable hand of President Bunce in the 1890s, Phoenix got its finances and management firmly in hand. At the same time, it addressed the problem of sales declines, hiring outsiders with fresh ideas: Archibald A. Welch and George S. Miller.

Welch's contributions to Phoenix and to the industry cannot be underestimated. He would become president in 1924, but from his first day as head actuary in 1890, he can be counted as an architect of the modern Phoenix. First, last and always Welch was an actuary, an individual who exemplified what one insurance historian observed: "The great achievements of life insurance are pretty apt to find their origins in the

Home Life's headquarters, built in 1894, once dominated Manhattan's bustling City Hall district, as shown in the postcard on page 25. The 16 men at left constituted Phoenix's entire home office staff in 1890, one year after the company was almost sold. But by 1897, Phoenix had grown to the point where it built and moved into "a home of its own" at 49 Pearl Street, Hartford.

Archibald A. Welch, president of Phoenix from 1924 to 1935, joined the company as chief actuary and modernized its practices. Welch had a great intellect, a pioneering spirit and a strong belief in the responsibility of the life insurance industry to adhere to high ethical standards.

actuarial offices of the business…looking far beyond figures to the realities of life insurance in its broadest application."

Like many Phoenix leaders, Welch was a Yale graduate. He spent his first eight years out of college as an actuary at The Travelers. From the start, Welch took a broad interest in his industry, with special concern over its ethics and turmoils. For example, he wrote about "Legislative Interference with Impaired Life Insurance Companies" for the Fackler Prize, a contest sponsored by the Society of Actuaries.

No doubt Welch could have worked for The Travelers all his life. But he knew about Phoenix because his grandfather had been the company's first examining physician. Welch also happened to marry the sister of President Bunce — a fact modestly deleted from the earliest company history, though the marriage was no secret — and soon an offer of employment followed. Whether it was awkward or advantageous to be the boss's brother-in-law didn't matter. Welch's brilliance stood on its own.

A THOROUGHLY MODERN MANUAL

Welch had the best kind of intellect: he was extremely smart and extremely practical. His first project at Phoenix was to revise the outdated "general manual" of policies, options and rates, substantially unchanged since American Temperance days. Welch phased out older mortality projections, some of which predated the medical knowledge created by the seminal work of Louis Pasteur — whose pasteurization process and other breakthroughs are taken for granted today — and introduced the far more reliable Combined Experience tables.

By 1896, Welch had developed a thoroughly modern manual. Policies were no longer limited to $15,000. There were no restrictions or contestability after two years, except in cases of military service in war. Claims were paid immediately and surrender charges — fees paid by customers who cancel their policies — were reduced. The manual enabled agents to illustrate not just premiums but extended insurance values, paid-up values, cash and loan values (at five-year intervals). *A policy with annual cash values* — no other company had anything like it, yet. From actuarial innovation came other new products, like a "3 by 20" policy, characterized by the waiver of premiums for the rest of the policyholder's life if he or she lived 20 years past the date of issue. The company also distributed a portion of the premiums back to the policyholder at three intervals.

AGENCY IMPROVEMENTS

Thus Phoenix, thanks largely to Welch, had something new and solid to sell. Now it needed a revitalized force to do the selling. During the years of retrenchment, distribution had shrunk to a handful of loyal agents in Connecticut, rural New York and Maine. The latter group also sold to customers in Canada.

George Miller rebuilt the organization, adding agencies in the rest of New England, Cincinnati, Pittsburgh, Chicago, Milwaukee, St. Louis and Denver, and raising the standards for recruitment and training as he went. His agents, in turn, increased Phoenix's sales volume tenfold from 1890 to 1900.

Both home office and field had an uphill battle, however, because times continued to be tough economically. And competition was ferocious. Life insurance agents tended to be part-timers and amateurs — they earned high commissions on initial sales, then moved on.

Prospects were skeptical of their promises, often for good reason.

Phoenix and Home Life doggedly emphasized professionalism at a time when the industry, for the most part, sorely lacked it. Phoenix's contributions are especially notable: in 1901 Miller introduced a company magazine called the *Field*, believed to be the first regular publication for life insurance agents, and in 1904, Winslow Russell, a Boston agent, moved into management. Later renowned as "a champion of the individual insurance man," Russell was vital to company growth. Under him, Phoenix offered the first conferences for agents and annual meetings for regional managers. They sometimes convened in pretty grand places, too: the first meeting of Western and Southern general agents took place in 1904 at the St. Louis World's Fair, a dazzling exposition that every American wanted to see.

HOME OFFICES OF THEIR OWN

Home Life had two short-term presidents, Charles A. Townsend (1890-1891) and George H. Ripley (1892-1893), before settling on George E. Ide as a company leader. A former banker and company secretary, Ide was, like Archibald Welch, an innovative thinker. In an increasingly scientific age, he was also something of a maverick. "We as a nation are too analytical," he told a conference of agents. "We are driving out of our daily life much of its sweetness and spontaneity. Artificial and cold-blooded calculation [should not take] the place of human judgment."

Ide's first responsibility was to preside over the construction of Home Life's landmark home office at 256 Broadway, which housed the company until the 1980s. The directors had capitalized on depressed real estate prices to buy the land adjacent to its existing four-story building for the bargain sum of $170,000. Using the original foundation as the cornerstone, Home Life completed its 16-story edifice in 1894. Officially domiciled in Brooklyn, the company continued to keep a small office there until 1906, when Brooklyn became a borough of New York and Home Life changed its charter to reflect 256 Broadway as its official home office.

A grand limestone structure adorned with balconies, the Home Life building was, for a short time, the world's tallest building. It towered over New York City Hall, which was just across the park, and offered clear views west to the busy Hudson River. Home Lifers didn't enjoy the best vistas, however. In thrifty fashion, the company occupied the first five stories and collected premium rents for the upper floors.

As Phoenix grew under Welch and Miller, it also needed more space, which fortunately it

Phoenix agency managers were joined by their wives at their annual Hartford meeting in 1906. Agent meetings, recruitment, training and the *Field*, below, were part of George Miller's effort to strengthen Phoenix's sales organization at the turn of the century.

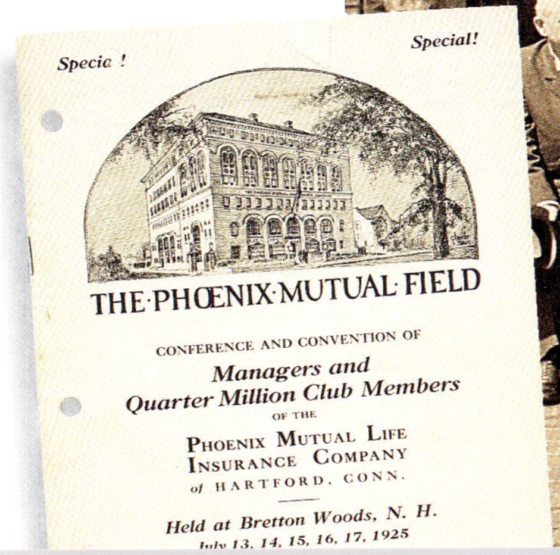

could afford to build. In 1896, the board broke ground at 49 Pearl Street in Hartford, across the street from its rented headquarters. Employees moved into the handsome new six-story home office in June 1897. Downtown Hartford had had electricity for 14 years; now Phoenix caught up by incorporating the marvelous "juice" into its home office. Most of the power went strictly to ceiling lights, because business machines such as typewriters were still hand-operated.

Home Life's new home withstood a great test. On a cold Sunday in December 1898, the building next door burned so thoroughly that it collapsed onto adjacent Warren Street. But 256 Broadway — one of America's first steel-frame skyscrapers — resisted the spectacular blaze. In fact, the structure helped to stop the fire from further destroying New York's main thoroughfare. *Leslie's Weekly,* a popular magazine, marveled: "The spectacle of the immense Home Life building still towering to its full height, while old-fashioned buildings beside it became heaps of blackened bricks in a gaping hole, is strong proof of the fire-resisting qualities of our modern, improved structures."

Companies in nearby buildings lost everything, but Home Life resumed business as usual the very next day — almost. Employees had to wear overcoats at their desks until heat-shattered windows were repaired.

ARMSTRONG INVESTIGATION

Soon another kind of heat threatened to engulf not just Home Life but virtually the entire life insurance industry — the Armstrong Investigation of 1905-1906, named for William W. Armstrong, the New York state senator who chaired it.

The investigation had its roots in the election of Theodore Roosevelt as U.S. president in 1900. Roosevelt was a self-described "trust buster" who wielded the big stick of government against

This six-story structure at 49 Pearl Street, completed in 1897, was the first Phoenix-owned headquarters building. It was home to Phoenix for more than 20 years.

industry monopolies, union abuses and consumer fraud. Newspapers, which were then the dominant media, eagerly took up the cause. Journalists called themselves muckrakers, after an image from the Christian allegory *Pilgrim's Progress.* Their persistent digging created a uniquely American tradition that gave us *60 Minutes,* uncovered the Watergate scandal and the like. Muckrakers focused on life insurance after discovering some young executives of a major insurer throwing lavish expense-account parties for themselves and their chums at one of New York City's priciest supper clubs. Was this how policyholders' premiums were being spent?

Parties aside, there is no question that the industry was then plagued by scandals and irregular practices. In the 1860s, most insurers washed their hands of the dubious half-note system. But to recover from the Panic of 1873, many offered a new device known as the Tontine Plan. It called for the pooling and reinvesting of earnings on participating policies and the distribution of accumulated funds to survivors after a 20-year period. These plans became immensely popular, mainly because of the speculation as to the amounts that would accumulate. Over the years, huge sums mounted in the coffers of companies that made no accounting until the 20-year period expired. Illegal stock speculation by companies was also part of the misuse of the funds.

Both Home Life and Phoenix had adopted the deferred dividend plan — Welch's "3 by 20" product was a variant — but with a critically important difference. Both companies handled the accumulated funds responsibly. Phoenix offered distributions at 5 and 10 years, not just at 20. Home Life did an annual accounting and set up full liability in its financial statements. Indeed, the item was included in the company's policy reserves and covered by the Certificate of Valuation of the New York State Insurance Department.

The life insurance industry came under fire during the Armstrong Investigation of 1906. Home Life and Phoenix were among the very few companies found free of accounting abuses and unfair competitive tactics. Phoenix had adopted an advertising slogan in 1904 that highlighted the company's reputation for fair dealings, below.

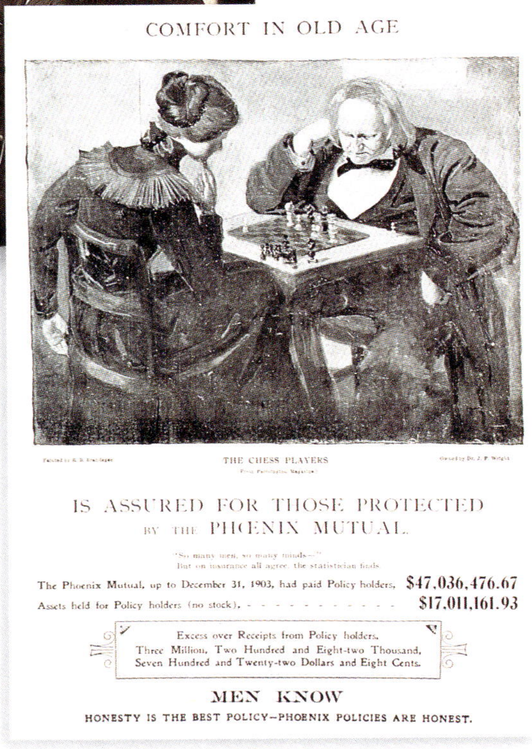

EXECUTIVES ON THE HOT SEAT

The Armstrong Commission probed into the practices of every life insurer based in New York or doing business there. For four months, Chief Counsel Charles Evans Hughes (who later became U.S. secretary of state and a U.S. Supreme Court chief justice) grilled one executive after another. The key questions: Were policyholders being treated honestly? Were companies competing fairly? The answers, mostly negative, made front-page news.

Home Life's President Ide took the witness stand for two days, followed by Chief Actuary William A. Marshall. Neither executive had anything to hide. Indeed, the day after Ide stepped down from the stand, people read the kind of coverage they hadn't seen before. "No mystery in accounts," said the *New York Globe*. "Home Life hasn't made any political contributions, its officers have not been involved in syndicates, the salaries of the officers are moderate," noted the *New York Sun*. From the *Brooklyn Eagle* came the ultimate compliment: Home Life officers were "the angels of Life Insurance" because the company's administration was "as clean as a hound's tooth."

Typically, Phoenix enjoyed less fanfare but was judged equally solid. President John Holcombe, who succeeded Bunce in 1904, did not have to testify because Hughes was satisfied with Phoenix's written responses to a preliminary questionnaire. Chief Actuary Archibald Welch did speak, at a private hearing. Hughes was so impressed with Welch that he used him as a consultant and appointed him to chair the committee that shaped the industry's first major legislation.

Out of the hearings came the landmark 1907 New York insurance regulations that became the model for other states. It is generally believed that these laws changed life insurance practices for the better. In brief, they corrected the worst industry abuses by eliminating Tontine Plans and introducing uniform accounting standards. They also clamped down on lavish incentives to agents.

Despite the reforms, Americans briefly lost some confidence in the industry — a natural reaction after seeing so many life insurers airing their dirty laundry. Unlike many competitors, however, Phoenix suffered only a slight sales decline, and Home Life actually saw a rise in sales. Urged to capitalize on the favorable publicity accorded to Home Life during the Armstrong Investigation, George Ide "quietly and without ceremony declined, because it wouldn't be the best thing for the business of life insurance," as President James A. Fulton later said. Nonetheless, in 1907, the first full year after Armstrong, Home Life's annual sales soared to a new high of $14,678,000. The achievement was especially remarkable because it came amid yet another panic in the financial markets.

Gerald K. Rugger, a former Home Life president and chairman, says the Armstrong heritage was still a tangible source of pride when he joined the company in 1937. "The quality of our company, the integrity of it, was embodied and vindicated by the way we came out of the hearings," he notes. "Within the Home Life family, we knew it, but we didn't go around beating our chest about it."

MORE INDUSTRY FIRSTS

Well before Armstrong, George Miller and Winslow Russell had been steadily improving Phoenix's agency system. Concurrent with the investigation, they introduced another innovation: the first agent training course in the industry.

Phoenix purchased the course, "A Prospectus and 10 Lessons," from agent Jay Dwiggins of San Francisco in 1906. Employee Charles W. Burpee, a former managing editor of the *Hartford Courant*, rewrote it. Burpee turned the 10 lessons into 12, but otherwise the course didn't need much work. The prose is old-fashioned but most of the information is as relevant today as it was 100 years ago:

I. Outline
II. The Policy.
III. Knowledge That Begets Self-Confidence.
IV. More Fundamentals: Surplus, Dividends, Ratios.
V. Character of Your "Goods" and Your Company.
VI. Peculiarities and Possibilities of Field of Prospects.
VII. Getting at Prospects.
VIII. The Kind of Policy and How to Interest.
IX. Our Circularizing System.
X. Objections and How to Meet Them.
XI. Closing.
XII. Competition.

Designed as a correspondence course between agents and a home office instructor, the lessons convey a wonderful straightforwardness and heart-to-heart quality. "There was never so favorable a time for entering the business as now," Lesson III assured new agents. "In [past] days a man was given a rate book simply and was sent out to train himself or be trained by the hard knocks of experience. It took him years to acquire what an agent today can get in a few weeks from our Educational Department and its adjuncts. This is saying nothing about the greatly improved policies today, and the absence — *in the Phoenix*

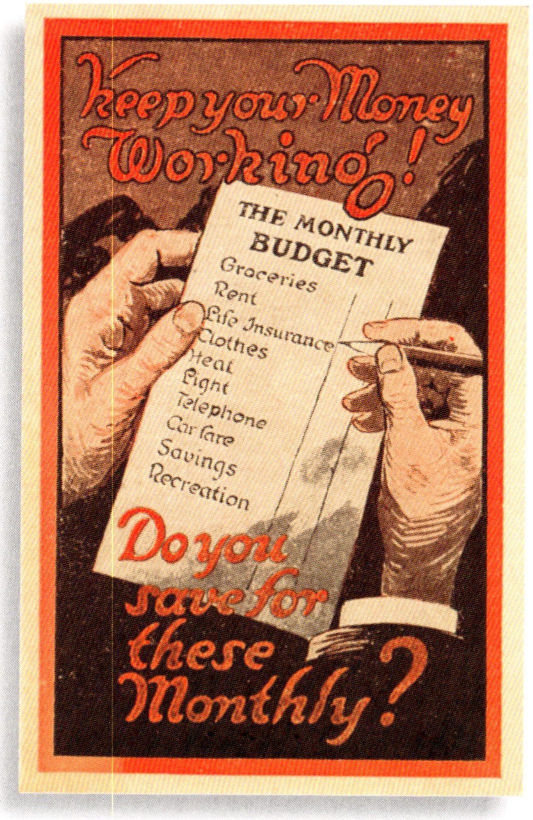

In 1912, Phoenix became the first life insurer to use direct mail to generate leads. This marketing aid included another pioneering tool for lead generation: a return postcard to be preaddressed by the agent and returned by prospective policyholders.

Home Life's Gala 50th Anniversary

Phoenix probably observed its 50th anniversary, but any formal celebration was so quiet that it was never recorded. Home Life, by contrast, threw itself an elegant banquet at the Plaza Hotel on May 10, 1910. By coincidence, President George E. Ide himself turned 50 that night.

The movers and shakers of New York society turned out for the gala affair. Among the guests were "one hundred and fifty men who are leaders in life insurance, journalism, law, literature and business," along with a number of "richly gowned women," according to the *Eastern Underwriter*. President William H. Taft sent his regrets.

Another invitee who had to decline was Archibald A. Welch, then second vice president and head actuary of Phoenix. Welch had a Yale class of 1882 reunion trip that week. Judging by his response, he clearly held Home Life and Ide — a fellow Yale alumnus — in warm regard:

My Dear Mr. Ide,
Nothing but an '82 party in the Michigan woods could hire me away from your anniversary dinner on May tenth. Unfortunately our plans have been made for months and it will be impossible to help celebrate your semi-centennial. It has not escaped me that the occasion is doubly important, and as I may not offer my congratulations on the day itself, will you let me anticipate the occasion by wishing for you and the Home all the happiness and success which have followed you in the past, which you are now deservedly enjoying and which can't help but come to you in the next fifty years.

Very sincerely yours,
A. A. Welch
April Twenty-Second, 1910

One prominent guest was William H. Hotchkiss, the New York State superintendent of insurance. Along with other speakers, Hotchkiss commended Home Life on its blameless record and sterling performance during the Armstrong hearings. Ide tactfully used the occasion "to express the hope that a change would be made in the regulation limiting the amount of business a company could do" in New York, a nagging aspect of the Armstrong legislation. Hotchkiss in turn asked the audience, which included many industry executives, to work more willingly with state supervisors.

Politicking aside, guests enjoyed not just "a splendid repast" — the menu included caviar, foie gras, rack of lamb, champagne and cigars — but "a feast of reason and a flow of soul such as rarely falls to the lot of those who sit at tables on occasions of this kind," said the *Eastern Underwriter* reporter.

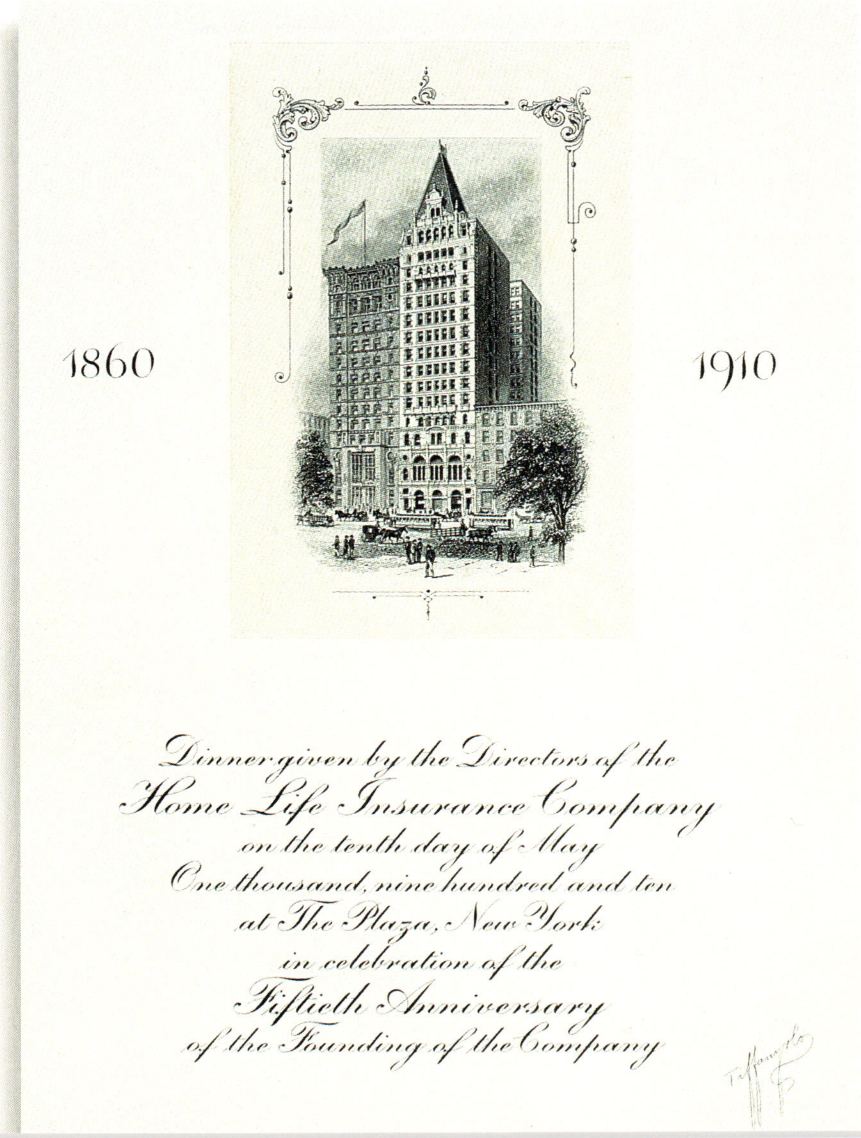
1860 1910

Dinner given by the Directors of the
Home Life Insurance Company
on the tenth day of May
One thousand, nine hundred and ten
at The Plaza, New York
in celebration of the
Fiftieth Anniversary
of the Founding of the Company

By coincidence, Home Life President George E. Ide was born on the day that the company was formed. The 50th anniversary celebration of this event drew congratulations from an impressive number of friends of the company.

At Work in the Home Office, Circa 1907

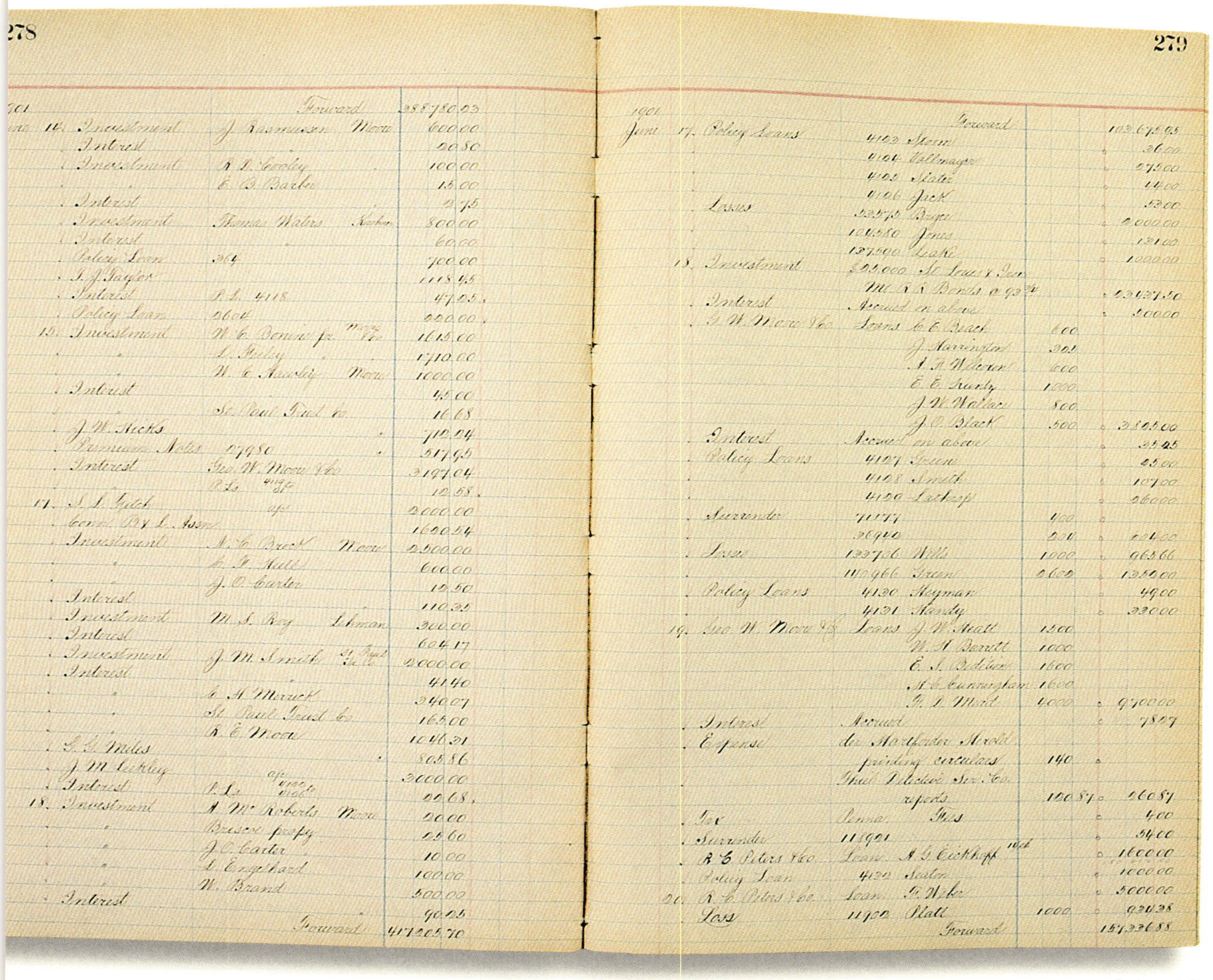

Imagine a workplace where everyone except officers sat in an open space and employees puffed on pipes if they so wished — a place where one floor with a gallery, like an old-fashioned library, held every single paper record for $97,583,000 of insurance in force.

Such was the Phoenix that Howard Goodwin joined as a policy clerk in 1907. He went on to become an underwriter and company officer. Fifty years later, Goodwin wrote down his recollections of a vanished past where Charles Dickens would have felt at home:

I reported for work at 49 Pearl Street. At that time Jonathan B. Bunce was President.... He continued to write his official correspondence in long-hand rather than to have his letters typed on a 'new-fangled typewriter.' [Typewriters had been invented 40 years earlier.] Copies were made in a wet press tissue book.

Employees worked for the most part at high double desks on each side of which was a high stool, on one of which I duly perched. Around the room were built-in supports on which were spread the old policy registers which recorded the individual policies and the status of each.

The day was spent by Mr. X in writing policies in long-hand and by Mr. Y in copying applications by pen for attaching to such policies. These two sat near each other and were not always in accord. Mr. X had very definite opinions to which he gave explosive expression. Mr. Y had an eruptive temper and answered Mr. X in vehement terms, sometimes supplementing his ardent comments by hurling any available article. And then there was Mr. Z, a cheerful soul who unfortunately was stone deaf....

I settled claims from the Province of Quebec.... Frequently [the beneficiaries would include] twelve to sixteen children, some of whom had been dead themselves for several years.... It was quite a puzzle to unravel the affairs. Yes, those were the good old days.

Mutual contracts — of anything that can bring the policyholder or beneficiary the slightest worry."

The highlighted phrase speaks volumes about Phoenix's own blossoming self-confidence — it's a gentlemanly jab at competitors, to be sure, but a jab all the same.

Phoenix further advanced the industry in 1912 with the first known use of direct mail marketing in the industry. As superintendent of agencies, Winslow Russell handwrote 300 post-cards to select prospects. His test led to Phoenix's "circularizing department" and the concept of lead generation, which almost every competitor copied. Decades later, agents and brokers still depended on their allotment of 100 free mailings per month to generate new business. "They worked marvelously," says William F. Kelly, New York brokerage manager from 1947 to 1983. "Every Monday we'd stay in the office until 9 p.m. and we'd phone, phone, phone to follow up. Boy, did those mailings work."

BIRTH OF THE CAREER SYSTEM

Russell brought a new era of agency professionalism to Phoenix. Most significantly, in 1914, the company became the first life insurer to do away with part-time agents. Simple math confirmed that part-timers did too little business for too much overhead. Of 1,700 agents, about 300 had been producing 80 percent of Phoenix's total sales.

Traveling the country to weed out nonproducers and recruit better ones, Russell said: "The part-time man, the helper and the broker have become an almost dominating factor.... The old idea of an 80 percent commission, $50 monthly guarantee, and a rate book as the basis for agents' success must be superseded by one of better understanding on the part of the public and of better apprehension and approach on the part of the field man." He whittled the field force to about 450 agents.

Thereafter, Phoenix agents underwent a close investigation of character and business practices. Only qualified, full-time, licensed agents with contracts on file could earn commissions. Anyone found rebating premiums to customers, a common practice at the time, would be terminated and fined. To support its agents and give them the widest advantage, Phoenix stopped selling through brokers (with notable exceptions for large cases and "recognized brokers doing solely a life insurance business").

Moreover, Russell emphasized "the scientific method of sales training," which rigorously tracked and measured results. He summoned managers from Phoenix's 10 largest agencies to the home office to discuss the new guidelines and agree to them in writing. They called the changes "a long step in the right direction."

These were extraordinarily aggressive moves, and some field agents chafed at them. Russell was not perturbed. By steps, he achieved his ultimate goal: to replace the general agency system with branch offices operating under careful home office supervision.

In short, under Russell, Phoenix developed a true career agency system — thus proving, once again, to be an industry pioneer. Other companies followed, including Home Life, which reorganized its agencies along similar lines 10 years later.

WAR AND GROWTH

Life insurers had a respite from turmoil in the years following Armstrong. But soon, like most Americans, these companies watched with alarm as war spread across Europe. The United States joined the war in April 1917, one year after Home Life directors voted to wholly mutualize.

Why would Home Life abandon the part-stock, part-mutual form chosen by its founders? The foremost reason was to guard against potential takeover, a very real threat, given Home Life's illustrious performance in the post-Armstrong years.

In a letter to agents asking them to urge policyholders to vote for the plan, President Ide described "many occasions" in which raiders had attempted "to control the organization by means of purchase of the stock. Such attempts often emanated from interests which appeared to the directors to be contrary to the best interests of the policyholders and in every instance have been met and frustrated by the present stockholders or their predecessors. While the defense has been sufficient in the past, we recognize the possible danger, especially as the Company has been growing in importance and size...."

The time was ripe in other ways. For "a long time," perhaps since the 1874 takeover attempt that resulted in dividends paid in pure gold, Home Life had considered mutualizing. In 1915, the insurance departments of New York and New Jersey had put additional legal protections into place for mutuals. These were so attractive that Metropolitan Life and Prudential both had promptly mutualized. "The announcement of [Home Life's] plan is regarded in insurance circles as further evidence of the trend of life insurance companies toward mutualization," reported the *New York Times* in a headline story on Home Life.

And as the fiscally prudent Ide reminded everyone, the longer Home Life waited to mutualize, the more funds it would have to appropriate from its surplus for the job. The vote passed, and the company retired its remaining stock out of surplus on May 25, 1916, for $450 per share, or a total of $442,086 — far less than speculators would have paid. The newly mutualized company also paid its dividends from surplus, another first.

It maintained the wartime tradition of holding the job of any employee who went into military service during the war.

World War I, as well as a devastating flu epidemic, emphasized the "absolute need of life insurance in stabilizing the affairs of the civilized world," to quote an anonymous historian of Home Life.

Phoenix managed to double its business from 1910 to 1920. Outgrowing Pearl Street, where the ever-vigorous Russell set up one of the first training schools for agents, it built a new home office on Bushnell Park in Hartford.

Like the boat building decades later, Phoenix's home office at 79 Elm Street was not a piece of conventional New England architecture. It is a fairly close copy of the Longa, a sixteenth-century stock exchange building in Saragossa, Spain. "It was like a big brick house," says retiree Edward A. Richardson, who started there in 1941 and eventually headed Administrative Services for the entire company. "Six stories, front hall, an attic and a basement. It was coal-heated until the 1950s, and that pile of coal frequently caught fire by spontaneous combustion. Building employees had to go in with smoke masks and hose it down." An in-house staff of 36, including a night watchman and 16 female housekeepers, handled the maintenance. One of the building's charms was its size. It was small enough for all the employees — about 400 in all — to know, or at least recognize, each other.

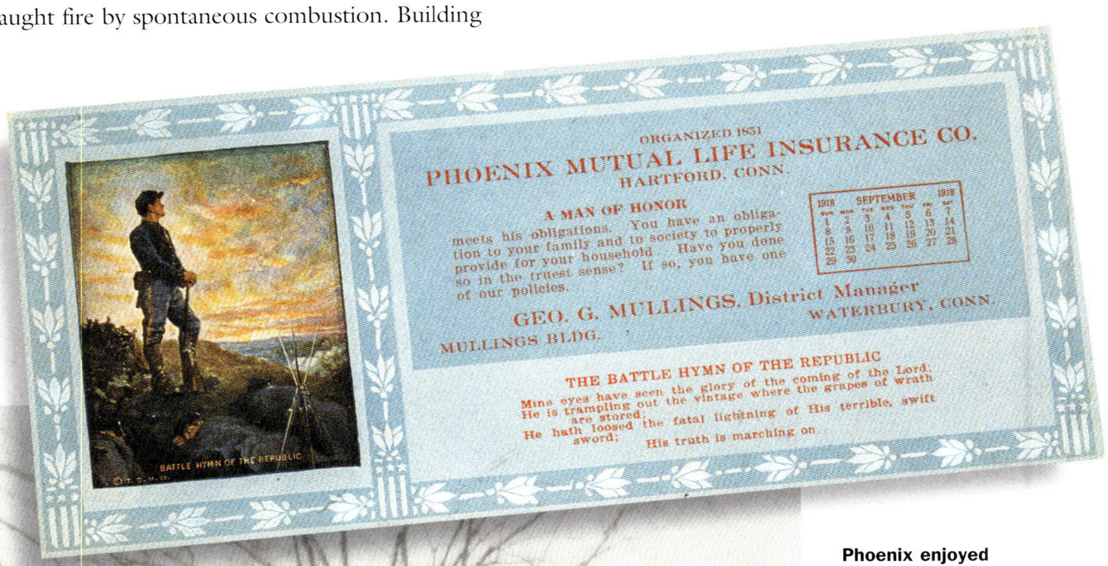

Phoenix enjoyed tremendous growth during the turn of the century. Total insurance in force more than quadrupled, from $57.9 million in 1899 to $253.3 million in 1919. The growing company commissioned a new home office at 79 Elm Street on Bushnell Park, seen under construction in 1920. The patriotic sentiments of the First World War carried over into Phoenix sales aids, including this blotter from 1918.

The Phoenix Mutual Club and Phoenix Players

The Phoenix Mutual Club is how Phoenix employees made friends, enjoyed themselves and did good works for decades. The origins of this volunteer-run club date to 1913, when the Phoenix men formed a sports association. Not to be outdone, the women started their own organization. In 1919, the groups merged. The club existed in this form until the Phoenix-Home Life merger, when it became the Phoenix Employees Club.

Club-sponsored social, athletic, educational and charitable activities were a highlight of Phoenix life. Club dues were minimal — just 10 cents a month at the start, and only 25 cents a month in the 1950s — and nine out of ten employees took part. For working-class men and women, especially those who were unmarried, the club offered a social life they couldn't find elsewhere.

Members who liked to put on plays formed the Phoenix Players, a club offshoot that flourished through the mid-1970s. They chipped in to hire well-known regional directors and would perform at the Bushnell Theater or Wadsworth Atheneum auditorium.

The club calendar revolved around reliables such as the bowling league and banquet, Christmas party, formal dance and summer picnic. In the 1940s and 1950s, club committees were also a proving ground for ambitious young managers. But generally, the club and players were ways to have fun with coworkers.

Here's what was on the club calendar in late 1953:

Month of October: Installation of New Vending Machines
October 7: Steak and Movie Party
October 20: Home Movies of Yosemite National Park
October 28: Halloween Costume Party

Vending machines? Yes, these were part of a kind of club-sponsored benevolent society. Before full-fledged medical benefits, club members helped each other through hard times with "premium-free sickness insurance." They pooled their profits from morning coffee sales and vending machine receipts into a Benefit Fund, thus turning pennies into grants of hundreds of dollars per year that were gratefully received by members who encountered unexpected illness.

Some Memories:

"I kept the accounts and was the collector of the Flower Fund. [The club sent flowers to members whenever the occasion demanded.] That was quite a job. I made many friends. Oh, I enjoyed being part of the club."
— Josephine Melusky, paralegal, law department

"I acted in the plays. I guess I was stiff, because they always seemed to cast me as a minister. But it was fun."
— C. Russell Noyes, retired company secretary and vice president, public relations

"Phoenix was a power in the table tennis area. The old auditorium at 79 Elm Street had five tables that we used all the time for tournaments and league play. When we moved to One American Row, we played in the parking garage. Phoenix also participated in other insurance company athletic leagues, like basketball, tennis, softball and baseball. This was before the days of national athletics, except for baseball, so these company sports used to get a lot of ink in the local press."
— Edward A. Richardson, retired second vice president, administrative services

"The club is still a great way to meet new people, get out and enjoy new experiences, and make a real difference within the community."
— Darlene Colapinto, associate manager, Hartford services, a member since 1968

Employees line up at a soda machine operated by the Phoenix Mutual Club at 79 Elm Street. This photo was part of a series of home office snapshots compiled and bound into monogrammed albums by the club and sent to Phoenix employees who were serving in the military during World War II.

AT THE DESK OF

Silas Cornwell

First job at Phoenix:
Clerk, 1868, age 16

Last job:
Vice president and company secretary, 1933

Remembered for:
65 years and eight months of continuous employment.

Where he worked:
49 Pearl Street and 79 Elm Street, Hartford. Pictured here under the electric lights that were an innovation at Pearl Street.

Unusual perk:
In Cornwell's later years, a building employee would bring crackers and milk to his desk each day precisely at 10:00 a.m.

"I AM AMBITIOUS..."

Home Life went into mourning when George Ide suddenly died in office in July 1919. Charles Evans Hughes eulogized him: "Life insurance has had no better apostle." William Marshall, the chief actuary who had testified with Ide at the Armstrong hearings, took over as president until 1923.

Following Marshall from 1924 to 1928 was Ethelbert Ide Low, a member of the Ide family and a company director for seven years. A captain in the war, Low was the first attorney to serve as Home Life president. Upon taking office, he said: "I am ambitious that this company shall not only give to its policyholders the ultimate in life insurance service, but that it shall be a good company to work for."

"I am ambitious...." Such bold statements may have raised some eyebrows on the Home Life board. So did, no doubt, Low's newfangled practice of rapidly promoting employees who showed promise. From the field, Low brought in James A. Fulton, a lawyer-turned-agent and agency manager. As superintendent of agencies, Fulton quickly set about developing products and building an organization of full-time agency managers, who in turn recruited full-time career field underwriters. Like Phoenix six years earlier, Home Life eliminated part-timers and emphasized new products. Both companies profited from these strategies.

The year 1924 was auspicious for presidents. At Phoenix, Archibald Welch replaced the retiring Holcombe. On actuarial grounds alone, Welch was a leader in the industry. He proved equally progressive as a president. In 1925, he allowed Phoenix to eliminate medical examinations for selected applicants — at first for policies up to $2,000, then for larger amounts. Given the obvious opportunity for fraud, only one or two other companies had attempted this. Applicants had to be carefully screened by agents, but Phoenix now had full faith in the professionalism of its field force.

Defunct Jobs: Scout

In pre-computer days, hard copies of applications and signed policies weren't just legal necessities; they were the company's lifeblood. Typical scenario from the first hundred years of Phoenix and Home Life: A policyholder sends a letter requesting, say, a policy loan. A mail clerk routes it to the proper department. A clerk there finds that another department is working with that policyholder's master file, which contains his policy and is needed to fill his request. Enter the scout, who physically tracked down and delivered files. The good ones developed tremendous contacts and could locate materials in a flash.

THE ROARING TWENTIES

Low and Welch were in tune with the 1920s, which were prosperous and broad-minded. Having weathered decades of economic upheaval and a sobering world war — and having absorbed waves of immigrants, who brought a new energy to the country — America was shedding its Puritan attitudes. The accent was on money, youth and fun.

Explorers like Charles Lindbergh and Richard Byrd captured the public imagination. Our love affair with cars had begun, with automobile ownership soaring from 8,000 in 1900 to eight million in 1920. Bootleggers cheerfully ignored Prohibition. (The government, like Phoenix, eventually realized that temperance was an impossible basis for business.) Women shortened their skirts, entered the paid workforce and exercised their newly granted right to vote. Newspapers and magazines were joined by the mass medium of radio, which could do marvelous things like broadcast baseball's 1926 World Series to 15 million listeners nationwide.

National magazines played a growing role in Phoenix's success. In 1923, the company created one of the first advertisements to sell Americans on the idea of life insurance. By 1926, it was the first mid-sized insurer advertising in popular magazines, initiating a campaign as "the retirement income company."

These were boom times for life insurers: total U.S. business in force rose from $40 billion in 1920 to $100 billion in 1929. Yet policy loans — the practice of borrowing against the cash value of a policy — were increasing faster than new business by half. Although life insurers had offered such loans since the 1890s, customers had regarded them as a last resort. That attitude began to change in the "Roaring Twenties." Some people borrowed modestly to furnish their new homes; home ownership was growing by leaps and bounds. But others drew down the cash value of their life insurance policies to invest in stocks. Speculation was rampant.

On October 29, 1929, the happiness came to an end. The stock market sank and, in its treacherous downward spiral, dragged down much of the U.S. economy with it — to the eventual sum of $50 billion in losses. Fortunately, Home Life and Phoenix were in better shape than most companies to survive the ensuing depression. The former was now under the intelligent vision of James Fulton as president. The latter had two formidable forces at work: President Welch, who understood life insurance as well or better than anyone, and an advertising campaign that was starting to break sales records.

Phoenix and Home Life had learned the whys and wherefores of the life insurance business. Indeed, they had helped shape them. These companies had come of age. Now the Great Depression would put them to a new test of strength.

This photo shows the 17th class of the sales training division of Phoenix Mutual, graduated on May 19, 1925. Phoenix placed great emphasis on training of and communication with field agents. The straight rows and spotless desks represented the typical office environment of the era.

CHAPTER THREE

1930-1962

Giants in Effectiveness

Our goal is not to be a giant in size, but a giant in effectiveness.

— Winslow Russell, superintendent of agencies, Phoenix Mutual Life Insurance Company

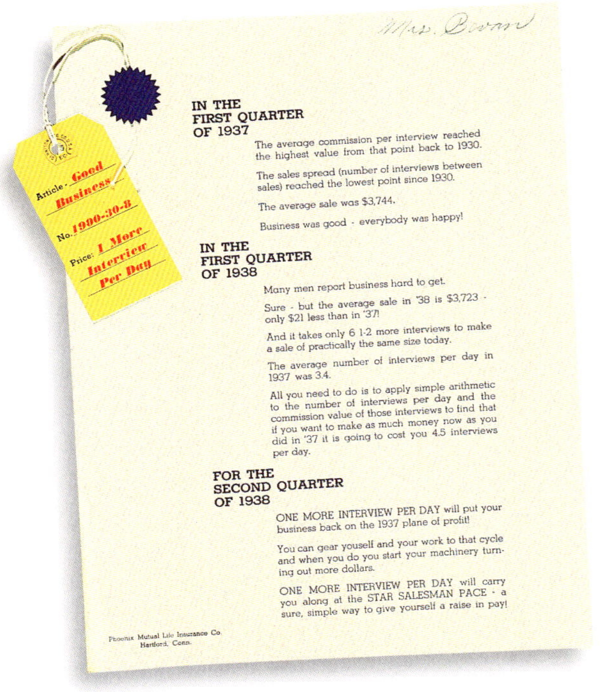

Article - Good Business
No. 1990-30-8
Price: 1 More Interview Per Day

IN THE FIRST QUARTER OF 1937

The average commission per interview reached the highest value from that point back to 1930.

The sales spread (number of interviews between sales) reached the lowest point since 1930.

The average sale was $3,744.

Business was good - everybody was happy!

IN THE FIRST QUARTER OF 1938

Many men report business hard to get.

Sure - but the average sale in '38 is $3,723 - only $21 less than in '37!

And it takes only 6 1-2 more interviews to make a sale of practically the same size today.

The average number of interviews per day in 1937 was 3.4.

All you need to do is to apply simple arithmetic to the number of interviews per day and the commission value of those interviews to find that if you want to make as much money now as you did in '37 it is going to cost you 4.5 interviews per day.

FOR THE SECOND QUARTER OF 1938

ONE MORE INTERVIEW PER DAY will put your business back on the 1937 plane of profit!

You can gear youself and your work to that cycle and when you do you start your machinery turning out more dollars.

ONE MORE INTERVIEW PER DAY will carry you along at the STAR SALESMAN PACE - a sure, simple way to give yourself a raise in pay!

Phoenix Mutual Life Insurance Co.
Hartford, Conn.

On the previous page, Home Life agent Hugh Meredith signs up Yankees pitcher Herb Pennock. Through field communications like the one above, Phoenix motivated its agents to keep up production through the Great Depression — and they did.

Banks failed…businesses folded…bread lines of hungry people stretched down city blocks. Triggered by the stock market crash of 1929, the Great Depression of the 1930s created waves of misery that pounded life insurers and policyholders from every direction. Yet both Phoenix and Home Life stayed afloat. They held the course by acting conservatively and putting their owners — their policyholders — first.

Home Life took the unusual step of addressing policyholders directly, through a 75th anniversary edition of *Home Life* magazine. Usually the magazine went only to employees and agents. In 1935, President James A. Fulton felt that loyal customers deserved more. He approved a special 16-page issue that was a forerunner of the modern annual report — informative, almost chatty, richly illustrated with photos and graphs. Its centerpiece and longest article was "How the Home Life Has Met the Depression."

RIPPLE EFFECTS

"The first effect [of the Depression] was on new business," Home Life admitted. Indeed, new business for both Home Life and Phoenix plummeted. It was no surprise given unemployment rates of 25 to 40 percent. Along with this decline was an increase in policy lapses and surrenders, inevitable for those caught between paying premiums and feeding their families. Yet many policyholders hung on, eager for every bit of stability they could afford in a society that offered few safety nets. The situation forced agents to focus on servicing and keeping existing customers as well as prospecting.

The loss of business, and the cash drain demanded by policy loans, were only half the picture. Home Life and Phoenix were also losing interest payments on bonds and mortgages in default. (Insurance companies generally invested little in stocks, regarding them as too volatile.) They found themselves the owners of foreclosed properties, many of which were deteriorating.

State insurance departments knew the severity of the situation. Encouraged by President Franklin D. Roosevelt, they sought to avoid any possible "insurance panic" like the bank panics of the Depression's first years. To that end, they offered a menu of liberalized accounting methods. For example, insurers could assume that overdue mortgage interest would eventually be paid. They were thus permitted to post it as income, or to add it to the value of properties acquired by foreclosure.

Fulton didn't bite. Nor did Phoenix's President Welch, who died in 1935, or his successor, Arthur M. Collens. These were the industry leaders, after all, who had emerged from the Armstrong hearings "cleaner than a hound's tooth." Theirs were the companies that did the right thing, even in hard times. Throughout the Depression they claimed losses as losses. They rehabilitated properties from real income and contingency funds, not phantom paper assets. They met policyholder obligations with ready cash. They suffered short-term downturns but would emerge from the greatest business depression in America's history stronger than ever.

If there was a bright side to the Depression, it was that talent was cheap and plentiful. "Companies picked up highly qualified people for the low dollar," says one retiree, with a mix of bitterness and gratitude still evident 65 years later. Even after Roosevelt's New Deal programs fueled

Until 1923, only a few giant life insurers were known for their advertising. Phoenix broke the ice for the rest of the industry with a sophisticated campaign of 24 ads, including this one, which appeared in *Literary Digest* and other major national magazines. The companion booklet below, a guide to household budgeting, was distributed by agents and available to everyone who mailed Phoenix their address and two dimes.

THE BUSINESS OF RUNNING A HOME

THE man and woman whose home is run upon a business basis have found the secret of contentment. Their happiness is not disturbed by financial misunderstandings. Whether it is large or small, their income is disbursed so as to bring them the greatest possible comfort and pleasure.

Perhaps the greatest element of contentment in such a home comes from provision for the future. This man and woman have banished the spectres of unemployment, sickness and death. They have made permanent prosperity certain. They have done this through the proper use of life insurance.

If you would learn how life insurance can bring contentment into your home, it will pay you to enlist the service of a Phoenix Mutual representative. You will find him an intelligent, competent adviser—a man who has been specially trained in the uses of life insurance; whose business it is to show you new ways in which you can protect your wife and children through life insurance.

When you have talked with a Phoenix Mutual counselor, you will understand more fully what life insurance can do for you and your family. To guarantee the independence of your later years, to provide a permanent income for your wife and for each of your children, to make certain that your children will be educated no matter what happens to you—these are but a few of the uses of life insurance which the Phoenix Mutual counselor can explain to you.

One of the best things you can do for your family is to talk to a Phoenix Mutual man.

PHOENIX MUTUAL
LIFE INSURANCE COMPANY

HOME OFFICE HARTFORD CONN.

First policy issued 1851

A Reprint from the Literary Digest of April 12th, 1924 and the April issue of the American Magazine.

This smiling fisherman, featured in various ads from 1929 until the 1960s, helped Phoenix earn its reputation as "the retirement income company." Advertising industry historian J. L. Watkins honored this particular version of the fisherman ad by including it in his classic book ***The 100 Greatest Advertisements.*** According to Cyrus T. Steven, who directed public relations for Phoenix in the late 1920s, the fisherman ad was the most successful of a series of reply-coupon ads, producing nearly three times as many inquiries as the others. Said Steven, "It paved the way for decades of successful advertising which followed."

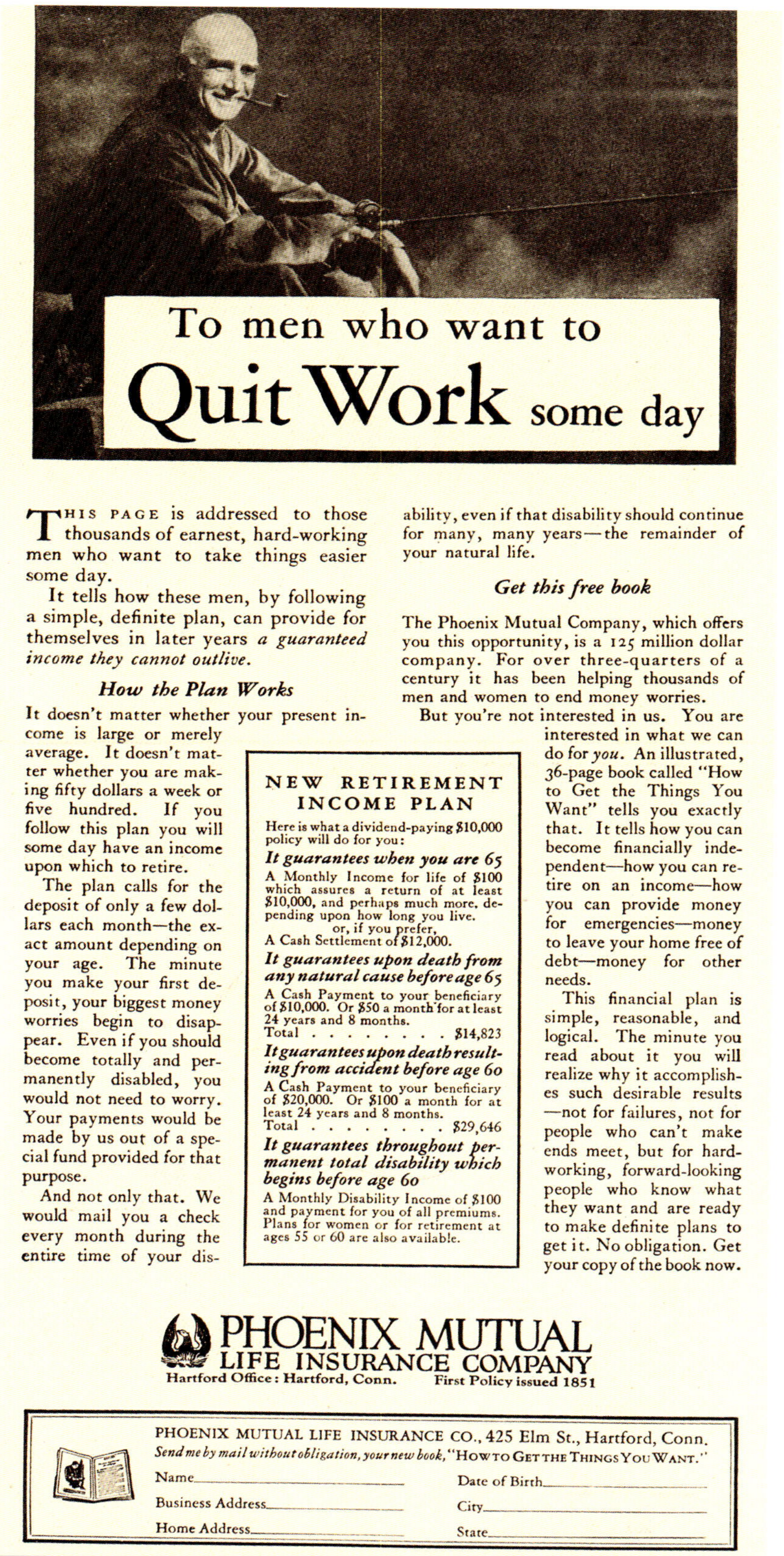

a slow turnaround starting in 1934, payrolls remained frozen. One Phoenix executive earned $26 per week from 1933 through 1941 — barely $1,400 per year — on which he supported his parents and five family members.

LEGENDARY ADVERTISING

In the 1920s, few insurers advertised at all, much less nationally. But with a 1923 advertisement in *Literary Digest*, Phoenix had begun turning itself into a household name on a par with Prudential or Metropolitan Life — companies with much larger sales forces. Its first ads focused on name recognition and the value of life insurance. Then, working with New York advertising agency Batten Barton Durstein & Osborne (BBD&O), Phoenix branched into ads that also produced enormous sales and made advertising history.

An advertisement featuring a fisherman, first used early in 1929, embodied the image of Phoenix as "the retirement income company." The basic formula of this ad — headline, text and reply coupon to send back to the company — was so potent as to require little alteration even into the 1950s. While the Depression made retirement income a harder sell, it also made financial security an even more coveted goal. BBD&O's copywriter, the legendary John Caples, simply adjusted the message for the times. "It makes no difference if your carefully laid plans for saving have been upset by the Depression," he wrote in 1932. "It makes no difference if you are worth half as much today as you were in 1929…." A campaign for working women promised a glimpse of eventual leisure in headlines like this one: "Just Wait 'Til I'm 60."

Such reassuring and upbeat words drew inquiries even in the leanest years. Furthermore, the message retained its power after President Franklin D. Roosevelt signed the original Social Security Act in 1935. Phoenix's retirement income ads spoke loud and clear to hardworking people who viewed Social Security and pensions, if any, as mere supplements to their own retirement investments (an outlook that would emerge again in the 1990s). C. Russell Noyes, who joined Phoenix's advertising department as a young assistant in 1930 and retired in 1972 as vice president of public relations, was in the thick of it all.

Advertising and direct mail always had to prove themselves. Though the company had different chairmen during this time — actuary Welch, president from 1924 to 1935; accountant Arthur M. Collens, president from 1935 to –1948; and lawyer Benjamin L. Holland, president from 1948 to 1961 — the opinion coming from the chairman's office was the same: "he didn't like advertising; he thought it was a lot of money to be spending. And with the New York ad agency, it was," Noyes says. But Phoenix and BBD&O took a scientific approach and tracked results so rigorously that even the sternest actuary was impressed.

By constantly testing, Phoenix learned precisely what made people read those ads and mail in their name and address on those coupons. Placement had to be "front-of-book," on a right-hand page. Headlines worked better above rather than below photos. Photos pulled better than artwork, and depictions of "leisure hobbies" — like fishing — trumped "working hobbies" like woodworking. The highest responses came in March, when income taxes loomed. The best magazines were *Life*, *Holiday*, *Coronet* and others reaching the target audience of middle-class men age 35 and up.

Although the ads were classics of direct response, Phoenix never sold direct. Agents were the link — and if they couldn't sell a retirement income policy ("an expensive product," according to Noyes), often they sold a basic life product. The more inquiries they converted, the more leads they received, according to a system carefully

Our Daily Bread

Just as the kitchen is the heart of the house, company cafeterias were centers of sustenance and friendship. Lunches were subsidized, as they are today, a benefit especially welcomed back when salaries were less competitive.

Phoenix started with two cafeterias — a big one for the women, a smaller adjunct for the men. Sex segregation broke down after World War II, while the custom of racial segregation disappeared in the 1950s. Both were aided by the space crunch at 79 Elm Street. Retirees fondly remember rushing down to the "caf" for coffee break when the 10 a.m. bell rang. Lunchtime got so crowded that staggered shifts became necessary.

Home Life's lunchroom had an in-house rival in the form of a Longchamps Restaurant in the lobby. But most employees opted for the company facility, which was air-conditioned at great expense in 1957. It doubled as a lounge that hosted more than a few intense bridge games.

Tastes have changed…except for desserts:

Phoenix's 1952 Favorites

Roast Beef
Chicken Pie
French-Fried Shrimp
Egg Casserole
Deviled Eggs
Chocolate Chip Cake

On the Menu in 2001

Top Your Own Burger
Chicken Francaise
Shrimp Sizzling Salad
Soft Tacos
Pizza
Chocolate Chip Cake

This photo shows lunchtime at Phoenix in the early 1940s. Retiree Dorothy Lagassey recalls: "We had a pastry cook so good that when Friday came, we were looking to buy whatever was left over."

Home Life presidents gathered for an executive dinner: Ethelbert I. Low and James A. Fulton are third and fourth from left; William P. Worthington is second from right. Fulton and Worthington collaborated on Planned Estates, an innovative marketing effort that transformed the industry.

worked out by Noyes and agency managers. "These leads had quite a reputation out in the field," he explains. "I was a very popular guy." The ads were more than "very popular." They were a Phoenix bedrock that eventually yielded an astounding $500 million in sales.

PLANNED ESTATES

Home Life also forged an industry benchmark in the crucible of the Depression. In May 1933, President Fulton launched Planned Estates. The brainchild of William P. Worthington, a dynamic young assistant superintendent of agencies recruited by Fulton, Planned Estates was a marketing program that became the very fabric of the company's culture. Decades ahead of its time, it turned agents into financial advisors.

"Bill was quite a guy," according to Jack Langdon, former senior vice president of sales, who came up through the ranks at Home Life. Every few Sundays, Worthington would invite Langdon and other young agents to his home "just to talk philosophy. Bill used to brag he only went to sixth grade. I don't know how he came up with the idea [of Planned Estates], but he believed in it very strongly. He could really, really motivate you."

What motivated Fulton and Worthington, in fact, was their desire to put agents on a professional footing. "So long as life insurance men are wandering around aimlessly, seeing people once and then forgetting them, the business can have little professional aspect," explained the agent training literature. "Contrast that with the intelligent servicing of a group of people by one man. This...puts you in the same class with the doctor or the lawyer. A lawyer or a doctor does not build his practice overnight. You too must start. Get out your card file and see that it has a place for five hundred cards...."

Those 500 cards represented 500 people who needed life insurance, were insurable and had the earning power to pay for it. Service by agents started with a fact-finding interview during which potential clients discussed their situation and identified their assets. Agents studied this information and returned with a Planned Estates chart, which blueprinted family needs and policy options to meet them. The chart covered 17 financial checkpoints, a comprehensive analysis for its day. In essence, it was surprisingly like today's computerized financial planning documents. Products were also ahead of their time in sophistication. Families could choose from policies and trusts that covered mortgage repayment, college funds, tax funds and more.

Above all, Home Life trained its agents in the fundamental conviction that their job was to "find problems to solve, not prospects to sell." Successful salespeople in all fields had always used this low-pressure, professional approach. The genius of Planned Estates was to codify it.

Planned Estates was widely copied. (Phoenix's versions, developed after World War II, were called "Personal Plan Service" and "Total Analytical Service.") Companies that committed to a similar approach reaped similar rewards: Higher sales — for decades, the typical Home Life policy purchase was usually twice the industry average — lower overhead and lower overall policy costs. "Fifty-odd years later, Planned Estates is still the cornerstone for our client building system," says John H. Langdon, co-manager of Phoenix's East Hanover, New Jersey, agency and the son of Home Life's Jack Langdon. "That's conviction."

As president from 1935 to 1948, Arthur M. Collens shepherded Phoenix through the end of the Depression and World War II. Under his leadership, the company achieved $1 billion of life insurance in force.

WAR YEARS

As the country entered World War II late in 1941, Phoenix and Home Life were on firm footing. Both had survived the Depression and were prospering under steady leadership. While Phoenix's Arthur Collens had a lower industry profile than Home Life's James Fulton did, he was a prudent businessman and company steward. Mainly the companies had to contend with reduced ranks, because so many employees went off to war. The companies generously paid their salaries on a percentage basis and promised to hold their jobs. Those on the home front anxiously followed their friends' progress and picked up the slack. The Phoenix Mutual Club was typical in suspending its usual roster of fun — bond drives and air raid training replaced picnics, sports and plays.

Having always invested in government securities, both companies naturally invested in government war bonds. To be able to say that money paid in premiums would support the war effort was a powerful sales tool. Some competitors, in fact, made it a central sales point — but not Home Life or Phoenix. The argument that "everybody else does it" rarely swayed these reliably conservative companies. In a speech to agents, Fulton plainly explained:

"It would be simple for a company to announce that an amount equivalent to every dollar of premiums on new business sold would be invested in War Bonds. Possibly that might give you a temporary lift

Home Life helped its policyholders track the whereabouts of their loved ones serving in World War II. Mildred McCourt and Richard Morse were among many Home Lifers who proudly enlisted; both Home Life and Phoenix provided generous allowances to salaried employees during their military stints.

"I Didn't Think I Should Ever Fuss"

William Hampton joined Phoenix in 1949 on the recommendation of his cousin, Homer Coleman, who was the company's doorman at 79 Elm Street in Hartford. Hampton worked as an elevator operator at the old building, then moved into administrative services data processing until retiring in 1975.

"I wanted a steady job," Hampton recalled at age 89. "I didn't like the pay" — Phoenix salaries were not high, regardless of race — "but it was steady work, rain or shine, hot or cold. I didn't think I should ever fuss." Hampton and his coworkers sometimes did odd jobs for other companies on Bushnell Park to supplement their wages. Their supervisor gave his tacit approval.

In Bill Hampton's heyday, Phoenix and other companies reflected the segregation of the United States at large. Certainly blacks faced exclusionary customs: at Phoenix they did not attend the annual country club picnics, although Hampton sometimes went as a cook, and black men traditionally ate after white men in the men's cafeteria at 79 Elm Street. (Women ate in a separate cafeteria, and there were no black women employees at all until the late 1950s.) Looking back, Hampton didn't dwell on this: "If you work with a group long enough, if you like yourself and the other people, you're going to blend in."

Bill Hampton is pictured in 1999. He says of his 26 years at Phoenix, "It was like a big family."

An experienced cook, Hampton became Phoenix's presidential chef, catering monthly executive lunches and other events. His work so impressed the contractors who ran the company's cafeterias in the 1950s that they tried to hire him away to work elsewhere. But loyalty won out: "Something grows on you. Money isn't everything." Hampton preferred "the good treatment, the friends and the job" at Phoenix, which, through the 26 years of his employ, enabled him to finish high school, buy a home in Hartford and send his children to college.

From the vantage point of today, it is clear that Phoenix (like American society at large) has come a long way on all matters involving diversity. The company's strong commitment to recruiting and promoting minorities and women is part of the larger story told in the next chapter.

but when you analyze it you would realize it did not mean anything.... As a minimum, an amount equal to our increase in assets will be directly invested in War Bonds. That may not sound as dramatic, but it is honest and it is genuine. The normal business of the country must go on.... To convert the entire investments [of life insurers] into government securities would produce disorganization and chaos."

The "good war" against Adolf Hitler and his allies was good for business. Home Life succinctly reminded agency staffs: "Men are working — money is plentiful — let's all redouble our efforts to *get the Cash.*" The general public didn't need much convincing; they went for ordinary life policies with high death benefits. Soldiers and would-be soldiers were a tougher sell. Standard underwriting practices specifically excluded coverage for death by war and even aviation. And the U.S. government was a powerful competitor, offering $10,000 of low-cost coverage against war hazards

Direct Mail

From the 1920s to the 1950s, Phoenix supplemented its advertising with hundreds of thousands of prospecting letters. Respondents received a free memo book or set of pencils — personalized on a gold foil-stamping machine at Phoenix — as well as an agent call. Some 400 replies per week poured in, requiring an evening shift of employees whose goal was to answer each letter within a day. In 1952, the company newsletter estimated that "for some years now roughly 45 percent of our total company business has been sold to people who have received these letters."

E. B. White, famed contributor to the *New Yorker* and the author of *Elements of Style*, *Charlotte's Web* and other classic books, answered his letter from Phoenix with a poem.

Memo for an Unclaimed Pad
No. HP618389C
THE PHOENIX MUTUAL LIFE INSURANCE COMPANY is reserving a genuine two-tone lambskin desk or pocket memorandum pad, "Things to do Today," for E. B. White, whose name will be embossed upon it in gold. It will be forwarded at once upon receipt of this card at the Home Office.

While years, like clocks, run slowly down,
And love lies curled in locket,
This patient pad in Hartford town
Awaits my desk or pocket.

This lovely, lambskin, two-tone pad
Whose pages are construable,
Promising what the Phoenix had,
To make my dust renewable.

This pad that shows at last a plan
By which, when I retire,
I'll have what Phoenix says I can
And things that I desire:

Money with which to do the things
And get the things I want,
And safety that this money brings
For son and wife and aunt.

Ah, lovely pad! Ah, lambskin pad!
Fashioned of genuine leather!
The only things I want I've had:
True love, and change of weather,

And one conviction, strong since birth,
Which still I find incurable:
That none was ever born to earth
Whose life was quite insurable.

No pad called "Things to do Today,"
Though two-toned and refillable,
Could make me anything but fey,
Or render me unkillable,

And though cold comfort for mine heirs,
Yet comfort let it be,
That never were a day's affairs
Predictable for me.

And let who finds the comfort cold
Be never made less sad
To find my name embossed in gold
Upon a lambskin pad.

under the hastily created National Service Life Insurance plan.

Fortunately, military personnel could place $10,000 of any existing insurance under the government premium guarantee plan. Alert agents handled the paperwork and thus headed off policy surrenders. They also pointed out other advantages of private insurance, like loan collateral value and broader conversion options. As a last resort, agency managers urged producers to resort to this visceral sales message to soldiers' parents or spouses: "He may be uninsurable when he returns, and while dollars will buy almost anything, the one thing they can never buy is insurability."

Home Life faced a vexing wartime problem when the federal government introduced wage controls in 1944 to forestall inflation. Since the birth of Planned Estates, trainees and field underwriters had received salaries and retirement benefits as well as production incentives — another industry first. The war had already thinned Home Life's sales ranks; suddenly remaining agents were hit with a salary ceiling of $5,000. Company lawyers doggedly filed Applications for Approval of Salary Adjustment to the U.S. Treasury Department. After almost a year's worth of negative rulings and appeals, Uncle Sam relented. The exemption allowed Home Life agents to earn up to $1,500 per month — at a time when home office vice presidents made about $200 per month — and many did.

BOOM TIMES

The postwar era was a boom time for America and for life insurers. Money flowed freely into new housing, new businesses and expanding industries. Yesterday's soldiers were today's new dads and moms, eager to protect their growing families with insurance. Inflation and higher taxes were a worry, but investments and salaries more than kept pace.

This super-heated economy worried Phoenix. So did America's new consumerism and the post-war government programs that picked up where FDR's New Deal had left off. With materialism and the cost of living on the rise, would Americans put money into savings — and life insurance? The 1949 year-end letter to policyholders by Phoenix's Chairman Collens and President Holland stated: "In these days of heavy spending by government…there have grown up so many pressures which discourage individual thrift. It is self-evident that security for our people can be obtained only by the conservation of wealth produced — and not by wealth consumed." The tone is oddly subdued for a company that had achieved $1 billion of life insurance in force the year before. (Home Life would reach this benchmark in 1952.)

Holland's rise to the Phoenix presidency in 1948 is a curious sidelight. He was a logical candidate, being general counsel in a company that has always valued legal talent. But his selection also sent an unwelcome message to 33-year company veteran D. Gordon Hunter, who desperately wanted to be president. Son-in-law of the revered Winslow Russell, the colorful "Colonel" Hunter — who earned his title in the Connecticut National Guard — was a brilliant superintendent of agencies. When "Ben Holland [became president], that just about killed the Colonel. He started holding [executive] meetings at his home in Farmington to discuss what a lousy president we had," recalls Russell Noyes. "We all felt this was really below our company. Holland was our President and we were devoted to him." The meetings eventually stopped, and Hunter became a West Hartford real estate mogul while continuing at Phoenix.

Leaders at Home Life shared some of Phoenix's postwar concerns, especially about consumer expectations and the dangers of inflation. The company refused to project dividends, for instance. "We have no crystal ball," Fulton sternly told field underwriters who clamored for such projections. "Whether it was good or bad for business, our course would be the same. Our experience is that the intelligent buyer prefers to deal with facts and not guesses." Producers complained but kept producing. Thanks to the brilliance of the Planned Estates strategy and the rising affluence of its customers, Home Life in 1948 could boast the highest average policy sale of all New York-licensed insurers — $14,139. Emphasizing class over mass marketing, it was a David to such Goliaths as Metropolitan Life, New York Life and the Equitable.

BRANCHING OUT

Home Life leaders also could be mavericks. Brilliantly, they moved the company into group insurance in 1949 — just as America's workers were starting to demand benefits such as substantial pensions and major medical coverage. By 1950, the sales force had a portfolio of new products to sell to employers and unions. For ambitious field underwriters like John A. Packal, CLU, ChFC, the expansion was a gold mine. A Cleveland career agent today, Packal sold Home Life's first group case, covering 1,800 employees of the National Advisory Committee for Aeronautics, which later became NASA. Forty years later, the policy, serviced by Phoenix Home Life, included more than 60,000 NASA employees and their dependents. As a result of his NASA contacts, Packal sold nearly 2,000 additional individual policies over the decades.

The death of President Fulton in 1950 shook Home Life. One of his last acts had been to testify before a Congressional committee investigating life insurance "monopolies." Although his own company was of medium size, Fulton spoke eloquently in favor of free enterprise and against any

Following the first manned voyage to the moon in 1969, NASA's Apollo 11 astronauts paraded along Broadway's "Canyon of Heroes" and past the Home Life building. The event was especially significant because NASA was a Home Life group client.

Insurance Girls

Insurance was a woman's world — sort of. "Insurance girls," as female employees were known, dominated as clerks, stenographers, secretaries and agency cashiers for decades. Some became supervisors, but few moved into management or sales until the 1970s.

As early as the 1920s, however, Phoenix sought to recruit and train women agents. "Miss Elizabeth C. Adams of the Cleveland Agency has earned the honor of establishing the first Women's branch that this Company has ever set up," the *Field* reported in September 1924. "She will have full opportunity to bring a type of woman similar to herself into her organization in a way that she and the officers of this Company have long wanted to see." Adams's efforts seem to have been isolated, but the Cleveland agency regularly ranked in the top 20 in subsequent years, suggesting that her contribution was notable.

Another pioneer was Dorothy C. Tennett, Phoenix's first woman officer. She joined the company as a clerk in the Providence agency in 1930, then worked as a cashier and supervisor in the midwest. After World War II she set up agencies nationwide, virtually living on the road in an era when women business travelers were rare. Tennett returned to Hartford in 1957 as manager of the personnel division and later director of personnel.

Impressions Through the Decades

Emma Metzler, Home Life policy renewal, on the 1920s:

"I went home and bawled my eyes out [after being called a foreigner by another new employee]. 'I'm not going back Monday,' I told my mother. I went back Monday and stayed for 42 years. I never liked to miss any days. Home Life became my home away from home."

Charlotte Noble, Phoenix agency department, on the 1930s:

"It was fun. But you were scared back then. Miss Sexton, in personnel, would stand behind the files and look at you. One day, she came along and slapped me on the back and said 'get your eyes examined!' when I didn't pull a file fast enough."

Esther Yules, Phoenix policy issue and auditing, on the 1940s:

"I went from the very bottom up, running, putting the policies together. We had runners bringing the work from desk to desk, department to department, division to division. It was a sociable place with hard work. It was family. From the day I started, I was working overtime. I would finish at 7 p.m., freshen up and take the bus to the social places."

Dorothy Lagassey, Phoenix administration, on the 1950s:

"The women I worked with in stenographic were like a family. Everybody took care of the other guy. We did work from all over the building. I did Ediphone work and copied. You typed everything that came through, big-figure jobs that they now put on computers. There were about 30 of us and maybe 10 or 15 on the night shift."

"The Average Insurance Girl," Circa 1953

In 1952, The Travelers Insurance Company profiled "the average insurance girl." Both Phoenix and Home Life found The Travelers survey sufficiently representative of their own female employees to feature it in their newsletters. Some highlights:

- Average age 31
- High school graduate with one year of business school or two years of college
- Roughly eight and one-half years of clerical or secretarial experience
- Single, "though one in four is wed"
- Lives with parents
- Pays $20 week in board, "one-third of her gross pay"
- Saves $425 per year
- Spends $300 per year on clothes
- "Goals: new car, vacation, marriage"

From Secret Marriages to Family-Friendly Practices

Once upon a time, all "insurance girls" were single. Until World War II, Phoenix, Home Life and most corporate employers did not hire married women and promptly fired those who wed. "In those days, they were seen as taking the bread out of some family's mouth," explains retiree Ed Richardson.

A woman could keep her job, of course, by keeping her marriage secret. The practice was not uncommon. Richardson recalled getting a Christmas card from a coworker who had retired after years at Phoenix. "The card had a different name on it…her secret married name. We didn't know who it was at first. She had been married throughout her career here and nobody ever knew it."

The rules changed when the core of the male workforce entered military service during World War II. "Then women could work and be married, but if you got pregnant, you had to leave at your sixth month," says Charlotte Noble, a retired Phoenix agency supervisor who was in that position herself in 1942.

Barriers continued to drop. Phoenix encouraged Josephine Melusky, a Phoenix employee since 1941, to work part-time while she raised her children from 1947 to 1962. A secretary at that time, Melusky still works in Phoenix's law department. When President

A sea of Phoenix stenographers at work in 1930. In that era, most female employees joined insurance companies straight from high school. Until World War II, industry practice was to hire single women only.

Dona D. Young graduated from law school in 1980, she chose Phoenix over a law firm because she wanted an employer who would value equally her ambitions for a career and a family. Obviously, she came to the right place. "My first promotion in the law department came when I was pregnant with my first child," says Young. "My second promotion, into reinsurance, came when I was pregnant with my second. My husband and I wondered if I would have to keep having babies to get promoted at that point."

In fact, in 1988, Young had just discovered she was pregnant with her third child when she learned she would be named general counsel at an upcoming board meeting. She quickly told the management and board about her pregnancy so that they might reconsider the offer if they so wished. They congratulated her warmly and proceeded without hesitation to promote her. When Young was named company president in February 2000, the press noted that her appointment reflected "Phoenix's creed that it is possible to blend work and family and still make it to the top," as the *Hartford Courant's* Matthew Lubanko put it.

Phoenix is renowned as a family-friendly company. *Working Mother* magazine has named it one of America's "100 Best Companies for Working Mothers" 10 out of the past 11 years, citing such criteria as opportunities for women to advance, child care support, and benefits such as job-protected leave for childbirth, flexible hours and job sharing.

AT THE DESK OF

Margaret Murphy

First job at Phoenix:
Mail Clerk, 1921

Retired as:
Accounting and Treasury Assistant, 1963

Remembered for:
Her steel-trap mind. Before computers existed, Murphy prepared Annual Financial Statements for each state where Phoenix did business, "all mentally and by hand."

Unusual background:
Joined Phoenix at age 14 to help support the family after her father's death. Always good at math and familiar with insurance accounting from her dad's work at John Hancock.

Memories of Phoenix:
"You could get an education there. I did. We women employees were scared of Miss Sexton in Personnel. But one time after she scared us, we heard her laughing. After that I was never afraid of her. I had very good times at Phoenix."

action aimed at diminishing bigger companies. Here, as elsewhere, he proved as influential as his predecessors during the Armstrong Investigation had been. By 1951, regulators would remove key restrictions and allow insurance companies to underwrite additional lines. William J. Cameron, the company's top actuary, succeeded Fulton briefly. But Home Life was always most comfortable with a sales executive at the top, and so in 1953, the board elevated William P. Worthington, the genius behind Planned Estates, to the presidency.

Phoenix's first growth spurt came on the individual front. It knew its years as "the retirement income company" were numbered. The cost of living (and retiring) continued to skyrocket, slowed only by artificial wage and price controls in effect during the Korean War. As the 1950s progressed, Phoenix's classic ads drew satire from sources as diverse as the *New Yorker* and *Mad* magazine. The company wisely turned its attention to new products, involving underwriters and actuaries in the accelerated activity. "It was an energetic time," says John Gummere, FSA, who joined Phoenix as a young actuary in 1949 and would eventually rise to become chairman. Many employees were back from World War II and eager, even restless, to move the company forward.

Soon Phoenix agents were offering "living benefits" for individuals and families — estate conservation, whole family/one premium plans, major medical coverage, college savings policies, mortgage protection and more. As fast as the new products emerged, the sales force sold them even faster. Purchases of new products skyrocketed by 11 percent in 1953, 17 percent in 1955 and 33 percent in 1956. On November 3, 1958, Phoenix reached the milestone of $2 billion of life insurance in force. "Everyone enjoyed a prime rib banquet in the cafeteria," reported the *Elm Log*, the company's newsletter.

Although agents barely needed a boost, they got a big one when Phoenix pioneered lower premiums for women in 1955. The reasons were actuarial rather than promotional: The new rates simply reflected women's longer life spans. But the notion that women could slice three years from their insurance age tickled the press. Phoenix's move inspired national headlines such as "Women Are Cheaper?" and "Women Licensed to Fib," as well as this verse in New Jersey's *Trenton Times:*

Letting a lady cut three years
Is a splendid policy
Provided you know the age from which
She should subtract the three.

"THE GIANT STIRRED"

Phoenix also expanded by aggressively pursuing new distribution channels. In 1954, it had entered the brokerage field, a rather radical move for a small mutual insurer. The board even hired an outsider, James Tapp, to build the new brokerage organization. According to Noyes and other executives of the time, these were significant turning points.

Brokerage — or life wholesaling — is essentially the practice of having other companies sell *your* company's products. Most insurers, in those days, preferred to "keep business in the family." Brokerage drove Phoenix to come up with unique products — ones that would give representatives of other companies a reason to sell Phoenix policies. This is partly why Phoenix became the first company to pioneer the aforementioned innovations, such as reducing premiums for women. Gradually the entire industry adopted these innovations. But back when companies took years rather than months to copy each other's products — partly because technology wasn't advanced, and partly because business was simply more "gentlemanly" — Phoenix's early innovations gave it a decided edge as well as forward momentum.

"The hiring of Jim Tapp to head brokerage was the beginning of bringing people in from the outside to do a really big job. For years, the company was a sleeping giant. The giant stirred," Noyes says. The giant also profited handsomely from the move. Within 10 years, brokerage would grow to 30 percent of all company business. (By the time of the Phoenix-Home Life merger, in 1992, the proportion was 50 percent.)

Success in brokerage paved the way for Phoenix's entry into group insurance. Group began in an alcove in the auditorium at 79 Elm Street in 1958, under the leadership of William Roth and Dennis F. Hardcastle, CLU, who had only been at the company for two years, as a sales supervisor. They recruited a field force of about 12 young agents, including Robert K. Griffin and John A. "Jack" Judge, who loyally served group for decades, both in the field and in management.

Most other insurers had gone into the group business earlier; Home Life, for example, had started some nine years before Phoenix did. "Being a Johnny-come-lately in group insurance," recalls Hardcastle, who later became company president, "we knew we had to do something different from the established industry. There were three ideas that did just this, and which were the basis of group's phenomenal growth within Phoenix."

The first two innovations came directly from Roth. Instead of writing basic health insurance, Phoenix instead cooperated with Blue Cross/Blue Shield organizations throughout the country to provide major medical insurance over their basic coverages. "We received cooperation to the point where many of our full-time group sales representatives were referred to us by Blue Cross," adds Hardcastle. "One was our first full-timer, Gene Christie of Kansas City, who later became our vice president of group sales."

Under Roth, Phoenix also centralized group service in the home office, rather than taking the traditional decentralized approach. "The success and acceptance of this program laid the groundwork for doing the same in individual insurance years later," Hardcastle points out. He credits New York group sales manager James Mazzeo for pioneering the concept of multiple employer trusts, also called "baby groups," which allowed small businesses to band together by industry for advantageous rates. Like other Phoenix innovations, this one soon became an industry standard.

Thanks to these creative tactics, Phoenix's group business became a nimble and growing contender. "After multiple employer trusts, we really took off," Hardcastle says. Within a year, the new operation had generated so much business that its home office staff filled the auditorium and spilled into the cafeteria for additional workspace.

Clearly, like so many American families outgrowing their starter homes, Phoenix needed more space. In 1952, the company purchased 58 acres of West Hartford farmland for new suburban headquarters. (Records show that a building department worker was dispatched from Hartford to plow and hay the land regularly; presumably Phoenix sold the hay.) Home Life was also cramped for space, despite having bought and spread into the adjoining skyscraper at 253 Broadway in 1947. Yet both companies managed to stay put for a while. Data processing machines, then in their infancy, helped Phoenix hold the line on hiring.

Life insurers had always embraced automation, from the Hollerith statistical calculators of the early twentieth century to the various Dictaphone devices used by fleets of stenographers. Starting in the 1950s, each year ushered in new miracles, such as the IBM Electronic Calculating Punch. The calculator was powered by 1,200 tubes, which figured dividend balances and handled premium billing. In addition, the Swift Bond Coupon Clipper's automated blades did in half a day what had taken 14 people with scissors a full day to do, and the IBM 650 saved Phoenix staffers from posting 14,000 monthly mortgage payments by hand.

Phoenix in particular was quick to invest in these money-saving technologies. Under Senior Vice President Eric Franzen and early technology mavens Al Botters and Glenden J. Dunlap, it even reorganized various policy, claims and agent services activities into one insurance service department designed around data processing. This was the company's first real reorganization, guided by the corporate consultants McKinsey & Company, and it set a pattern for later efforts. "We like to do things ourselves," explains Carl T. Chadburn, CLU, executive vice president. "If we do use consultants, usually we have them look over our shoulders and give us a general model to work with, but then we do the work ourselves."

"BIGGER THINKING"

Turning 100 years old in 1951 and 1960, respectively, Phoenix and Home Life marked the anniversaries in their own styles. Phoenix held an open house for employees' families and a sports day at the Hartford Golf Club. Home Life staged a lavish, black-tie gala at the Waldorf-Astoria Hotel. These old-line companies deserved to celebrate. They had diversified and kept themselves vital. Business was better than ever. But farsighted leaders took nothing for granted.

In a prescient speech, Worthington predicted the 1960s would be "the decade of seconds": Americans would buy second cars, second homes, second telephones and TV sets. Would families double their life insurance protection as well?

Not with mutual funds competing for their money and term insurance encroaching on traditional products, he argued. If the postwar era had stirred the sleeping giants, the immediate future demanded "if not *new* concepts of the overall job of selling life insurance services, certainly far bigger thinking than we've been accustomed to."

Phoenix was already thinking bigger. It had sold the farmland in West Hartford and commissioned a revolutionary new Hartford headquarters literally unlike any other building in the world. Home Life would look toward a new president — its first who was not home-grown — and vigorous expansion of its formidable Planned Estates empire.

Phoenix treated its employees to a 100th anniversary picnic and sports day at the Hartford Golf Club in 1951. Home Life commemorated its 1960 centennial with an informal gathering in City Hall Park (left) and a black-tie dinner at the Waldorf-Astoria Hotel.

82
81
79
78
68
69
70

CHAPTER FOUR

1963-1991

Comfort Zone to Combat Zone

The 1960s were fun because we were always coming up with something new. The 1970s were fun because we were always increasing dividends. Then came the 1980s — turbulent. Dealing with them was like digesting an elephant.

— John Gummere, retired chairman, CEO and president, Phoenix

Ship Shape: Setting the Record Straight

The exact shape of Phoenix's two-sided "boat building" was the subject of lively debate, as shown by this excerpted letter and editor's reply. It appeared on September 12, 1977, in Phoenix's employee newsletter, then called the *Communicator*.

To the Editor:
While I was in college and working part-time for Phoenix I often heard the assertion that the building's ship shape was technically that of a lenticular hyperboloid. But, the recent newspaper clipping which appeared on the bulletin board outside the cafeteria has inspired me to speak out in defense of the building: assertions to the contrary notwithstanding, the Phoenix tower definitely is not football-shaped! Now, before confusion sets in, perhaps I should point out that a lenticular hyperboloid more closely resembles a football than it does the Phoenix....

The Phoenix tower is actually an elliptic lenticular cylinder — or more precisely, a right elliptic lenticular cylinder. Any surface (the tower) traced by a straight line moving parallel to a fixed straight line (say, one of the elevator shafts or the vertical line at the bow or stern) and intersecting a fixed curve (the line around the base of the tower) is by definition a cylinder. The lenticular (i.e., biconvex) shape of the fixed curve forming the base of the surface determines the type of cylinder; since each side of the lenticular curve is essentially a portion of the ellipse (with semi-major and semi-minor axes of approximately 219 ft. and 188 ft., respectively), we have an elliptic lenticular cylinder. The tower is a right cylinder because, happily enough, the walls are perpendicular to the floors....

It is no doubt too late to ask for our money back or to request a change in the architect's plans, so I would suggest an alternative: let us recognize that the tower is a cylinder — a fancy cylinder, but a cylinder nonetheless. The layman will scarcely note the difference, and perhaps the burial of the hyperboloid myth will help should we ever attempt to sell insurance to the American Mathematical Association.
Fred Sawyer
Group Actuarial

Editor's Reply: "...or just calling it the 'boat building' is good, too. It saves time in explanations, and avoids any embarrassment from getting tongue-tied over 'elliptic lenticular cylinder!'"

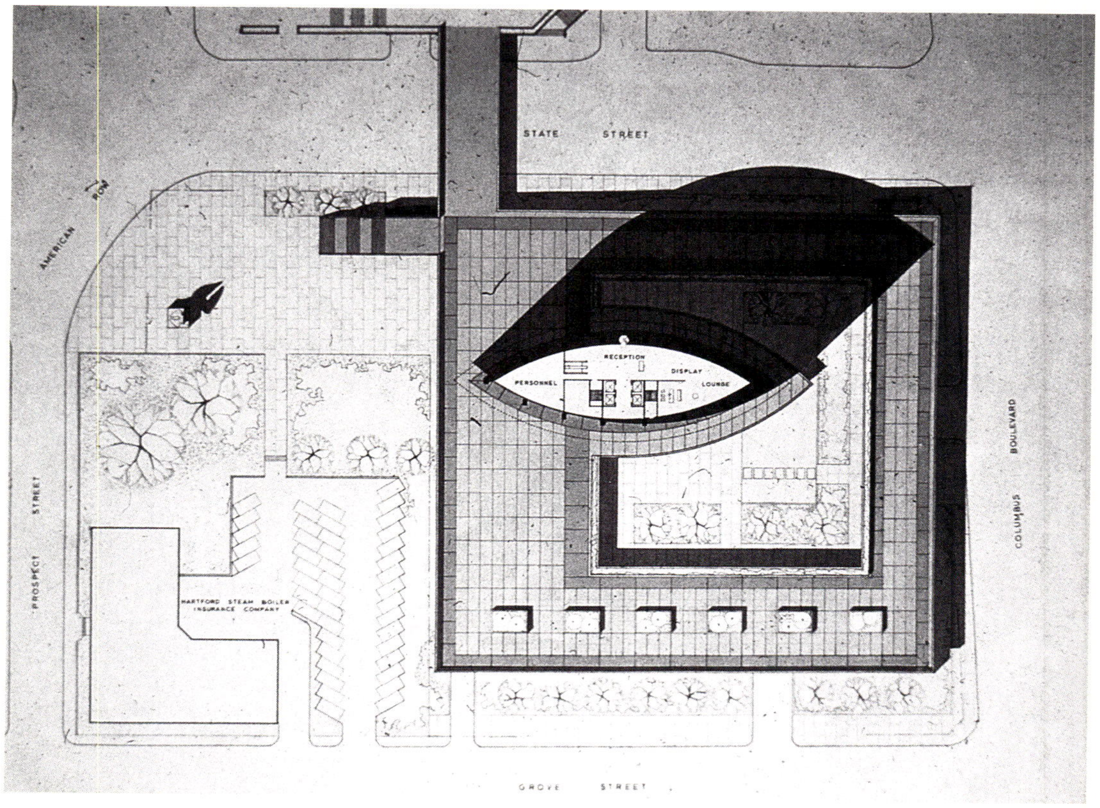

Designers assured employees that they didn't have to be wedge-shaped to fit into the "bow" and "stern" of the unique "Boat Building."

When the architects first unveiled the scale model of Phoenix's revolutionary headquarters — the world's only two-sided building — at a board meeting, President Holland said nothing. "He sat there for a very long time and let them sizzle," says John Gummere, recounting a company legend.

As Holland pondered the design that was so at odds with Phoenix's conservative image, he may have been thinking back to a conversation from a year or two before. "Phoenix had come out with its innovative high cash value policy and preferential rates for women," Gummere explains. "We had entered the brokerage market and were doing business like crazy. Holland was feeling very good because we were really causing ripples through the industry. And he was at lunch one day at the Hartford Club with a group. Sitting next to him was the CEO of Connecticut General (now CIGNA). Holland turned to him and said, 'I suppose we're providing some competition these days.' This man replied, 'Why, we never consider you to be competition.' Phoenix was competition-oriented, so to have that slap just energized us further."

One American Row, seen on page 58, cut a distinctive figure in the Hartford skyline. The unique building cost no more to construct than a conventional building, but was 82 percent more space-efficient. The architects overlooked no detail in their design.

EMBRACING THE UNCONVENTIONAL

Holland enthusiastically approved the unconventional architecture. So did Phoenix employees, who gathered at the Statler Hotel for a briefing. "When the artists' projection flashed on the screen, everybody stood up and clapped. We could not believe Phoenix would do anything like the boat building. It's still the most impressive building in Hartford. It changed the image of the company so markedly," recalls retiree Ed Richardson, who would be in charge of moving

Launching the Boat Building

January 1960:
Phoenix announces it will be part of Constitution Plaza.

February 1961:
Architectural plans are unveiled.

July 12, 1961:
The ground is broken by Chairman Benjamin Holland and Lynn Batty, Phoenix's newest policyholder.

June 28, 1962:
The framework is complete. Rhoda Haggard, the wife of Executive Vice President Paul Haggard, christens the "ship" at a topping-out ceremony.

November 24, 1963:
The official opening is postponed by the assassination of President John F. Kennedy.

December 2, 1963:
A brief dedication ceremony is held.

January 12, 1964:
An open house is held.

the offices from 79 Elm Street to One American Row on Constitution Plaza.

Executives at rival insurers could only have envied the attention and excitement generated by One American Row. Locally, the move won praise because it reflected Phoenix's commitment to downtown Hartford. Nationally and internationally, the building drew kudos for the innovative architecture of Harrison and Abramovitz, the same firm that designed the United Nations headquarters in New York.

For the grand opening, the company invited visitors from around the world. "We trained a group of guides and bought them uniforms," recalls C. Russell Noyes, retired vice president, public relations. One guide was Eileen Hollingsworth, Noyes's former public relations assistant.

"The opening event was going to be the last weekend in November 1963, then President Kennedy was assassinated," says Hollingsworth. "We were in the empty new building, practicing our tours, when the announcement came on Friday afternoon. I'll never forget it. We went back to Elm Street and had to send telegrams to everybody flying in [saying the event was cancelled]." A subdued dedication ceremony took place a week later, and the open house was rescheduled for January 1964. The building became a major draw. In the first year alone, 12,000 people toured it.

CAREFUL EXPANSION

Amid the growing social upheaval of the 1960s, and facing competitive inroads from mutual funds, Phoenix and Home Life moved ahead at a reasonable speed. Their respective presidents were Lyndes B. "Dan" Stone and J. Harry Wood. Stone, a company director since 1956, was a Yale-trained lawyer and investment specialist who strengthened Phoenix's already firm financial base.

Dennis Hardcastle, a sales and marketing executive who would eventually serve as president himself, calls Stone "the first president to open up the company...a very good president in that he encouraged other people to develop. He was genuinely interested in talent." Hardcastle elaborates: "Dan was quite happy, for instance, to let Robert T. Jackson [who would succeed Stone as president] take the initiative in product development at that time. Bob Jackson was his rising star. He was happy for me, too, to take the initiative in sales, so he didn't have to be up in the forefront all the time."

Wood, former head of the Life Insurance Agency Management Association, aimed to take Home Life's success even further. "Harry capitalized on Planned Estates and introduced good products at competitive rates," says William B. Wallace, CLU, ChFC, MSFS, who would succeed Wood as president almost 30 years later. "Harry also hired Leland Waggoner as chief marketing officer, and Lee was the best cheerleader a field force ever had. Harry energized us to take risks." In Wood's six years as president, Home Life's insurance in force grew from $2 billion to $5 billion.

In the 1960s, companies still had the luxury of

President Benjamin L. Holland and Lynn Batty, then Phoenix's newest policyholder, broke ground for the new home office on July 12, 1961. Stories about the building, and Holland's devotion to it, abound. Here's one that retired group executive Paul Hellenga liked to share — call it a Trojan Horse tale. "Why is our home office shaped like a boat?" a Phoenix agent once asked. "Because Ben Holland liked boats," he was told. "Too bad he didn't like horses," the agent quipped. "Then we could have pushed the building across the street on rollers and attacked the Travelers."

Phoenix ran a series of ads in the 1980s highlighting its achievement as "one of the lowest net cost companies in the business." While Ted Tansi, retired vice president, data processing and planning, consistently supported and encouraged new systems development at Phoenix, his negotiating skills ensured that the company met all of its computing needs at the lowest possible cost. Below, an artifact from a 1966 sales contest.

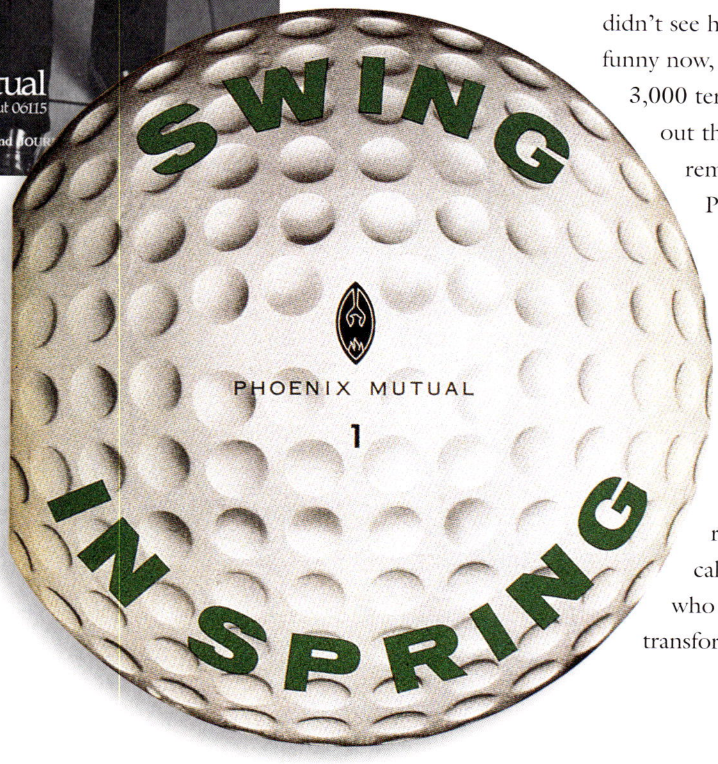

taking their time to decide on new directions. Individual life insurance remained the main focus, with many agents bettering themselves by earning Chartered Life Underwriter (CLU) and other industry designations. Group business continued to grow significantly at both companies: In 1967, Phoenix pioneered nonsmoker discounts for all life insurance products, an industry first that further demonstrated Phoenix's willingness to innovate. The move was seen as radical, but Home Life and most other competitors soon followed suit.

The mid-1960s were notable for Phoenix. The company made its first foray into reinsurance, which generated revenues with little increase in operating costs. Phoenix also created its own computerized policyholder service system called ServiData. Version I of this pioneering system was developed in conjunction with IBM by Phoenix's Glenden Dunlap and released in 1966. Version II, created by Glen Harris Jr. ("the most thorough man I ever met," says current chairman Robert W. Fiondella), went live in 1972. According to Harris, the "guiding administrative light" was Senior Vice President Eric Franzen. "Ric had this early vision of how to corral computers in an effective way," Harris says. "Phoenix beat everyone else to the gate." In fact, IBM adapted ServiData into a generic system used by Aetna and other insurers."

ServiData II went on line around the time Edward P. Hourihan Sr. joined the company. Hourihan, who retired as senior vice president, information systems, recalls: "I wrote a memo in 1972 recommending that we purchase 50 terminals. Ted Tansi and Al Botters, my bosses, didn't see how we could ever use so many. What's funny now, of course, is that there are probably 3,000 terminals out there." Hourihan points out that a modernized version of ServiData remains the technological foundation of Phoenix's individual insurance business, storing data on almost 450,000 policies.

Other bold moves came in this era. The personnel department, ably led for many years by Olin Budd and Dorothy Tennett (Phoenix's first woman officer), branched out from its traditional functions of payroll, benefits administration and clerical recruitment. William MacLachlan, who joined Phoenix in 1966, guided its transformation into a modern-day human

Flexible Hours: A Difficult Birth

Today many employees take flexible hours for granted. The people who championed the concept in the 1970s, however, had to fight for it.

Phoenix was one of the first companies in the country to embrace "flex time." William MacLachlan, former head of human resources, brought the idea to then-president Dennis Hardcastle, who was highly receptive. Flex time fit perfectly with his desire for increased decision-making by employees.

"Bill was very enlightened," Hardcastle says. "I presented his idea of flex time to the board of directors and was hooted down. 'Everyone is going to take advantage,' the old-timers warned." Rather defiantly, Hardcastle and MacLachlan put the new policy into effect — and found that it worked astoundingly well. In fact, absenteeism went down, because people who had to be an hour late no longer had to take a full sick day to do so.

"Flex time was one of many innovations, such as the eventual creation of our onsite child care facility in Enfield, that characterized Phoenix as an especially attractive employer," MacLachlan adds. "As was the case with flex time, not all of the innovations were easily adopted; some were even resisted. But they proved to be cost-effective and to help the company attract and retain a strong workforce."

The era of benign paternalism, symbolized by handwritten time sheets and bells that rang to start and end the workday, was clearly vanishing. Displaying a bit of his characteristically irreverent humor, Hardcastle adds: "Eventually even the old-timers accepted that people want to be treated like adults. More people than not want to do a good job. For one thing, it makes the time pass faster."

resources department that handled management recruitment and introduced a series of innovative programs such as flex time.

In 1968, Dennis Hardcastle separated brokerage from career agencies, setting the stage for the clearly defined distribution channels of the future. To enhance field training and home office communications, Phoenix became the first insurer with an in-house video production department.

Equally aggressive strategies on the investment side of the business — the legacy of Dan Stone and future president Robert T. Jackson, FSA, CLU — would help Phoenix weather difficult years to come. Phoenix staked its claim in the mutual fund business in 1968 with the creation of Phoenix Equity Planning Corporation (PEPCO), the forerunner of Phoenix Investment Partners (PXP). The force behind the PEPCO concept was Bob Jackson, then executive vice president. Launched under the leadership of Edward P. "Ted" Ward, a vice president for strategic development, PEPCO moved Phoenix into the world of mutual funds, just as they were approaching critical mass in the U.S. market. That was anathema to some agents and home office employees, who argued that mutual funds had been cutting into life insurance sales for years. Others immediately saw the advantage of adding equities to Phoenix's product line and allowing them to be sold through outside broker/dealers as well.

Characteristically, Phoenix gave the subsidiary ample time to prove itself. "PEPCO was a strategic development, not limited to mutual fund sales," says PXP chairman and CEO Philip R. McLoughlin, who joined PEPCO fresh from law school in 1971. "We did pension work, and new ideas were filtered through. It started as a loss leader, frankly, a way to concentrate some losses."

McLoughlin fondly recalls the early days — "a dozen or so employees, an incredibly collegial office" — when PEPCO acquired a fax machine. This exotic new technology permitted same-day mutual fund transactions. "You put the paper in a cylinder disk, dialed the number and waited four minutes for the page to transmit," McLoughlin chuckles. "Then we waited for the confirming fax back. More often than not, we'd have a fire. The motor would overheat in those eight minutes. We all stood around and watched, from Ted Ward on down. That also tells you how much business we had. One sale today! Wow! We'd run around the office and cheer."

Like other started-from-scratch subsidiaries, PEPCO grew by a combination of in-house initiatives and acquisitions. Its first major purchase was the investment advisory firm of John P. Chase Company of Boston, later named Phoenix Investment Counsel, Inc., in 1975. By the early 1980s, the firm had $325 million under management — a small fraction of the $60 billion under management in 2000, but a benchmark for its time. Traditionally strong in mortgages, Chase, as Phoenix Investment Counsel, also became a partner in numerous real estate developments. PEPCO also developed its own fund family, the Phoenix Series Fund.

These moves showed foresight. "Bob Jackson always positioned us," Bob Fiondella says. They also stimulated an expansion in staff and a much wider and more dynamic view of jobs.

As Phoenix expanded, its law department grew significantly. The executive who guided its growth was retired senior vice president and general counsel Hugh S. Campbell, who had been at Phoenix since 1933. "For decades, until Phoenix got into group insurance, just four attorneys handled all of the company's business — Hugh, Albert 'Bert' Saunders, Merritt Lane and myself," recalls retired senior vice president Richard P. Smith, who succeeded Campbell in 1973 as general counsel. "By the 1960s and 1970s, as we got into new areas, we grew to a staff of 40. Hugh knew what we needed and moved us along."

"Hugh was very much the professional lawyer," Dennis Hardcastle adds. "When you first met him, he could be intimidating. But when you got to know him, he was quite the opposite. Hugh was extremely encouraging toward new ventures. In fact, he had a characteristic that Bob Jackson had and that Bob Fiondella has — he was very open to diversity, both of ideas and personnel."

Indeed, the growth of the law department brought Bob Fiondella to Phoenix. He came on board in 1969, a young lawyer from Bristol, Connecticut, with a background in systems analysis and local politics. "They hired me on the investment side of the law department," says Fiondella. "Because I knew some data processing, because I was always onto new things, I gravitated toward corporate development. Early on, I was asked to computerize estate planning and develop the innovative product that is the forerunner of the variable annuity — all in my first three years. I was fortunate to have had a critical set of skills and background at an early age, at a time when over half the officers were within five years of retirement."

CHANGING IDENTITIES

While Phoenix was enlarging its focus beyond insurance, Home Life tried to provide a broader selection of insurance products. It introduced business insurance products and variable annuities. Shrewdly, it also targeted its traditional products to organizations of young professionals on the rise, such as the National Association of Residents and Interns. But some executives worried that their company, which they loved so much, was resting on its laurels. In Lee Waggoner's 1972 MBA case study on Home Life's challenges, this dedicated senior vice president described a field force blessed with brilliant agents but lacking in agency managers skilled enough to recruit and retain such agents. A crucial level was largely missing. "The word had spread to other companies that anyone wishing to take a good man from Home Life could do so," Waggoner lamented, "for Home Life would not put up much of a fight to hold him."

Just as Phoenix had shed its identity as the retirement income insurer, Home Life had to reinvent itself. The beloved and profitable Planned Estates concept was no longer enough, a painful realization. Waggoner's ironic observation: "Everyone wanted progress, but at times it appeared some did not want change." Gerard K. Rugger, an actuary and group sales executive, had succeeded Wood as president in 1969. In his own words, he aimed for "good, sustained, balanced growth" and "stayed out of every new venture that came down the pike."

With inflation rising in the 1970s, cost control was a necessity and a priority throughout Rugger's tenure; though some felt that it was carried too far. "Gerry was bright, hardworking and treated every dollar like it was his own," says Wallace. Such thriftiness extended to corporate improvements. Under Rugger — and his predecessor Wood as well — building maintenance and technology upgrades were put on hold.

Both companies worked to transform themselves without losing sight of their core businesses. Unlike Home Life, Phoenix continued to invest in data processing, which yielded efficiencies and permitted the design of more flexible products. "I remember writing programs for punched cards and how labor-intensive that was," recalls Robert Merritt, FSA, MAAA, an actuary still working part-time at Phoenix in 2001 at age 91. "A lot of the complexities in insurance products would not be possible without the financial expertise aided by computers."

Glen Harris offers the example of Ordinary Life Special (OLS), a popular policy with premiums that increased in steps over the first 10 years. Before computers, clerks had to pull individual punch cards from giant decks that contained about 500,000 cards each. They would remake each OLS card to reflect the following year's premium, then painstakingly refile the cards. "It's very likely the OLS product would have broken the back of the punch card system if computers hadn't come along and saved the day," says Harris.

Computers saved employees valuable time as they took over all the painstaking calculations required. Once, there had been dozens of "doers" and "checkers" at Phoenix, Home Life and every mutual insurer. They made all policy changes by hand, such as adding riders or reducing face amounts. "The doers did the work and the checkers checked the work," says Diana Allen, retired director of compliance. She joined the Phoenix actuarial department as a young "math doer" in 1968, shortly before technology began rendering such jobs obsolete. The computerization of policyholder services freed employees such as Allen for more creative work.

ARCHITECT OF THE MODERN PHOENIX

The driving force at Phoenix was now Bob Jackson, who became president in 1971 after 32 years at the company. "Brilliant" and "entrepreneurial" are the words most often used to describe this introverted actuary and lawyer. "Bob Jackson decided to become a lawyer in mid-life," Fiondella notes. "His wife didn't want him to be out four nights a week. He said, 'How about three?' She said okay. So he rotated cutting a different law class every week. This is the way his mind worked."

Instrumental in putting Phoenix into mutual funds, Jackson positioned the company in other new areas. Under his leadership, Phoenix added many subsidiaries. "His theory was that if you think you might need something 10 or 20 years down the road, you're better off positioning yourself now, with an investment you can tolerate," says Fiondella. "Jackson also broadened the company while keeping expenses down by hiring many young people. I was fortunate to be one of them."

Dennis Hardcastle credits Jackson with making Phoenix "less paternalistic" and allowing "decision-making to be passed farther down the line." Jackson had an exceptionally strong group of executives under him: Hardcastle at the marketing helm; John Gummere, who had risen through the actuarial ranks and moved into the top spot in underwriting; Arthur "Ed" Erickson, CLU, who headed actuarial operations and had other finance responsibilities; Bill Roth, the creator of the group business, who had taken on wider product development responsibilities; and Irving Wolfson, a relative newcomer to the company, who focused on investments and product planning. "The four of us, and later Irv Wolfson, were the legs of the stool, so to speak," Hardcastle says.

Wolfson exemplifies the changes that were taking shape at Phoenix in the early 1970s. Unlike the other "legs of the stool," he had spent his earlier career at another insurer, MassMutual. Recruited to bring fresh energy into product planning, Wolfson drew on his expertise in investments and pensions to move Phoenix ahead in those directions as well.

"Irv's contribution was that he reorganized our investments and made us more aggressive and effective," Bob Fiondella says. When Phoenix made its first move into the investment business by buying John P. Chase Company, a Boston asset management firm, Wolfson negotiated the deal. It was the very beginning of the company reinventing itself as a money manager.

"If we hadn't reoriented our investment operations under Irv, we probably would not have gradually built the capability to be money managers," adds Fiondella, who was Phoenix's in-house lawyer on the John P. Chase deal. Wolfson also headed the task force that paved the way for Phoenix's entry into reinsurance and property-casualty insurance. All five "legs of the stool" figured vitally in Phoenix's future. Hardcastle eventually became president; Gummere became president, CEO and chairman. Roth developed sophisticated, tax-advantaged products and served as executive vice president for strategic development. Wolfson became chief investment officer before his untimely death. Erickson, who also perished

Robert T. Jackson headed Phoenix from 1971 until his death in 1983. Introverted in personality but bold in business vision, he moved the company forward in new directions.

Another Phoenix first: toll-free centralized policyholder service, pioneered in the mid-1970s at the Greenfield, Massachusetts, home office. Until then, the company had kept dual records on more than 400,000 policies — one set on a mainframe in Hartford and duplicates on card files in field agencies.

suddenly, was in line for the presidency. Their deaths were a great loss to Phoenix. Both men, however, left a legacy of lasting accomplishments.

FOCUS ON SERVICE

The 1970s were a time of physical expansion for Phoenix. In 1971, the company opened a new policyholder service facility in Greenfield, Massachusetts, under the direction of Eric Franzen. Why Greenfield? Labor markets were tight in Hartford, according to John Chmielewski, CLU, who later took over the Greenfield operation. "We had competition from factories and other insurers," he recalls. "Greenfield was on the I-91 corridor. The education level of potential employees there was quite high. And the town wanted us."

During construction of the Greenfield facility, people worked in makeshift rented locations. "My first office was in a newspaper building," says Vice President Tricia Ethier, CLU, FLMI. "Every afternoon, when they started the presses, the whole place would shake." Ethier exemplifies the career opportunities created by company expansion. She started in Greenfield as a clerk and steadily took on more responsibility before becoming vice president and general manager of the Albany Operations Center.

With the call center in Greenfield, Phoenix became the first major insurer to offer toll-free centralized customer service — a move so innovative that AT&T (then America's sole long distance telephone company) published a case study about it. Directing agents and policyholders to an 800 number for policy information was a turning point, one that rankled some producers. Previously, field offices had kept copies of all client records and functioned like miniature home offices. They worried about losing control.

"I wasn't convinced that the home office would be adequately responsive to the field," says Chmielewski, who had agency management experience himself. "Well, Hardcastle solved that for me. He said, 'You're in charge. Make it work.' I had a quick change of faith." Chmielewski visited every agency to get input and ease the transition. Starting from scratch, the people at Greenfield developed the customer service call center into a model for the industry.

And agents accepted the change, says Chmielewski, "once they saw the quality of the service, the better and more current information. The sales office became truly a *sales* office." At the same time, Phoenix created a staff of customer service specialists second to none.

This growth was especially remarkable given the erosion of the life insurance industry at large. According to A.M. Best statistics, the industry's aggregate surplus fell 20 percent in the first half of 1974, a signal of declining business. Banks and brokerage firms were encroaching on traditional life products. The entire financial services industry was less insular, more market-savvy and focused on the end consumer.

Donald E. Bertrand, vice president, insurance and investment products counsel, remembers rewriting policies as his first project at Phoenix. The "plain English" movement had just been enacted into state law. Fresh from the Yale Law School class of 1973, Bertrand and a team of underwriters pored over "every single insurance contract Phoenix had." Word by word they asked, "What does it mean? Why is it there? Must it be there or can we take it out?" As a social activist, Bertrand welcomed the opportunity to simplify contract language. He also benefited professionally: "Can you imagine the depth of knowledge one acquires? The plain English movement was the greatest grounding any lawyer could possibly get in the insurance business."

DEATH OF AN HEIR APPARENT

Beginning to suffer from the emphysema that would eventually take his life in 1983, Bob Jackson planned carefully for his succession. His reputed choice for president of Phoenix was Ed Erickson, who was widely acknowledged to be as brilliant as Jackson himself. On February 5, 1976, the 45-year-old Erickson died in a car crash. "I remember so vividly learning of Ed's death," says Bob Merritt, who had shared an office with Erickson on Elm Street. "Someone came to me in the parking garage and told me what had happened. I leaned against the wall and said, 'We just lost our next company president.'"

"A lot of careers changed the day Erickson died," Chmielewski explains. "Mine certainly did," Gummere affirms. But Gummere was not yet the next in line. In 1978, Jackson appointed Dennis Hardcastle president. His background in sales and marketing was a first for the president's office at Phoenix. Fiondella regards Hardcastle as "truly a mentor" because "he drew me into helping to manage the growth of our money management business."

DIVERSITY EFFORTS BEGIN

However, Hardcastle may be best remembered for bringing consciousness-raising workshops on gender and race to Phoenix. Anita Putnam, retired assistant vice president, human resources, was instrumental in selecting the facilitators: Kaleel Jamison and Associates, a Cincinnati-based firm. The sessions, designed to be confrontational and cathartic, drew wildly mixed reactions. Stressing personal examples and feelings, they were quite unlike anything ever experienced at quiet, conservative Phoenix. While people still argue about the methods used, no one doubts the value of the outcome. The workshops crystallized a commitment to open up the organization to everyone.

Participants remember these workshops, which spanned two years, as if they happened yesterday. "They broke you down and built you back up again," Hourihan says. "You were not going to come out unscathed. Being a white male, at both workshops [on gender and race] it was 'get into the middle here because it's your

Diversity Update

"Collaborative" and "powerful" is how Wyrot M. Ward, second vice president, human resources, describes Phoenix's current diversity initiatives.

Small-group discussions have replaced the controversial workshops of the 1980s. "That effort served its time; now society approaches things differently," Ward says. Through a series of "Community Conversations on Race," part of a program in the Hartford area, groups of 12 employees meet regularly for facilitated two-hour sessions. They get to know one another, consider different points of view, explore disagreements and work together to act on issues they care about.

"We discovered that people really want to talk about race and race relations in order to build a greater understanding and a common ground," says coordinator Monique Grissette-Banks, director, office of diversity. "And we want to be part of the solution to improving the social and economic viability of the metro-Hartford area. We want to create an environment where everyone in this organization can be successful."

Creating such an environment has always been an informal but important part of Phoenix's culture. Donald Bertrand, who joined the law department in 1973, recalls special mentoring from Personnel Manager William Dowdy and Group Marketing Manager Herb Wheeldin. "Herb was very hospitable and gracious to us as minorities and fellow employees," Bertrand says. "He was also quite candid about company difficulties and company challenges." Bertrand has mentored younger employees in the same way.

The company continually strives to improve recruitment and retention of employees of color. One highly focused effort is the Phoenix Actuarial Passport Program. It targets historically black colleges, which traditionally have strong mathematics departments, to awaken students to the possibility of an actuarial career. The program has annually placed at least one person of color in an actuarial department summer internship and has subsidized exam fees for students at Howard University.

Progress in all departments comes more slowly than everyone would like. "We're a lot better off than we were, but there's still a long way to go," admits Ed Hourihan. "There's lots of competition," Ward explains about minority recruitment. "But Phoenix has a genuine conviction. We had it when I was recruited — I was impressed that Phoenix voluntarily had developed a formal Affirmative Action plan — and we still do."

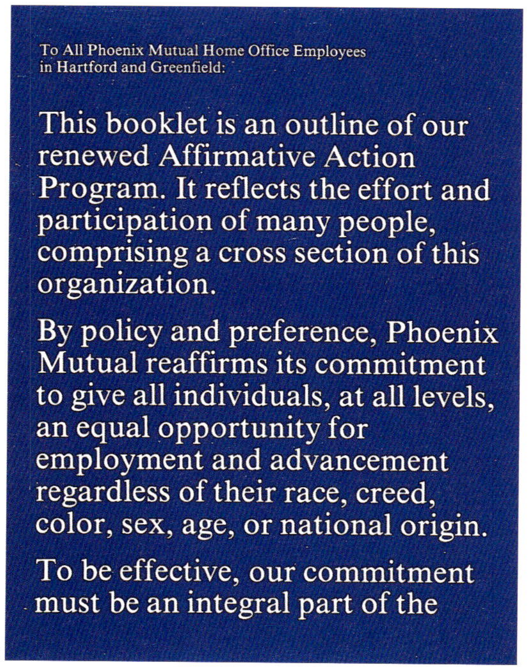
To All Phoenix Mutual Home Office Employees
in Hartford and Greenfield:

This booklet is an outline of our renewed Affirmative Action Program. It reflects the effort and participation of many people, comprising a cross section of this organization.

By policy and preference, Phoenix Mutual reaffirms its commitment to give all individuals, at all levels, an equal opportunity for employment and advancement regardless of their race, creed, color, sex, age, or national origin.

To be effective, our commitment must be an integral part of the

Phoenix took vigorous steps toward Affirmative Action. This 1978 booklet spelled out the action plans, which included workshops designed "to heighten awareness of the concerns" of minorities and women and "to recognize misconceptions and biases that affect behavior and working relationships."

time, your turn in the ring.'"

"[It was] intrusive," says Bertrand, who also took part. "I am a minority and I am politically liberal, but I know intrusion when I see intrusion. Racism needs to be dealt with by companies. I am not against that. What I am against is the style. There is such a thing as an intrusive, disrespectful style when somebody is in your face, correcting you on attitude.... I want real work on it, but it has to be *real* work."

Blanche Campbell, retired supervisor, underwriting services, and the first black woman supervisor at Phoenix, calls the workshops "sensitivity training" and believes that, in the end, they aided understanding. Some sessions were difficult, she says, "because you had to sit there and tell people what you didn't like about them. But it made you sensitive to other people's feelings, because a lot of times we act the way we do because we don't think about how the other person feels. So it was hard, but it was enlightening."

Jamison also ran "all-woman workshops that were much more supportive," Ethier recalls. "The man/woman workshops helped the men understand...that women have the same kinds of ambition that men do. But I found it very tough on the men. It moved us ahead in those areas, but with a lot of pain."

"We had no idea what we were getting into," admits Hardcastle, who visibly supported the workshops by taking part in them himself. "I learned a hell of a lot about myself," he says. Well-liked throughout the company for his easy-going and irreverent style, suddenly he found himself taking flak over these hard-nosed sessions. "'What's happened to Dennis? He's lost his sense of humor' is what I started to hear," he recalls.

Hardcastle cared deeply about diversity. As early as 1976, he had sent a letter to the field with this message: "The measure of success will be when no talent is wasted because of gender or race, and when women and minorities in top positions at Phoenix will no longer be a novelty." In his view, these goals couldn't be achieved until the era of paternalistic management ended.

"The ultimate purpose of the diversity workshops was to have all of us recognizing each other as adults, responsible adults," he stresses. "Not men, not women, not black, not white, but as responsible adults. In spite of the pain, I think the workshops helped. I think they put Phoenix ahead, and from a business point of view, Phoenix has profited from talent it might not have used otherwise."

John Gummere, who became president when Hardcastle retired from Phoenix in 1982, continued Phoenix's diversity efforts in his own effective style. "I talked with groups of new officers as they came in," he says, "to emphasize the importance of developing minorities and women throughout the organization."

"John's sensitivity program for officers astounded me," says Maura L. Melley, senior vice president, public affairs, who joined Phoenix in 1989 after being the highest-ranking woman officer at ITT-Hartford. "John would talk about his first boss at the company [Actuarial Supervisor Zenia McLean], who was really smart and couldn't get ahead. Gummere's presentation "reinforced my decision to come here," Melley adds.

The workshops and sensitivity programs were like a tidal wave whose ripples can still be felt, albeit more quietly, as Phoenix has maintained its commitment to diversity and equal opportunity.

DECADE OF CRISES

The big upheavals of the 1980s, increasingly, were financial ones. "The 1980s gave us a landscape we hadn't experienced in 40 years," Fiondella emphasizes. "Right after World War II, interest rates started to rise. For four decades, we

Product Innovation: Second-to-Die Insurance

"Phoenix was one of the first companies to come up with 'second-to-die' insurance," Bob Fiondella says. "It allowed us to sell in very large amounts and was one of the innovations that helped us to survive the early 1980s." Still a premier component in Phoenix's sales portfolio, it accounts for about 25 percent of individual in-force business.

Also called "survivorship life insurance," second-to-die was a creative response to changes in federal tax law. It facilitates the transfer of wealth to heirs by couples facing large estate tax liabilities. On the first death, proceeds from the policy pass to the surviving spouse tax-free under the marital deduction. On the second death, the proceeds pay the estate taxes. Leon L. Levy, CLU, RHU, longtime sales leader at Phoenix, elaborates: "Second-to-die is fundamentally a single policy on two people, available at a lower premium than two separate policies."

Simon Y. Tan, currently executive vice president of life and annuity products and operations, helped design Survivor Legacy, Phoenix's original whole life survivorship product. "I never dreamed it would be so successful," he says modestly. "I didn't think we had that many affluent people." The survivorship portfolio has expanded to include Estate Edge, a variable universal life policy, and Estate Legacy, a universal life product.

Even in the difficult 1980s, Phoenix had all the right strengths to take an early and commanding lead in second-to-die. Dona Young tells why: "We had distribution that was sophisticated for the product, which is designed for the affluent market. We had internal capabilities geared to support that market, mainly advanced marketing attorneys who are experts in estate planning. We had the complete package. As a consequence we remain one of the top 10 providers of second-to-die.

"That's how you compete," Young says. "You pull it all together, package it and serve it to the market that is going to value what you have."

simply increased dividends or reduced prices. Then we hit the 1980s."

"The comfort zone disappeared," says Senior Vice President Joseph E. Kelleher, FLMI, then in underwriting at Home Life, using a popular phrase of the time. "We got ourselves in too much trouble trying to be all things to all people."

The notion of one-stop shopping had gripped the financial services industry. Insurers competed with recently deregulated banks, mutual fund giants and direct sellers as well as each other. At the same time, inflation, mortgage rates and interest rates spiraled into double digits — near-mortal blows to an industry so sensitive to rising interest rates — and rating agencies were getting tougher.

Policyholders saw that dividends were only 4 or 5 percent while money market funds paid 15 percent or more. Some surrendered their policies; many others took advantage of the spread to borrow against their policies at bargain rates. "Life insurers had to borrow money to lend it out," Wallace says. "Borrowed money was going out one door faster than premiums were coming in the other door."

Insurers had no choice but to seek higher returns on their investments. They invested more heavily in equity ownership of real estate — a direction Phoenix had taken since the mid-1970s — and high-yield, high-risk bonds. They also began to sell "guaranteed investment contracts," or GICs, which guaranteed attractive interest rates on employee pension plans or savings plan monies put under insurers' management. The payout usually came due in five years. Mortgage-backed GICs were being sold "in the industry in spades, and you either did it or got out of the business," Gummere says.

"Not everybody was prudent and in control of GICs; Phoenix was," Fiondella points out.

Phoenix's growth in the 1980s necessitated a third home office, in Enfield, Connecticut. The complex was designed with expanded training facilities and childcare provisions in mind. "Enfield was completed on time and under budget," retired human resources vice president and Enfield project manager Bill MacLachlan proudly recalls.

"They wouldn't have been such a time bomb if not for the fact that mortgages instead of bonds were now being used to back GICs. Fortunately, we had only $200 million a year [in payback obligations] to wrestle with. If you had $900 million coming due in one year, as Home Life did, what did you do?"

OTHER CREATIVE STEPS

Phoenix took other creative steps to navigate the storms. As general counsel, Fiondella had developed a "vision for the law department that was a departure," says Young, who joined the department full-time in 1980. "It was a vision that we lawyers, as counselors, should be integral to the business. We should be engaged, not the department where everything stops and people say 'no,' but fully integrated and involved with business strategy and decisions."

The transition of the legal department from its traditional watchdog stance to a consultative role is exemplified by the creation of Phoenix's first "survivorship life" ("second-to-die") products in the early 1980s. Attorneys who were experts in estate planning were essential to the team that developed and marketed these products. Today, Phoenix's advanced marketing unit — staffed with attorneys with expertise in estate, gift and income tax planning techniques — works directly with producers and high-net-worth clients to advance the company's services to the affluent market.

With less access to capital than is enjoyed by stock companies, mutuals such as Phoenix had to resort to buyouts and budget cuts to help finance necessary expansions. In Phoenix's case, one expansion was physical. Starting in 1981, the company built a third home office location, in Enfield, Connecticut, about 20 miles north of Hartford. By the end of the decade, this spacious corporate campus had grown to include three connected buildings and a separate childcare center. Certain operations, such as underwriting and human resources, relocated there while some floors of the boat building were leased out at favorable rates.

Phoenix also expanded its product line prudently in these years, entering the survivorship life market, for example, and adding dental insurance to the group product portfolio. But the times increasingly called for vigilance. In 1983, Gummere put Fiondella in charge of the individual line and soon asked him to oversee the reduction of $25 million in expenses companywide. For the first time, employees were offered an enhanced early retirement program based on length of service. "Phoenix was always very proud of the fact it never laid anybody off," Gummere points out. "In 1984, we absorbed a lot by attrition, but out of the 300-plus positions eliminated, we did lay off 45 people." The move was so surprising it made the front page of the *Hartford Courant*, next to news of far bigger layoffs at The Travelers. "It was the only time in my experience we got equal billing," Gummere notes wryly.

The emergence in the early 1980s of "universal life," a forerunner of variable products, shook the industry. This new type of policy offered market-level returns, flexible premiums and cash values. "It came on the scene with a vengeance," says Dona Young, recalling how rival companies used universal life to replace and "cannibalize" huge chunks of their traditional business. Gummere resisted this trend. Eventually Phoenix sold universal life products — but with major differences.

"We responded to the universal life challenge by creating our Maximum Life Protector plan, for example, an innovative product that eventually was widely copied," recalls Fred Sawyer. Sawyer had been chosen by Fiondella to revitalize individual line product development, a role he would fulfill for almost 10 years. "And our agents, unlike those of many other companies, were paid *no commission* should a client switch from a traditional policy to universal life," he emphasizes.

Phoenix also responded to the challenges of the marketplace by reducing rates on standard products and offering existing policyholders up to 15 percent added coverage with no increase in premium. "In all, it was a decisive time for Phoenix," Sawyer says. "Once again, we bucked the trend and did the right thing."

This was also the era of "one-stop financial shopping," when investment firms, banks, insurers and other financial institutions experimented with large, multifaceted organizations designed to meet all types of financial services needs. Phoenix responded to this trend in its own way. To expand and diversify the company's distribution options, it created new subsidiaries. Two in particular would grow notably: American Phoenix Corporation and Phoenix Re.

American Phoenix was a network of property/casualty insurance agencies. President Martin L. "Mell" Vaughan nurtured it from scratch, primarily through acquisitions, eventually propelling it into the top 20 property/casualty agency groups in the nation. Phoenix Re, a property/casualty reinsurer also developed from scratch, was a logical adjunct. It grew under the leadership of President Gerald L. Radke; when the business demanded more capital than Phoenix as a mutual could provide, the company spun it off as a public company in 1986. Known since as PX Re, it has benefited from significant price increases in reinsurance. Phoenix has benefited in turn because it has continuously owned a minority percentage of PX Re's stock.

"Other life insurance companies that started property/casualty operations lost a lot of money," Chief Financial Officer David W. Searfoss, CLU, comments. "All of ours turned out acceptably or spectacularly."

These ventures, masterminded by Bob Jackson and engineered by Bob Fiondella, helped position Phoenix to withstand financially difficult times. And the 1980s would continue to be full of upheaval. The Tax Reform Act of 1986 effectively devalued real estate overnight; then, in a one-two punch, the stock market crash of October 1987 deflated high-risk bonds and spooked investors. The absurdly high interest rates of the early 1980s crashed back to earth, and the United States fell into a recession. While all insurers were affected by this roller coaster of economic events, mutuals with their limited access to capital and slower recovery times were hit especially hard. Some competitors of Phoenix and Home Life, most prominently Newark-based Mutual Benefit Life, did not survive.

"We spent a lot of time in the 1980s deciding what we should and shouldn't do," Fiondella summarizes. He had been named president in 1987. "We decided to stay the course with traditional life insurance and not go wholesale to universal life. We emphasized retirement accumulation and our mutual funds business." The new emphasis brought PEPCO to a landmark $1 billion in assets under management during the decade.

"In short," says Fiondella, "we made decisions that avoided risk or narrowed the focus or marshaled the capital."

HOME LIFE IN THE 1980s

Home Life approached the troubled 1980s differently, aiming to be a broad-based financial services organization. This vision emanated from Kenneth C. Nichols Sr., CLU, a former Prudential executive who served as Home Life's president from 1978 through 1987 and as its chairman from 1988 to 1991. "People would say he was trying to turn Home Life into Prudential," says Robert G. Lautensack Jr., FSA, who worked for Nichols and is now senior vice president, corporate structure, at Phoenix. "That was never the case. It was too small." But Nichols did introduce "trappings of corporate power, like limousines, for the first time."

Under Nichols's ambitious expansion plans, Home Life introduced its first money market

AT THE DESK OF

Olivia M. Shaw, ACS

First job at Home Life:
Group pension clerk, 1981

Currently:
Senior benefits service representative, Enfield.

Cherished memory:
Celebrating Home Life's 125th anniversary in May 1985. All home office employees marched across the street to city hall, where Mayor Edward Koch proclaimed Home Life Day, then paraded to the World Trade Center for a reception.

What she loves about her work:
Helping colleagues and retirees. "It's like they become family members. You remember when they got married, when their first child was born. When a significant event takes place in their lives, that becomes part of your life, too."

Home Life had explored merger options for several years before William B. Wallace became president in 1988.

fund. More dramatically, it purchased Orange State Life of Largo, Florida, a stock life insurance company, and renamed the subsidiary Home Life Financial Assurance Corporation. HLFAC, as it would be known, became the umbrella for numerous acquisitions and growth initiatives. At one point, it represented 22 affiliated financial services companies.

Bill Wallace credits Nichols for turning around group insurance — that line of business had lost $17 million in 1987, partly due to cyclical lows — but believes Nichols "didn't recognize the brilliance of Planned Estates and felt the future lay elsewhere." Home Life suffered a constant turnover of senior executives. "One year, I had five bosses," Joe Kelleher recalls.

Like Phoenix, Home Life decentralized. In 1987, it sold its grand but now outdated headquarters and transferred all operations to new facilities at 75 Wall Street and Piscataway, New Jersey. Russell Berry, CLU, in data processing at Home Life and later at Phoenix, recalls one practical reason for leaving the aging building: "There was no freight elevator at 253-256 Broadway, and computers wouldn't fit in the passenger elevator."

Under a changing management team, Home Life grappled with mounting GIC obligations and troubled real estate. A merger with Pacific Mutual, announced to employees and agents as a "done deal," ended up falling through. Despite the internal and external havoc, Home Life's steadfast field force continued to produce: in the mid-1980s it boasted 375 agents in the industry's prestigious Million Dollar Round Table, the highest proportion of any life insurer.

STAGE IS SET FOR MERGER

Bill Wallace had been at Home Life since 1952. A longtime agency manager in Washington, D.C., Wallace had also been a personal producer and had spent several years at the home office under J. Harry Wood. Warm and effusive, among the industry's most beloved and honored leaders, Wallace was held in high regard by the field. Nichols needed field support. In September 1987, he asked Wallace to take over the presidency. Nichols would continue as chairman. Wallace said no — at first.

"Ken asked my advice," Wallace says. "'Whatever you do, don't look outside the company,' I told him. 'Then who?' he asked." Clearly, Wallace himself was the ideal choice. "I was tossing and turning in bed at 2 a.m.," he says. "My wife, Sallie, knew I was awake. She spoke first. She told me if I didn't accept the presidency, she suspected I'd always regret it."

As early as 1985, the Home Life board had quietly established a standing committee to explore merger possibilities. With the right partner, Home Life management hoped, the company could address its deepening fiscal troubles while continuing to grow.

While mergers among publicly held companies were (and are) common, they were almost unheard of among mutuals. Valuation of mutuals

Unisex Pricing Controversy of 1983

"If nothing else is on my gravestone, I want 389 to 102 engraved on it!" John Gummere proclaims with glee.

An odd request — especially for a minister's son? Not really, because the numbers represent one of Phoenix's most notable moral triumphs. In 1984, by a vote of 389 to 102, members of the American Council of Life Insurance headed off efforts by the U.S. Congress to ban rate distinctions by sex. The well-meaning but misguided push for unisex rates originated with equality groups, and the vote was set to go in their favor. Activism by Phoenix turned the tide.

At the forefront was Barbara J. Lautzenheiser, FSA, a former senior vice president. Accustomed to firsts, such as being the first woman president of the Society of Actuaries, Lautzenheiser didn't mind taking an unpopular stand. "I couldn't be accused of being a male chauvinist," she told the *Hartford Courant*. "I'm an actuary. I believe strongly you have to base price on cost."

Lautzenheiser alerted Gummere that the board of ACLI, a prominent industry lobbying group, was about to cave in on unisex pricing. "I had to decide only about three weeks after becoming CEO whether we were going to try to fight this," Gummere says. In 1955, "Phoenix had been the first company to differentiate between rates for men and women, and give women a break, and we couldn't let that go without a fight."

Company lawyer and vice president Raymond Coburn pored over the ACLI charter and discovered Phoenix could call a meeting if enough fellow members took part. The company joined forces with Berkshire Life, Standard of Oregon and Transamerica Occidental to round up the magic number. Gummere relishes the memory: "We made our case and defeated the biggies. It was really one of the high points of my career." (At Gummere's request, the figures of the final vote, "389-102," were subtly painted into his official company portrait, which hangs in the Phoenix boardroom in Hartford.)

"Like David and Goliath," Dona Young exults. Then assistant vice president of reinsurance administration, she witnessed the vote. "I lobbied and watched my then CEO — he was proud in that meeting, speaking in a packed room in a hotel in Washington, D.C. It was another example of Phoenix standing up for what was right. And it was so much fun."

After Lautzenheiser left Phoenix, she continued to oppose unisex legislation attempts that arose at the state level. Her rallying cry resonates today: "If this law passes, women will receive only the right to pay more than their fair share."

is difficult because there is no stock to exchange. In addition, insurers domiciled in different states operate under different regulations.

Aside from those complications there are the usual deal killers: irreconcilable disagreements over the leadership, location and even the name of the merged company. A combination of the latter factors had annulled the Home Life-Pacific Mutual merger. Was a merger the only way out for Home Life? That question will be debated as long as Home Life employees are alive. Bill Wallace will tell you that he accepted the presidency, effective January 1988, with the conviction that a merger was inevitable for the survival of his company.

Phoenix had also explored a few mergers in the 1980s, less urgently, and saw them falter for similar reasons. "One potential partner outside of New England seemed ideal," says John Gummere, "but in the end they just didn't want to give up their regional identity." Through his activity in the industry, Wallace knew and respected Phoenix and Gummere. He felt confident the two companies could be a good match and that they could resolve the kinds of issues that had thwarted earlier merger attempts.

The die was cast.

CHAPTER FIVE

1991-1992

The Historic Merger

Everybody who merges consolidates. Some integrate. Very few align. It's like two people getting married. If they still behave the way they did before, then they really haven't created a new life. They aren't one. Phoenix and Home Life became one.

— Robert W. Fiondella

PHOENIX

Measured against any standard, the merger of Phoenix Mutual Life Insurance Company and Home Life Insurance Company was an exceptionally successful union.

The merger enabled the new company — officially Phoenix Home Life Mutual Insurance Company — to prosper in a stubbornly "capital-poor, low-margin, high-risk environment" of the early 1990s, as the industry newsletter *Probe* described it. The merged company lowered expenses, expanded distribution, improved earnings and capital, set aside a bigger reserve to handle troubled assets and diversified investments. Most important of all, perhaps, it was able to stay mutual — not for sentimental reasons, but to preserve policyholder value while pursuing growth.

At first, the industry questioned if Phoenix and Home Life could achieve such a feat. "The merger was a giant risk," acknowledges David Searfoss. It was seen as "very much an out-of-character move, but one, I think, that was very consistent with mutuality. It was certainly a controversial decision. Outsiders wondered about the ability of mutual companies to execute it."

They didn't wonder for long. "A marriage made in heaven," wrote Don Barnes in *National Underwriter,* summarizing the industry's general response. Susan Pulliam of the *Wall Street Journal* neatly analyzed the factors for the success: "Phoenix and Home Life are, in many ways, unusual. Both chief executives are near retirement age, making succession questions less complicated. The two companies are also considered to have complementary distribution systems and products."

INGREDIENTS FOR SUCCESS

The merger was distinctive in many respects. First and foremost, it succeeded not just in fact but in spirit. Most mergers don't. In studying hundreds of merged companies since 1985, major firms such as A. T. Kearney, Mercer Management Consulting and J. P. Morgan have found that 44 percent to 58 percent of merged companies "have not added value" based on financial gains or improved performance. In another study, by Right Management Consultants of Philadelphia, fewer than one-third of 179 merged companies said they had truly combined. The rest admitted to being hobbled by clashes of executive egos and company cultures. Phoenix and Home Life enjoyed a different scenario.

"Both chairmen and CEOs, John Gummere and Bill Wallace, had spent their entire careers in their respective organizations and had a deep passion about their respective companies," says Dona Young. "Both, through different sets of eyes and experiences, cared fundamentally about policyholders and doing what was right. Bill sat on top of a company he saw deteriorating and felt an enormous obligation to strengthen it for the policyholders and field force. On John's side, the merger was a natural. He was very rooted financially and very committed to policyholder value."

The merger moved forward at every level because Bob Fiondella, responsible for implementation, set up a team structure that got people involved. "Alignment won't happen unless whoever is driving the company is actually engaged in causing people to come together. You cannot order it," Fiondella emphasizes.

SETTING THE STAGE

Gummere, Wallace and Fiondella sat together for the first time to explore merger possibilities in February 1991. They met for breakfast in the Vista Hotel in downtown Manhattan, near Home Life's Wall Street offices. At sundown, they were still talking.

Curiously, Gummere had kept informal tabs on Home Life since joining the industry 32 years earlier. As a kind of homework assignment, Bob Jackson had encouraged the newly hired Gummere "to identify who the good mutual companies were. I remember noticing Home Life as very good. I said, 'how can this company be so good when they're so much smaller than we are?'"

In 1991, Home Life was still smaller than Phoenix:

HOME LIFE

Assets	In Force	Policyholders	Employees
$4.6 billion	$30 billion	300,000	1,200

PHOENIX

Assets	In Force	Policyholders	Employees
$6.4 billion	$76 billion	400,000	2,500

However, the companies were virtually equal in a crucial way. At about 750 agents each, their career field forces closely matched each other in size and productivity. Anything else would have been a deal-breaker for Wallace: "I didn't want us to be swallowed up."

Moreover, the companies' distribution systems complemented each other well, down to the geographical overlay. Home Life was clearly field-oriented; all its agents were career agents. Phoenix

Bob Fiondella (standing), Bill Wallace and John Gummere played unique roles in the merger. The industry research organization LIMRA lauded the merger as "a tremendous success, resulting in significant cost savings, a stronger distribution system and a more solid market presence." The photo on page 77 displays the double diamond logo created to symbolize the merged company.

focused more on products; it sold through career agents and career affiliates (now called personal producing general agents or PPGAs) but, since the late 1950s, had traditionally emphasized brokerage, or life wholesaling. Bob Lautensack saw the merger as an ideal blend of "Home Life's field culture and Phoenix's strong products and operating expertise."

In many ways, the companies already knew and admired each other. Phoenix data processing manager Russell Berry, who once worked in reinsurance at Home Life, remembers, "Phoenix was one of our biggest reinsurers — a good, solid company with a good, solid contract." At Home Life's retail broker/dealer, WS Griffith & Co., Inc. (named after the first president of Home Life), the feeling was the same. "Phoenix was one of our top three or four fund families before the merger, because they were a quality fund provider," says Gerard Rocchi, who went on to be the first president of the broker/dealer when it became a wholly owned Phoenix subsidiary. WS Griffith is an excellent example of the synergies stimulated by the resources and talents of the merged company, having grown more than tenfold from 1991 to 2000, when it achieved $90 million in revenues.

WRITING THE BOOK

Merger talks continued quietly into the spring of 1991. The companies had to negotiate delicate issues — the kind that had killed many other companies' merger efforts. Where would the merged company be located? Who would stay? Who would go? Who would lead?

Young recalls realizing "this isn't going to be like Noah's Ark. We are not taking them two by

A New Policyholder Service Center in Albany

What happens when you combine the policyholder services of two companies that have different information systems, products and management styles? You work together to take the best of both and build a better entity.

To satisfy regulatory requirements, the merged company of Phoenix Home Life had to establish individual policyholder services in New York. East Greenbush, near Albany, was the location of choice. Vice President Tricia Ethier, CLU, FLMI, a longtime Phoenix employee, left Greenfield to help run the Albany operations center, eventually becoming general manager. She recalls the ups and downs of this merger-within-a-merger, achieved mainly in the second half of 1992.

"Was it going to be the Home Life way or the Phoenix way? We took seven people from each company and went off-site for a week to develop a program," Ethier says. "Home Life had done a really good job of developing their customer service. Their field force was very happy with the service. Phoenix had also done an incredible job. Unfortunately, the two models were very different."

Phoenix's policyholder service had long been centralized through the toll-free call center in Greenfield; Home Life had computers in each field office. Greenfield employees worked in self-directed teams, with overlapping responsibilities, while Home Life had a more hierarchical support staff in Piscataway. Both groups had worked hard to design and improve their operations. In fact,

Created as a condition of the merger, the Albany operations center moved to its permanent home in 1997. Tricia Ethier, vice president and general manager of the facility (front row left), joined with Chairman Bob Fiondella and Julie O'Hara of client services to cut the ribbon at the official opening.

Greenfielders had just spent two years redesigning and streamlining their workflow. "That was the best turnaround I've seen in my time here," Fred Sawyer says. "We were full of that self-directed team religion," affirms John Chmielewski, retired general manager of Greenfield.

So the core group of 14 squared off at first. Facilitator Barbara Fernandez, now an assistant vice president of strategic development, finally told them to step back and start over. That broke the tension. The objective, as Ethier says, "was to figure out how to make this work, instead of trying to prove which model was best."

We-and-they feelings subsided as people realized how much they had in common. Some 40 employees relocated to Albany from Greenfield and Piscataway, all highly experienced and attuned to the needs of agents and policyholders. Together, they devised a training program for about 160 new hires that would satisfy everyone.

The new operation first followed Home Life's model "because we needed to be functionalized — no way could we take brand-new people and train them to do all the various functions," Ethier says. As the staff gained experience, they evolved toward self-directed teams. Each team now services specific agencies, which makes for better efficiency and stronger field relationships.

For all 200 pioneering employees in Albany, the merger presented "an opportunity to build something new," Ethier points out. "That was appealing and exciting. You don't get a chance to do that too often in your career."

two. Only one is getting on in each category." Sitting alone for a few minutes in Phoenix's law library, reflecting on the enormity of what might happen, "I felt sorry for myself," Young admits. Then she rallied. "I said to myself, 'I love this company. I love the people on this floor, the eleventh floor, the law department. I owe them something, and what I owe them is this: No matter what happens to me in the end, they deserve my leadership and they deserve for me to do the best I can do to represent the company.' And with that in my mind, I said 'okay, here goes. *I am in this.*' And I was in this."

Young literally engineered the legal and regulatory "roller coaster" of events. "We had to write the book as we went along," points out Fred Sawyer. There was, in fact, no precedent to follow. "Dona ran circles around our counsel throughout the process," Wallace says.

Senior executives and counsel of the two companies met face to face in May 1991. Young recalls it as an uneasy meeting — "sizing up your counterpart" — that nonetheless yielded initial "game plans." One month later, key players convened in secret during the NAIC convention in Indianapolis. Also present were the respective insurance regulators of New York and Connecticut, Superintendent Salvatore Curiale and Commissioner Robert Googins. "We got agreement there to the restructuring that ultimately prevailed," Young says. "Phoenix Home Life, the resulting entity, would be a New York domiciled company. But its corporate office and headquarters — all the positions and functions that currently resided in the state of Connecticut — would stay in Connecticut. And we would build a policyholder service center in New York," which would keep a minimum of 200 jobs in that state.

In strict legal terms that did not reflect the spirit of the merger, only one company could be the "survivor." But as always, dedication to policyholders was the yardstick. Phoenix became the survivor because the merged company would sell primarily Phoenix products, which had been the envy of the industry during a decade of solid product development directed by Fred Sawyer. "The Phoenix product portfolio gave us so much more to offer than what we had as just Home Life," notes Joe Kelleher.

Individual policyholder service would be in New York, even though it meant breaking up Phoenix's operations in Greenfield and Home Life's in Piscataway. Remaining under New York's jurisdiction brought forward a vital Home Life tradition, Wallace says: "We'd always taken great pride that our policyholders were protected by the toughest insurance laws in the country."

MOVING OVER THE HURDLES

Although the plans were public by the summer of 1991, the merger itself was still far from official. The companies needed the approval of their boards, subsequent enabling legislation in their respective states and affirmative votes from policyholders. Thus began months of long days on "the intense legal work of putting the structure together," in Young's words, and preliminary steps toward integration.

Some longtime employees deeply loved Home Life and wished to see it stay independent. Others, who loved Home Life just as strongly, accepted the merger realistically. "We were sad to see something like that happen, but we obviously knew the decisions were being made for the best interests of the policyholders," said the late Mary Berry, who had joined Home Life in 1969. As senior administrative assistant to Bob Fiondella and Bill Wallace during the period of joint leadership, Mary Berry would become a valued "bridge" between employees of the merging companies.

As the process went forward, the leadership of

the merged company was resolved. The agreement provided that the board of directors would consist of 19 people, eight each appointed by Phoenix and Home Life, plus three senior officers: Gummere and Wallace, then chairmen and CEOs of their respective companies, and Fiondella, then president and chief operating officer of Phoenix. Once officially merged, the resulting company would have a period of shared leadership with Gummere as chairman and CEO, Wallace as vice chairman and chief operating officer, and Fiondella as president and principal operating officer.

In December 1991, the boards of both companies voted to merge. But the deal was still far from done. "The day we voted to merge, it was still not legally possible for us to merge," Fiondella points out. "The statutes of both states would not permit us. I said if it's in the best interest of policyholders, then we should be able to persuade the regulators." Under Young's direction, Phoenix's legal and government relations teams got the necessary legislation enacted and obtained regulatory approvals. Fiondella focused on business integration.

"It became a classic case of mutual respect resulting in the building of a new company," says Randall Giangiulio, former senior vice president, group life and health. "Everybody at Phoenix was very sensitive to the fact that Home Life had a culture it was proud of. I challenge any two entities to do it better."

TEAM APPROACH

Fiondella lives by a piece of wisdom he acquired as a third-year law student. "A lawyer is an architect of ordered change," he quotes. "That's what a lawyer ought to be. I've never forgotten it." The merger was an opportunity to put this philosophy in action. "We had 70 task forces working at the same time on the integration plan," he says. "Sixty-nine did not have a head." (The one that did was Fiondella's own steering committee.)

"We put groups of Home Life and Phoenix people together to find a way to combine the operation and come forward with staffing plans and timetables," says Lautensack. The groups made consolidation plans for such areas as individual operations, data center, investments, reinsurance, law, human resources, facilities, finance and pensions. "We didn't define leaders; we let them do their own thing," Lautensack continues. The sole requirement for each task force was to keep minutes of their meetings, so the steering committee could know their decisions and follow their progress.

Teams traveled back and forth to the main locations — Hartford, Enfield, Greenfield and Piscataway — for meetings. As they got to know

Through a series of ads in industry publications, Phoenix spelled out the benefits of the merger. The first-year savings of $70 million was the crowning proof of success.

each other, trust blossomed. “The people from Home Life had to start their lives over again, for business reasons, and I shared their pain and distress,” Don Bertrand says. But the companies were determined to handle personnel issues humanely. To that end, Carl Chadburn left his position as head of the human resources department at Phoenix to work at Home Life’s Piscataway office for most of 1992 as head of human resources and corporate communications. He was now legally a Home Life employee and a “consultant” to Phoenix. “The objective was to have someone who could answer questions for the Home Life people about what Phoenix was like to put people’s minds at ease. And to handle the placement of the individuals who couldn’t join the new company, either because we didn’t have positions or because they decided they couldn’t relocate,” Chadburn explains.

JOINT COMMUNICATIONS

Throughout the merger, the team approach also extended to communications. Jo-Anne Leventhal, the assistant vice president who headed Phoenix’s public relations department, partnered with her Home Life counterpart, Geraldine O’Brien, to handle internal and external communications. Their goal was nothing less than a consistent, timely flow of information through print and video media. The companies hoped to head off rumors and misinformation, of course. But first and foremost, they wanted each and every affected person to be accurately informed.

“From the day we announced the merger until the day it was complete, the same information went to key audiences in both organizations,” Leventhal emphasizes. “Through video updates, newsletters and other mailings, everyone was hearing the same news at the same time.” And “everyone” was a huge constituency — most prominently 400,000 Phoenix policyholders, 250,000 Home Life policyholders, 260,000 Phoenix mutual fund shareholders, two workforces totaling 4,000 employees, two field forces totaling 4,500 agents, two boards of directors, numerous legislators, more than 50 regulators and the media.

The efforts of Leventhal and O’Brien were so successful that they were highlighted in a 1996 merger case study by LIMRA, an industry “think tank” that conducts research and educates insurance executives worldwide. “During such a complex process, what does it take to get the message — the right message — out to the right people to minimize stress and maximize support?” wrote the study’s creators, Dorothy Kramer-Kawakami and Robert Allio. “For the Phoenix Home Life public relations team, it meant sending out a few communiqués. Make that close to a million communiqués to 18 discrete groups, on a one-time, weekly, monthly and annual basis.... Constant, proactive communication was the glue that held it all together.”

“All companies like to talk about the importance of communications, but Phoenix and Home Life made the commitment,” Leventhal says. “I think the success of our efforts during the merger gave senior management a new appreciation of the role of communications in strategic business issues.”

This message reinforced the advantages of the merger for policyholders and emphasized the single company identity, “Phoenix Home Life.”

PERSONNEL ISSUES

Especially at the start, the mood in Piscataway was understandably somber. Yet Home Lifers "couldn't have been nicer, more open or friendly to me," says Chadburn. "That told me immediately what type of company they were, and hopefully I reciprocated." In keeping with the goal of treating people fairly, "we tried to make personnel decisions as quickly as we could. We also worked hard to convince Home Life's human resources team to join the new company, and they did — almost intact."

The fact that Home Life's Mary Martinez would move to the fledgling Albany operation and Olivia Shaw would come to Enfield was a plus. (Martinez is now Albany's director of human resources; Shaw is a senior benefits service representative.) Janice Mazzallo, a Brooklynite, moved to rural Greenfield, Massachusetts, to head human resources there; Art Spiro took over HR systems; Steve McCusker headed employee benefits; and Ian Bowers, an iconoclastic Ph.D., became overall head of employment and training for the new company. "We wanted the Home Life folks to take some comfort that their own employees were going to be setting personnel policy," Chadburn says. In addition, Phoenix's Wyrot M. Ward, second vice president, human resources, made several trips to New Jersey, where she met with all employees and in particular talked "to the people of color at Home Life, indicating what I felt about the culture at Phoenix and its openness to them."

In January 1992, Home Life had 1,200 employees. About 400 soon took an early retirement package. At O'Brien's suggestion, Fiondella traveled to New Jersey to talk firsthand to the others. Characteristically, he spoke from the heart. He sympathized with employees faced with the prospect of uprooting, and so he assured Home Lifers: "If you cannot be part of this because you can't move or there isn't any place for you, we will treat you humanely. I am one who could not move. I still live in the town where I was born, so I understand it. If I were confronted with this choice, I would probably have to quit."

"We were targeting 100 Home Life employees to join the new company," says Carl Chadburn. "We hit that number right on the nose — 100 of the cream of the crop eventually came." Additionally, a significant number of employees were able to stay in Piscataway as part of Home Life's group operation. ("Phoenix kept that intact and later sold it as an ongoing business," Giangiulio notes. New York State did not want the merged company to continue two group operations, and in any event, "they were in the under-10-life business and 80 percent medical, where we didn't want to be.") Ultimately, job fairs and outplacement services helped to place all but 61 of Home Life's employees.

People at Phoenix also felt upheaval, and more than 100 chose an early retirement option. "There had to be choices made," says Ed Hourihan. "America was changing as well. People weren't staying in jobs as long. It hadn't affected Phoenix much until that point. We had been pretty insulated."

About 40 Greenfield and Piscataway employees moved to the new individual policyholder service center in East Greenbush, New York. The company kept the balance of jobs in Greenfield by internalizing its mutual fund transfer agent function, which had been contracted out — an unusual move that once again demonstrated Phoenix's commitment to its employees.

After the merger, individual policyholder services moved from Greenfield to Albany. The Greenfield facility, pictured here in 1996, remained the customer service center for group claims, variable products operations and mutual fund transfer agent operations through the 1990s.

REACTIONS IN THE FIELD

After the upheavals of the 1980s, Home Life's agents generally greeted the merger with relief.

At the same time, they grieved for "the old Home Life." John Packal, who joined Home Life in 1946 fresh from the U.S. Navy, expresses the range of feelings. "When I first heard about the merger, I was sad," he says. As Packal considered what Phoenix had to offer, he says, "I was elated. I realized what the merger would bring to me and the field people in terms of new product. For the first time, I would be with a company that would allow me to meet everybody's needs."

An early move gave Home Life agents extra confidence: Joe Kelleher came to Phoenix as head underwriter, even before the merger was official. "That sent a message to the field that they had a friend in Hartford," Wallace says.

Home Life agencies lost their direct computer access to policyholder records after the merger. That was a sore point, just as it had been for Phoenix agencies losing their manual record-keeping to the Greenfield system back in 1971. "We eventually gave the agents all the old capability and more, through the system that we developed in the post-merger years," Hourihan says.

"We welcomed them," says Phoenix career agent Leon L. Levy of his Home Life colleagues. "It gave Phoenix the opportunity to get additional talent." A task force of agents from both companies advised on the process to adjust differences in compensation and pensions. Phoenix standardized and adjusted these benefits toward a midpoint, another favorable outcome.

"ELECTRICITY AND EXCITEMENT"

Months of hard work by thousands of employees came to fruition on May 21, 1992 — when policyholders of both companies approved the merger — and then on July 1, 1992, when legal papers were filed. Finally the 70 task forces' game plans could officially go into effect.

Like all well-laid plans, of course, some

A Voice of Approval

The much-loved J. Harry Wood was chairman and president of Home Life in the 1960s. He avidly followed the company's progress throughout his life. After his death, Wood's widow, Kathy, gave Bill Wallace a section of Wood's unpublished memoirs.

Wallace was astonished to discover that Wood had recorded his thoughts on the day of the merger. Wood, then almost 90 years old, wrote as if he were speaking directly to Home Life employees:

July 1, 1992
Today marks the culmination of the work of William B. (Bill) Wallace to protect Home Life policyholders and to invigorate the field force by supplying them with additional and more competitive products to sell.

I doubt that any other individual could have gone through all that was necessary with his board of directors, two insurance departments, financial advisers, rating agencies and backbiting by a few of his own officers. If he had once thought of himself first, it would never have materialized....

If the old Home Life had remained independent, 'supposedly' maintaining the old employment, here would be some of the results:

1. All of its hundreds of thousands of policyholders would have paid by having lower dividends;

2. The field force would have continued to decline in number and productivity;

3. Unit expenses in the field would have increased;

4. Employment would have decreased year by year, good people would have become less willing to accept jobs, salary increases would have been smaller;

5. The best and youngest officers would have left as rapidly as they could, thus

6. The overall quality and efficiency of the entire organization would have deteriorated. Once begun, it would rapidly accelerate.

For Wallace, there could be no better blessing. Wood had been his cherished mentor. "Harry was completely for the merger," Wallace says. "Just seeing what he thought about it alone was good enough for me."

$14 Seals the Merger

After 18 months of intense work, payment of a token $14 filing fee officially consummated the merger between Phoenix and Home Life.

"Because Bob Fiondella was unavailable at the last minute, I drove to the Rensselaer County Courthouse in Troy, New York, on July 1, 1992," recalls Fred Sawyer. Sawyer was tapped because he had been responsible for finding Phoenix's first site in New York, the state where it had to be domiciled as a condition of the merger.

Back in Hartford, Maura Melley, then vice president of public affairs, sat by her telephone. As soon as the company's New York City lawyers announced that all the papers were approved, Melley relayed the news to Sawyer. He stepped up to the counter with the fee — "five crisp new bills, a 10 and four ones" — and a one-inch stack of documents that county officials

date-stamped and filed.

Local television stations recorded the historic moment; politicians were on hand to point out that Phoenix's new location brought over 200 new jobs to the region. For Sawyer, the simple transaction capped "an extremely complicated event. For a year and a half, we had negotiated and planned the future of the two companies. Finally, all objections to the merger had been set aside, all approvals obtained."

In typically cost-effective fashion, the first purchase of the newly combined companies was $2.85 for a breakfast "celebration." "We went out and had bagels, then drove home," Sawyer says. "There was no ticker tape parade waiting for us back in Hartford. But, without question, it was the most productive $14 Phoenix ever spent."

changed. And that was fine — indeed, expected. Retired vice president John Chmielewski, who directed Greenfield operations, believes the alignment happened successfully *because* it allowed for uncertainty: "Fiondella's whole focus was let's get this thing merged. Let's get it together and get it functioning. I don't care if you've got three VPs of this or that. Let's get it focused and later we'll sort it out."

"Sorting it out" took more hard work, of course. Just one example: Real estate accounted for one-third of all assets of the merged company. In the year immediately following, John Gummere and Chief Investment Officer Philip R. McLoughlin made it a top priority to decrease this exposure and address nonperforming holdings. For the legal and real estate departments, then, "business as usual" quickly became a thing of the past. "During the merger, it was a madhouse in real estate," says Josephine Melusky, a devoted and plainspoken Phoenix employee since 1941. "After the merger it was not easy. There were many, many documents to assign from Home Life to Phoenix, which meant working late hours and weekends." Melusky, a paralegal, credits Laurence Fleming II, vice president and real estate counsel, with "taking care of things. Larry set the routine and helped everyone accomplish their goals." Again, teamwork paid off. By June 1993, Phoenix had sold $100 million of real estate at a profit.

For many people, the merger was like running a marathon for the first time. They were amazed by their strengths. "It was exciting because you really, really saw the potential of the company," Kelleher says.

"I loved the electricity and excitement — the merger put a premium on concentration and creativity," attorney Don Bertrand says.

MERGER OF CULTURES

As for cultural differences, Wallace neatly summarizes the consensus. "Phoenix was more analytical, independent, product-driven," he says. "Also a stable culture. At the merger, all the Phoenix senior officers except one had 20-plus years there." He contrasts Home Life as "more market-driven" with a "more 'feeling' type of management" that had experienced many more changes at the top.

It's fair to say that most Home Lifers found Phoenix "a top-down culture rather than a bottom-up culture — it just seemed to take longer to get anything approved," says Russ Berry, who was under tight deadlines to implement Home Life's superior data system used for pensions and other repetitive payments. "Much more centralized decision-making at Phoenix," Bob Lautensack agrees, "but there had been a vacuum at Home Life, so that would have happened with any merger partner."

What counted, ultimately, was that people felt comfortable with each other. And that didn't take long, in Jo-Anne Leventhal's experience: "The people who came over were great additions. They were very friendly and knew how to get things done. They fit in, and we worked together really well."

The name was a tender subject at first. "We were really careful at the beginning never to say just Phoenix; it was always Phoenix Home Life," Leventhal notes. "A lot of Home Life people would say just 'Phoenix' but we never would." Eventually people relaxed and felt free to "just be proud of where you came from."

SCORECARD

After the merger announcement, Gummere told the *New York Times* that the merged company expected to save $70 million a year by reducing staff and consolidating data systems and offices. That raised eyebrows in the industry. "Several people I talked to were skeptical about Gummere's chances," John C. Angle, FSA, wrote in *Probe* in January 1992. Having retired as CEO of The Guardian in 1989, Angle was in a unique position to comment. He differed with the skeptics: "Even $30 million a year would make the exercise worthwhile.... I expect them to find pots of money.... Phoenix has a culture of spending money as carefully as any hard-bitten Yankee of the last century. That culture seems to be just the ticket for the decade ahead." The merging of data centers into one location at Enfield saved $10 million in expenses the first year alone.

Eleven months after the official merger date, Gummere had the deep satisfaction of reporting the post-merger "scorecard" to the field at their 1993 conferences. The data center's remarkable performance was just part of the good news. The sales force had doubled in size. Surplus was up by 7.5 percent. The ratio of surplus to assets had risen to 8.2 percent. GICs were gone. The company realized a profit on sales of $100 million of real estate and enjoyed a capital gain on the sale of Home Life's group business. Capital increased to $600 million. In all, the company

AT THE DESK OF

Satish Bangalore

First job at Phoenix:
Systems analyst, 1977

Current position:
Managing director, Phoenix Global Solutions (India) Pvt. Ltd.

Merger Achievement:
Participated in the technological merger of Phoenix and Home Life, which took six months, less than half the time allotted. "Within the first year, we saved the merged company $10 million. This was substantial evidence not only to us, but to the outside world, that it was worth the effort to merge."

Merger Memories:
"Getting all the teams together, especially from the two different companies, let us focus on the work and the goal."

Special Olympics: Coming Together As One Compa

When Special Olympics needed volunteers to organize its 1995 World Games softball competition in New Haven, 1,500 Phoenix employees responded. They brought 1,000 of their family members and friends. And they turned one event over a four-day holiday weekend into a defining moment in the company's history.

For the first time since the merger, employees from the four home offices worked together on a single, massive volunteer project. Field people took part, too. They traveled from as far as California to lend a hand in person and raised $125,000 to benefit local athletes and send hometown teams to the World Games. One volunteer summed up the involvement and excitement: "We worked for 13 months on a plan and found out the plan works. I think we can do anything now!"

President Bill Clinton opened the ceremonies, and Bob Fiondella threw out the first pitch at the softball competition. But the celebrities who really captured the hearts of the volunteers were the athletes and their families. And so the 1995 games were just the beginning.

As the first Official Worldwide Partner, Phoenix will sponsor Special Olympics International through 2004. Employees continue to get involved year-round in their states and towns. Like the merger itself, the partnership has proven an ideal match. The mission of the Special Olympics — to help people with mental retardation achieve their dreams through athletic competition and training — echoes Phoenix's goal of helping individuals and businesses achieve their financial hopes and dreams through focused wealth management.

G. Jeffrey Bohne is vice president and general manager of Greenfield operations. He worked throughout 1994 on Phoenix's Special Olympics World Games planning committee and, with his wife, Nancy, volunteered at the 1995 event. Excerpts from his diary capture the spirit of that unforgettable time.

June 30: The banners, the fields, the fresh paint, the tents, the satellite dishes, the people running around doing last-minute tasks. This is really going to happen! Now the torch is coming. Each of us has goosebumps.

July 1: As the athletes file down the sidewalk to the fields, the Phoenix Home Life (PHL) volunteers stand on both sides and spontaneously cheer.

July 2: All around me I hear PHL volunteers talking to each other. Many people have never met before and yet they have talked to each other by phone for years. A face with a voice. It will make a difference.

July 3: Texas is beating Illinois 20-12 in the last inning. Illinois rallies. It finally hits me. These are athletes like anyone else. Illinois wins 21-20.

July 4: Home. Have the day off and I need it. I'm really tired. But I wish I was in New Haven!

July 5: Free day, no games. I walk into work and can't move three feet without someone telling me how wonderful their experiences at the games have been. People are asking to sign up for more time. I love these people.

had achieved its projected $70 million savings.

Despite this stellar performance, Phoenix was downgraded by rating agency A.M. Best. The "threat that they'd downgrade us if we merged" was explicit all along, says Gummere. The actual news, delivered to him as he addressed top producers at the conference, made him weep. While it recognized the major cost efficiencies created by the merger, A.M. Best had reservations about Phoenix's remaining exposure to underperforming commercial mortgages and real estate. "Rating agencies were downgrading companies throughout the industry for the same reason," Gummere notes. "Still, I was naive enough to think — and I might have been as old as 62 — that I might have all those problems solved by the time I retired."

The retirement of Gummere and Wallace in February 1994 marked the end of an era and a historic process. "My objective was to bring the company to a soft landing, and I think I did," says Gummere. "We found the strategies to survive, and we executed them. It paid off better than we planned," adds Wallace.

Fiondella became chairman, CEO and president. He would later say (and still does) that the two companies truly united as one when employees from all locations volunteered at the Special Olympics World Games in New Haven in 1995. That is true. But the alignment began much earlier.

Young captures the essential reason for the phenomenal success of the merger: "So many transactions look great on the table. That is the world of investment bankers. The world of management in a company is making it work, making the people work, making the organization work. All the mergers in the world won't ever happen if you don't get that."

The people of Phoenix and Home Life "got" it. They made the merger work.

Employees from all the home offices "merged" in an unforgettable volunteer effort: organizing the 1995 Special Olympics World Games softball competition.

July 6: The other day we met a couple who adopted 20 children no one else wanted. Today one of those kids won a gold and two bronzes. Her mother says: "There is nothing but acceptance here. For 51 weeks, Katie is different. For this one week, she is treated like everyone else."

July 7: I'm asked to hand out awards after one game. I have never felt more honored.

July 8: It's over. The End. And then I see it. As the athletes get on their buses, every volunteer cheers and applauds. And so it ends as it began. Fitting.

CHAPTER SIX

1993-2001

Expanding and Redefining

This company started from an idea in 1851 to become what it is today in the face of a lot of bigger companies around here, many of whom do not exist today. What allowed us to get here is innovation.

— Robert W. Fiondella

WALL ST

The post-merger years were a tumultuous time in the financial markets and a time of enormous change for Phoenix. For the company, the decade culminated in three profound events that came in rapid succession: the establishment of a laser-sharp focus on wealth management; Dona Young's appointment as president; and authorization by the board of directors to develop a plan to convert Phoenix from a mutual to a publicly traded stock company.

The timing of these events was fitting: they clustered around the threshold of the twenty-first century and anticipated Phoenix's 150th year, confirming and solidifying a course of action that took shape throughout the 1990s.

"The steps toward wealth management and demutualization reflect our roots," Young affirms. "Like the phoenix symbol itself, Phoenix has always reinvented itself for the next stage of our growth."

"Our goal is in keeping with our history," Fiondella adds. "The objective of wealth management is to help clients accumulate, preserve and transfer assets. These are capabilities Phoenix has been perfecting over its 150-year history."

A PRACTICAL VISIONARY

If the architect of the modern Phoenix was Bob Jackson, the architect of the postmodern Phoenix is Bob Fiondella. His ability to move the company forward in giant steps stems from his realization that such steps are composed of smaller, more painstaking steps — and occasional missteps as well. "I call it taking a Taoist approach," Fiondella says — a surprising phrase from a second-generation Italian with blue-collar roots, a steel-trap legal mind and no New Age airs. "The best you can do is muddle through with a purpose, because things change."

Ask people to describe Fiondella, especially in reference to the post-merger era, and the word that arises most often is "visionary." Fiondella resists the characterization, or tries to. "I am a bit more involved in the details and operations than is typical of a visionary, whatever that word means," he says. When pressed, he interprets the label in his own way. "I can see ideas and the inevitable shift of events," he explains. "I can see the shapes that things can take." The shape envisioned by him and his executive team for the post-merger Phoenix — a global company intensely focused on wealth management, best able to pursue that path as a public company — has positioned it for the twenty-first century.

At the same time, if being visionary includes making long-term forecasts, Fiondella isn't playing. "If you think you can see exactly what will happen three or four or five years out, then you're deluding yourself, because you don't know what will happen," he emphasizes. "Think back three years on what events have occurred. Would you have been able to predict them? In 1998, for example, we considered demutualization but concluded that we weren't ready then. Phoenix has always had a one-year plan and a four-year to five-year projection. Our approach tends to be conservative as opposed to a stretch."

DIVESTING AND REALIGNING

Does a particular line of business or subsidiary actively strengthen Phoenix's wealth management position? This is the litmus test that prevailed post-merger. It has identified which businesses to expand and which ones to sell, activities that sharply accelerated in the late 1990s. "Our expertise, built up over 150 years, is managing risk and managing money. We do those things really well," says Bob Fiondella. "Our challenge has been to come to grips with which businesses we should be in."

Strategic fit aside, divestitures can be painful. It is not easy to turn away from a line of business that figured prominently in the company's history — or to part with a robust and profitable subsidiary nurtured from scratch. Also, Phoenix has always prided itself on being a stable company. It has grown by adding rather than subtracting. The marketplace demanded changes in the 1990s, yet the company fought to preserve its commitment to employees. While some other companies boast to their shareholders of job cuts, Phoenix takes great pains to avoid them. Whenever possible, it structured business transitions so that jobs were not lost. It worked with employees to find them new positions within Phoenix, a challenge made easier by periodic early retirement programs that found favor with numerous employees.

American Phoenix is a case in point. Founded in 1981 and headed by President Mell Vaughan, this subsidiary had grown from the nation's 67th-largest property/casualty distributor to the 13th-largest by 1998, as measured by revenues. It ultimately reached $65 million in commission revenues.

When American Phoenix no longer fit into Phoenix's evolving focus on wealth management, Bob Fiondella didn't simply sell it to the highest bidder. Instead, Phoenix entered into a strategic relationship with Hilb, Rogal and Hamilton Company (HRH), a publicly held insurance broker. HRH purchased the thriving subsidiary

A Block of Business That CLICked

When Phoenix won the bid on the individual life and single-premium deferred annuity blocks of business from the former Confederation Life Insurance Company (CLIC) U.S. in 1997, it marked the biggest acquisition in the company's history — and a "perfect fit" for both sides, according to Bob Fiondella.

CLIC, a Canadian mutual insurer, went into liquidation in 1994. Its U.S. branch operation was then placed into rehabilitation. Because CLIC sold mainly to upper-income professionals and business owners, its block of business suited Phoenix extremely well. There was also a good overlap in distribution; many brokerage representatives who had sold for CLIC also sold for Phoenix.

Incorporating 42,000 CLIC U.S. policies with their $166 million of in-force premium into Phoenix's base, however, involved much more than data entry. Conversion teams worked for a year to restructure CLIC's 75 types of policies, create new policy illustrations, calculate updated values and notify customers. At that point, policyholders could legally opt to take their business elsewhere. Ninety-seven percent chose to stay with Phoenix.

Jo-Anne Leventhal, a retired assistant vice president, found that skills cultivated in the merger of Phoenix and Home Life came in handy for CLIC. "Phoenix was in competition with some very good companies, so just the fact that we won the bid was impressive," she says. "Then to implement the business was no small feat. I'd say our Confederation Life acquisition was another defining moment in our history."

in 1999 for an attractive price that included some convertible notes and shares of HRH stock. "The relationship provides Phoenix with a potential strategic marketing opportunity through HRH's distribution network," Dave Searfoss points out. "In addition, the company was preserved." Vaughan and other American Phoenix staff members made the transition, ensuring continuity and specialized expertise. Vaughan, Fiondella and Searfoss serve on the company's board of directors.

Traditional life reinsurance was another line that Phoenix nurtured and carefully "harvested" at the right time. Phoenix entered this highly competitive business, which involves the sharing of risk among insurance companies, in 1965. Reinsurance thrived, then hit some rough times in the volatile 1980s. "My challenge was to see if I could turn the reinsurance business around, grow it and make money," says Fred Sawyer, who managed the line in the 1990s. He succeeded in raising the total volume of in-force business from approximately $25 billion to $119 billion, making Phoenix the seventh-largest life reinsurer in the United States.

By 1999, however, Phoenix concluded that

While other mutual life insurers went public in order to become broader financial services companies, Phoenix pursued demutualization in order to maximize its wealth management focus. Phoenix shares now trade on the New York Stock Exchange, seen on page 91.

Rating Agencies

Rating agencies assess the financial condition of insurance companies. Company ratings are not recommendations or warranties of future performance; they are independent opinions of a company's financial strength and claims-paying ability. Phoenix is proud of its very high ratings from the four major rating firms: AA (Very High) from Fitch IBCA (formerly Duff & Phelps); A (Excellent) from A.M. Best; Aa3 (Excellent) from Moody's; and AA (Very Strong) from Standard & Poor's. These firms formulate reevaluations of a company's rating each year, as well as during times of significant change, such as demutualization. According to Chairman Bob Fiondella: "While we can't predict the actions of the rating agencies, we believe the financial flexibility Phoenix has as a public company will enable us to improve our ratings over time."

Insurers have been graded by rating agencies since the A.M. Best Company started its reports in 1899. But not until the mid-1980s, when life insurance companies began selling Guaranteed Insurance Contracts (GICs), did ratings leap into prominence. GICs buyers, mainly institutional pension managers, wanted a way to compare providers. "They said 'where are the S&P and Moody's ratings?' Those two companies used that as an opportunity to include insurance companies' financial data in their financial reports and roster of rated companies," CFO David Searfoss explains. He recalls a definite learning curve for the newer rating agencies: One issued its highest rating, AAA, to a company that soon went into receivership.

"Over the years, the rating agencies began to be much tougher," Searfoss observes. "They don't just evaluate solvency or capital levels now. They want to see a vibrant business that is growing capital and earnings." He points out that agencies base their grade on subjective assessment of management as well as on quantitative measures.

Phoenix believes that a company's financial strength and vibrancy goes beyond its ratings as well. Informed consumers consider a company's record of growth, its liquidity, an appropriate risk profile and overall operating performance. On all these measures, Phoenix remains a company upon which policyholders and customers can depend — continuing a 150-year tradition of innovation, consistent growth and the prompt fulfillment of all financial obligations.

it made sense to sell this franchise. Even if life reinsurance had been in line with Phoenix's wealth management goals, the gap between the top few reinsurers and other strong players was widening. The aggressive price-competitiveness of the marketplace increasingly favored the biggest players. Phoenix had built a solid book of traditional life reinsurance, which brought an attractive offer from ERC Life, a highly respected global subsidiary of GE Capital's Employers Reinsurance Corporation. The sale was completed in 1999.

Sawyer admits that it was also a bittersweet decision to divest the subsidiary Financial Administrative Services, Inc. (FAS), which he oversaw from its purchase in 1994 to its sale in 1999. A third-party service business that handles life and annuity administration for many other insurance companies, FAS grew from $3.4 million of sales in its first year to $15 million by 1999. The company's relatively small size made it easier to minimize impact on employees; FAS president Belinda Monat and her staff continued in their jobs.

The sale of Phoenix's group business in 2000 was similarly bittersweet. Since 1958, this profitable arm of the company had sold life, disability and health benefits to employers. "As we began shifting our focus to wealth management, we could no longer make the required investments in group," Bob Fiondella explains. "Also, in light of industry consolidations, our operation didn't have the scale to compete adequately in group markets." For staff and customers alike, however, the transition was smooth. The buyer, GE Financial Assurance Holdings, Inc., hired most group employees and has maintained and expanded the business.

REAL ESTATE

Once upon a time, life insurance companies and real estate ownership were synonymous. From the 1920s onward, Phoenix and Home Life proudly helped to house Americans and to build, mortgage and manage their office parks, shopping malls and medical centers. Phoenix also specialized in farm mortgages; for decades, in fact, it kept an office in Davenport, Iowa, dedicated to that lucrative business. "When I first began to know people in the investment department in the early 1970s, real estate was dominant," says Chief Investment Officer Philip McLoughlin. "Certainly, it was the focus in terms of excitement."

The excitement died down with America's real estate traumas of the 1980s, but that was not the reason Phoenix ultimately sold all of its real estate businesses in 1998 and 1999. "It was a decision based on diversification of risk," McLoughlin emphasizes. "Owning brick-and-mortar real estate became punishing for an insurance company." Years of overbuilding in the office market had led to ample supply and thus to a leveling of prices — a trend supported by the relative lack of inflation in the 1990s. The inherent illiquidity of real estate, which even in the strongest markets can't be bought and sold overnight, was a special concern for mutuals with their limited access to capital.

"Equity real estate is a very poor asset class for matching up against insurance liabilities," confirms CFO Searfoss. Another deciding factor, perhaps strongest of all, was that Phoenix would have had to triple its capital devoted to real estate in order to meet rating agencies' relentlessly rising standards.

Phoenix rejected a few subpar bids and packaged its properties to maximize return. The main transaction, which took place in 1999, involved the sale of 53 commercial properties to a real estate fund managed by Donaldson, Lufkin & Jenrette Inc., a major investment-banking firm. This transaction, along with other sales in 1998, yielded Phoenix a substantial gain. The company also sold the various real estate businesses it owned.

"We haven't walked away from real estate," McLoughlin summarizes. "We invest in it in different ways, through real estate funds and investment products." The company's mortgage investments now generally take the form of mortgage-backed securities issued by the Federal National Mortgage Association (Fannie Mae) and similar bodies.

Without doubt, the divestitures of the 1990s were critical turning points. From a bottom-line perspective, they have enhanced liquidity and freed the company to pursue its wealth management strategy through several new initiatives.

THE EVOLUTION TO WEALTH MANAGEMENT

"We're looking to make this company a recognized name," Dona Young said a few years ago. "Not in every household, but certainly in the households we want to serve."

Increasingly, the households served by Phoenix are affluent, defined as those with incomes in excess of $100,000 or net worths in excess of $500,000. Specifically, the company has chosen to focus on a subset of the affluent: individuals and business owners whose net worths exceed $1 million.

Why the tight focus on this particular market? Walter H. Zultowski, Ph.D., senior vice president, marketing and market research, explains: "We don't have the resources to play in all markets. The high-net-worth market is large and growing — in fact, it's the fastest-growing segment of the U.S. population. From 1990 to 1998, the number of pentamillionaire households (those with $5 million or more in net worth) doubled. This market will grow as America's 78 million baby boomers not only move into their peak earning years but begin to inherit their parents' estates." Nearly $12 trillion is expected to be transferred to the baby boomer generation over the next 20 years.

"High net worth is a market that plays to our strengths in insurance and money management, and one in which we are already well-positioned," Young emphasizes. In fact, the company has had historic success among affluent individuals and business owners since the days of Home Life's Planned Estates concept and Phoenix's retirement income policies. In those times, of course, producers met customers' needs with ordinary life insurance products alone. Now they have more specialized tools to customize and deploy, second-to-die insurance being a prime example. Purchased mainly by the affluent, this product now represents 25 percent of Phoenix's in-force business and almost one-third of its new premiums. At the same time, 60 percent of the company's overall life premium comes from policies with face amounts of $1 million or more — and the average face amount of second-to-die policies grew from $1 million to $2 million between 1994 and 1999. Obviously, Phoenix and high-net-worth individuals are no strangers to each other.

Zultowski also likes to point out a surprising statistic. "Fewer than 20 percent of affluent and high-net-worth households currently have a written financial plan in place," he says. "These consumers need a certain level of customization in their products, and they will pay for personalized service. In short, they're ready and waiting for sophisticated insurance and investment products that Phoenix can provide through its advisors."

Creative methods of distribution and marketing are required to reach and cultivate the upper income market more efficiently. The rules keep changing, Young says, in accelerated ways: CPAs have moved into fee-based wealth management; banks now sell significant amounts of variable annuity products; and fewer individuals are buying life insurance, whether traditional or variable, from career agents. Phoenix has responded by strengthening and deepening its traditional

Phoenix. It's just not what it used to be.

Forty-five percent of today's millionaires are younger than 55, compared to 26 percent in 1990. To reach these individuals with Phoenix's wealth management message and raise the company's profile in a highly competitive marketplace, the company unveiled a bold advertising and public relations campaign at the end of 1999.

Advertisements appear in publications read by the high-net-worth market, including *Fortune*, *Art & Antiques*, *Golf Magazine* and *Forbes*. The ads also appear in major trade publications, such as *On Wall Street*, *Financial Advisor* and *Registered Representation*, reflecting the company's focus on the advisors to the high-net-worth market. Distinctive promotional programs sponsored by the publications, ranging from gallery openings to golf tournaments, give potential customers and Phoenix producers opportunities to meet.

The first round of ads, created by New York agency Post & Partners, has already won first place honors for corporate image in the Financial Communications Society's prestigious Portfolio Awards competition, edging out such entrants as Andersen Consulting, Goldman Sachs, Allstate Insurance and CitiGroup.

It's heady praise, but the ultimate measure of a campaign is how it extends into business practices. "Everything we do reinforces the same message," says Michele U. Farley, vice president, corporate communications. "No matter how our customers encounter Phoenix — whether on the Web, in the annual report, through operators on our 800 numbers or attendance at an event — we communicate our understanding that today's affluent individuals look and act differently from the old money stereotypes."

distribution channels and making alliances with nontraditional producers such as stockbrokers.

With Phoenix's support, both affiliated and nonaffiliated producers are evolving toward full-service wealth managers who provide a range of services that span a lifetime: retirement and post-retirement planning, investment planning, estate planning, business planning, charitable planning and executive benefit planning.

PRODUCT EVOLUTION

Throughout most of Phoenix's history, product innovation drove the company. It is still an important factor in the company's success, but the approach has changed. "It used to be that when you introduced a hot product, you had the field to yourself for at least a few years," Simon Tan explains. "With today's technology, however, it became very easy for others to copy products. Now the window of any innovation in product feature is perhaps five or six months." Thus the focus has shifted to fewer products more closely tailored to specific market needs.

A prime example is the shift in emphasis from traditional whole life insurance to variable products, which allow policyholders to invest the cash value of their policy in stock mutual funds, bonds or money markets (after covering expenses for administration and death benefits). With the full encouragement of Bob Fiondella, Sawyer, Tan and other members of Phoenix's product development team began to develop variable products in the 1980s. The company believed that customers could be entrusted to manage their own money, an idea that some other life insurers regarded as heresy.

As it turned out, variable products have been hugely successful because they meet the demands of savvy consumers. These pioneer investment vehicles gave policyholders a chance to enjoy the surge in the stock markets that were the hallmark of the 1980s and 1990s. They currently account for more than $15 billion of Phoenix's life insurance in force, with Phoenix now ranking 20th out of 51 companies in total variable universal life assets under management as of September 30, 2000.

"People want options and choices," Tan affirms. With Phoenix's variable products, they enjoy 42 choices from Phoenix's seven affiliated and eleven nonaffiliated asset managers. That represents a broad array of choices in investment options and fund managers.

Recognizing another growing trend, Phoenix has built a distribution channel dedicated to variable annuities (VAs). "There are many who might think the VA marketplace is crowded, but there's enormous opportunity there," Young asserts. "Think of all those individuals, including senior executives, who have amassed significant amounts of money in their 401(k) plans. When it comes time to retire, they're going to have to take that defined contribution plan and convert it to something that can translate into an income stream." As with variable life policies, variable annuities offer dozens of investment choices from Phoenix and outside fund managers.

Phoenix's Largest Case

COLI isn't an obscure crossword term. It's an acronym that categorizes the largest case in the history of Phoenix, one that currently generates about $29 million in annual premium.

COLI stands for corporate-owned life insurance, a generic term for employer-paid, highly customized policies that cover key executives. In 1995, Jim McFarlane, then an Illinois brokerage manager, heard about a COLI opportunity brewing at a Fortune 50 company. He asked Simon Tan, now executive vice president, life and annuity products and operations, to brainstorm ways for Phoenix to take part. Realizing that such a case would attract aggressive competition, Tan and Paul M. Fischer, CLU, CLFC, vice president, put together a top-level strategy team.

Typical for COLI business, the initial stages took several twists and turns. Some 18 months later, Phoenix emerged with the prize: a case that includes 145 life insurance policies covering 124 executives through Phoenix's Executive Equity Accumulation product.

When all was said and done, 100 Phoenix employees pitched in on this massive effort. McFarlane himself worked on it every day for almost two years. "To be successful in the COLI market you must be patient, flexible, creative and innovative," says Dona Young. "You also need nerves of steel. The people who worked on this case demonstrated all those qualities. I was humbled by their effort."

Philip R. McLoughlin (left), chairman and CEO of Phoenix Investment Partners (PXP), shakes the hand of Roger Engemann, chairman of Roger Engemann & Associates, Inc., a PXP partner. PXP's partnership model provides portfolio managers the support they need to be able to focus on what they do best without distraction.

To this end, in 1999 Phoenix purchased the private placement variable life and annuity subsidiaries of The Guarantee Life Companies, Inc. An emerging leader in its market, which encompasses high-net-worth individuals and sophisticated corporate life insurance purchasers, this Philadelphia-based group had built almost $100 million in assets under management in just two years. The investment provided Phoenix with additional distribution and growth opportunities. It also dovetailed beautifully with the renewed focus on Phoenix's variable annuity businesses, which in 1999 added a team of high-level professionals and rolled out two aggressively competitive products.

"All of our products help people deal with financial dependencies," Fiondella comments. "And there are a heck of a lot more financial dependencies today than 20 years ago, with more to come. You have two-income households, split households and multiple generations," all pointing toward the need for astute wealth management.

EVOLUTIONS IN INVESTMENT

A cornerstone of Phoenix's wealth management focus is Phoenix Investment Partners, also known as PXP. This investment management subsidiary traces its roots to Phoenix Equity Planning Corporation, or PEPCO, which was formed in 1968 to manage and distribute investment products.

Today's PXP is progressing in strategic directions set by Phoenix leadership in the mid-1990s, including McLoughlin, Fiondella and Richard Booth, a former executive vice president. "We envisioned a diversified model consisting of two business divisions, retail and institutional, each offering access to the investment skills of a variety of talented money managers," McLoughlin says. To successfully achieve this model, Phoenix took the operation public in 1995 by combining its securities division, then under the name Phoenix Securities Group, with Duff & Phelps Corporation, a publicly held institutional money management company. The new company, which adopted the name Phoenix Investment Partners in 1998 and reverted to a private structure in early 2001, built on its base of homegrown mutual funds by acquiring additional money management partners.

The very name Phoenix Investment Partners, Ltd., reflects the core of McLoughlin's strategy. "Our founding principle is that portfolio managers who operate with minimal outside distractions are most likely to produce consistently above-average results for investors," he emphasizes. To that end, PXP provides its eight investment partners with a consolidated platform of distribution, administrative and technological support. "This model differentiates us," McLoughlin notes. "There are other multi-managers, but no one incorporates all the managers and products with centralized distribution."

"We free our fund managers to concentrate on what they do best, which is investing money," says G. Jeffrey Bohne, head of mutual fund customer service. The strategy has paid off: PXP has achieved steady growth in operating earnings and increased assets under management to about $60 billion by year-end 2000.

But investment companies, like the funds they manage, cannot rely on past performance to predict future results. Having "covered all the bases" in investment philosophies, as McLoughlin

Investment Partnerships

Under its innovative "multi-manager/single platform" structure, PXP has eight distinct asset management partners:

Aberdeen Fund Managers, Inc. (Fort Lauderdale, Florida), subadvisor to Phoenix-Aberdeen international and global retail mutual funds. Not owned by PXP. Investment focus: *International*

Duff & Phelps Investment Management Co. (Chicago, Illinois), institutional manager and advisor to the Duff & Phelps closed-end funds, Phoenix-Duff & Phelps retail mutual funds and managed accounts. Investment focus: *Core and Value Equity and Fixed Income*

Phoenix Investment Counsel, Inc. (Hartford, Connecticut), institutional manager and advisor to the Phoenix-Goodwin retail mutual funds. Investment focus: *Sector-Rotation Fixed Income*

Phoenix Investment Counsel, Inc. (Sarasota, Florida), institutional manager and advisor to the Phoenix-Hollister retail mutual funds and managed accounts. Investment focus: *Classic Value*

Phoenix Investment Counsel, Inc. (Scotts Valley, California), institutional manager and advisor to the Phoenix-Oakhurst retail mutual funds. Investment focus: *Systematic Value*

Roger Engemann & Associates, Inc. (Pasadena, California), advisor to the Phoenix-Engemann retail mutual funds, managed accounts, private clients and institutional accounts. Investment focus: *Classic Growth*

Seneca Capital Management LLC (San Francisco, California), institutional manager and advisor to the Phoenix-Seneca retail mutual funds, managed accounts, private clients and institutional accounts. Investment focus: *Earnings-Driven Growth Equity; Value-Driven Fixed Income*

Phoenix/Zweig Advisers LLC (New York, New York), advisor to the Phoenix-Zweig retail mutual funds and Zweig closed-end funds. The wholly owned subsidiary Euclid Advisors LLC serves as investment advisor to the Phoenix-Euclid retail mutual funds. Investment focus: *Risk-Averse Asset Allocation*

puts it, the new challenge, then, is to develop a branding strategy that distinguishes the existing money managers and their investment styles in a competitive and crowded marketplace. Fortunately, in addition to its mutual fund success, PXP also boasts solid expertise in managed accounts and mutual fund wrap accounts, which are rapidly growing product choices among high-net-worth individuals. PXP's managed account sales have been doubling year over year — from $500 million in 1997 to $4 billion in 2000 — and the company participates in an increasing number of select money management and wrap programs at nonaffiliated broker/dealer and financial planning firms. "While there is no accurate industry measure, we estimate that we are among the top five companies nationwide in sales and assets under management offering these specialized and increasingly popular accounts," says Jack Sharry, president of PXP's Private Client Group.

"To be as effective as possible in wealth management, we've also introduced several advisory training and investor education programs in print and on the Internet," McLoughlin adds. "Our trusted advisors are well-educated advisors." PXP is also taking deeper root in the institutional money management business, with many of its investment partners now managing institutional assets in addition to retail products.

In January of 2001, after five years of being traded on the New York Stock Exchange, PXP once again became a wholly owned Phoenix company when Phoenix purchased the publicly held common shares. This change in structure did not alter PXP's mission or its operations: McLoughlin and his management team remained in place, as did the array of investment partners. "The decision to take PXP private was in the best interest of both Phoenix and PXP," Fiondella explained. "It provided immediate enhanced value to PXP shareholders and it allows us to work more collaboratively to execute our wealth management strategy."

IN TRUSTS WE PROSPER

Phoenix's entry into the trust business "was Marketing 101, if you think about it," says Martin J. Gavin, who retired as senior vice president, trust operations. The move was a natural one precisely because it *is* so fundamental to the company's direction. While many companies claim to be involved in wealth management, they usually offer only investment management and wealth accumulation services. Phoenix defines wealth management as accumulation, preservation and transfer of assets — and sees the largest long-term potential in the wealth transfer component. And as life insurance plays a critical role in the transfer of assets, so do trusts.

Gavin explains further: "About 50 percent of the face value of the insurance we sell goes into trusts for estate planning. And about 60 percent of the assets we manage are held in trusts, usually 401(k)s or pension plans." Realizing that all this money was being held by outside trust companies, Phoenix built its own trust operations from scratch, creating the Phoenix Charter Oak Trust Company in 1996.

Its first president, Richard Booth, articulated the "rightness" of the plan: "It creates opportunities for our agents and brokers to provide real stability for clients and their families through multigenerational financial planning." By offering a broad array of trust services — including living trusts, investment management, securities custody, future will appointments, personal and institutional not-for-profit funds and escrow arrangements — Phoenix Charter Oak allowed Phoenix to provide a level of service well beyond what was traditionally available through life insurance companies. Later in the 1990s, other insurers scrambled to catch up.

The growth of Phoenix's trust and custodial capabilities parallels the aging of the baby boomers, an important demographic trend. Boomers — those 78 million Americans born between 1946 and 1964 — have accumulated significant wealth through investments and pensions. They are also projected to inherit huge sums of money, estimated as high as $12 trillion, in the next two decades.

THE WORLDWIDE PHOENIX

Scotland ... England ... Bermuda ... India ... Argentina ... Luxembourg ... Japan ... Oman ... Brazil.

Every time you turn around, Phoenix seems to be entering a new country. International expansion through strategic alliances was a new strategy of the 1990s, the brainchild of Bob Fiondella. Phoenix's founders would have approved; they, too, looked outside the United States for opportunities. Rather than copying other Hartford insurers of the 1850s, they studied British companies and built the American Temperance Life Insurance Company — a promising adaptation of an idea that had worked abroad.

Phoenix is committed to establishing a presence in selected international growth markets when opportunities arise to enhance its wealth management strategy. Phoenix has enjoyed no small portion of its success by being able to gauge markets sometimes 10 or more years into the future. As Phoenix demonstrated with its exploration of variable products in the 1980s, a moderate investment at an early stage in a market's development can mean solid financial success down the road. "It's a long-term building process," says Bob Fiondella.

Fiondella has defined his philosophy of international growth in these words: "Develop a global business strategy now and business opportunities will come to those who are patient." Phoenix has implemented this approach by making relatively modest and manageable investments in different parts of the world. In so doing, Phoenix is not only diversifying risk, but is preparing to take advantage of international business opportunities as they develop from a grassroots vantage point, rather than as an outsider looking in. "More countries are privatizing their financial services sector and permitting American companies to participate," says Fiondella. "With the global economy a given and more and more wealth being generated outside the United States, a strong global presence is key to our wealth management strategy."

International inroads started on a small scale in the late 1980s, when Senior Vice President Terence N. Towry, FSA, MAAA, began exploring the possibilities. Towry, who suffered an untimely death from cancer in 1995, held several key positions in his 30 years at Phoenix. As head of reinsurance, he had cultivated contacts worldwide. In the 1990s, Senior Vice Presidents Richard Shaw and Joan Herman picked up the international banner and embarked on several smaller ventures to give the company experience in foreign marketing and distribution.

In 1996, Fiondella leveraged Phoenix's growing knowledge to forge a pioneering alliance with Aberdeen Asset Management, PLC (formerly Aberdeen Trust, PLC), a Scottish fund manager founded in 1897, listed on the London Stock Exchange and renowned for its expertise in the Far East and Latin America.

Through a series of transactions, Phoenix obtained a fully diluted 27 percent interest in Aberdeen. This relationship goes far beyond the ownership interest. The companies have actively pursued opportunities that benefit both. One of the first was to launch the Phoenix-Aberdeen

mutual funds for sale in the United States.

More recently, as an investor in Lombard International Assurance, Aberdeen introduced Phoenix to the principals of Lombard, which led to Phoenix's investment in that firm. Phoenix currently holds a 12 percent equity interest in Lombard, a rapidly growing pan-European life insurer based in Luxembourg. Lombard's unit-linked life insurance products are designed exclusively for the high-net-worth market and give Phoenix a unique perspective on its target market in Europe.

Among South American nations, Argentina represents a logical, strategic and attractive starting point for Phoenix to build on its wealth management resources.

After exploring a number of possibilities, Joan Herman and Vice President John Herndon developed a relationship with Emprendimiento Compartido, S.A. (EMCO), a Buenos Aires-based investment company with pension management, life insurance and annuity operations. After a very positive first year, which included the acquisition of another pension management company, Herndon negotiated an evolution of the partnership. As a result, Phoenix now is a 50 percent shareholder and its partner is TCW/Latin America Partners. Phoenix has representation on EMCO's board and assisted in the development of EMCO's life insurance subsidiary, which received an AA rating from Fitch IBCA in its first year. EMCO is specializing in credit life and group products through

Phoenix Global Investments, K.K., established in April 2000 is run by (left to right) Assistant Manager Rie Konno, Executive Officer Akira Yamamoto (standing), President Naoyuki Inada, Director Kouichiro Otani (standing), Chairman Yasumasa Ishizaka, and Director Takeshi Katsuyama, who are pictured here in the Tokyo office.

Breaking Through Work Barriers

Most companies strive to "work smarter" but don't have a plan to get there. Phoenix has adopted a continuous improvement process, known as Breakthrough, that is making its operations measurably more efficient and cost-effective.

"Breakthrough is based on a Japanese management technique called kaizen, introduced to us by board member Arthur P. Byrne, a nationally recognized kaizen expert. Continuous improvement is not new at Phoenix, but Breakthrough is a very different approach for Phoenix," says Executive Vice President Carl Chadburn. "It focuses on work processes, not just people or costs. Ultimately, it allows us to redirect our people to activities that are more critical to our wealth management strategy and our bottom line."

Breakthrough brings together diverse groups of people to study a current business process and then implement significant changes within an intensive, five-day period. "The results are carried out without delay. There is no 'analysis paralysis' or further approvals required," points out André Jett, second vice president and head of the company's Center for Continuous Improvement, established in 1999.

During the pilot period, one breakthrough team reduced a time-consuming 63-step procedure to a single, streamlined process. Another team identified 286 forms being used in different staff areas, eliminated 105 of them as obsolete and put 118 of the remaining forms online for instant, company-wide desktop printing. In a major breakthrough, Enfield's mailroom, supply department, data processing output department and print center were merged. That freed 40,000 square feet, allowed new time-saving procedures to be implemented and resulted in projected savings of $1 million annually. Encouraged by such successes, the company has rolled out the process into the individual insurance line of business.

"Over the years we've used a number of means to continually make our operations better," comments Chairman Bob Fiondella. "The breakthrough method is yielding impressive results quickly and efficiently. Most importantly, it directly involves those individuals who are on the front lines in improving their own work product and environment. Continuous improvement is invaluable in helping us execute our wealth management strategy.

Argentine banks with whom it has relations. Its principal business — pension management — was further expanded by a second acquisition in 1999.

In 1988, Phoenix established a relationship with Dai-ichi Mutual Life Insurance Company of Japan, then the world's second-largest life insurer, through its group operation. When group head Charles J. Paydos, FSA, MAAA, toured the Dai-ichi office in Japan, he met a young Venezuelan woman who had been educated in the United States and Japan, Veronica Maldonado, now director of strategic development with Phoenix. Paydos recruited Maldonado from Dai-ichi to Hartford, initially to help Phoenix manage its relationship with Dai-ichi. When Bob Fiondella met Maldonado, who is fluent in English, Spanish and Japanese, he was impressed with her ability to "think and act globally." In getting to know her, Bob came to understand Japanese culture better and to consider the business opportunities for Phoenix if it could build the right operation.

In 1999, Maldonado introduced Fiondella to Yasumasa Ishizaka, a savvy and urbane Japanese entrepreneur educated in the United Kingdom and the United States. Fiondella asked Senior Vice President Dave Pepin, Maldonado and Ishizaka to locate the right opportunity for Phoenix in Japan. They sought top talent in the Japanese financial services industry and helped Phoenix establish Phoenix Global Investments, K.K., an institutional money manager based in Tokyo, incorporated in April of 2000. PGI has a talented staff headed by Naoyuki Inada, and once it completes the licensing process, it has good prospects for bringing in significant assets to be managed by PXP, Aberdeen and other third parties.

This story exemplifies Phoenix's philosophy of maximizing the market-specific expertise and connections of in-country staff to get a foot in the door of an international market. Another example can be found in India.

When *Newsweek* drew up a list of the world's top 10 high-tech havens in 1998, only two non-U.S. cities made the cut. One was Bangalore, India — and Phoenix was already there. Like many other subsidiaries, Phoenix Global Solutions (India) Pvt. Ltd., got its start when an individual saw an opportunity, did his homework and won support from senior management. Here the individual was Satish Bangalore, a 24-year company veteran born and raised in the city whose name he coincidentally bears, and the initial opportunity was Year 2000 (Y2K) remediation.

Managing director of PGS and former head of emerging technologies for Phoenix in Hartford, Bangalore evaluated several Y2K planning vendors on Phoenix's behalf in the mid-1990s. Many such vendors had offshore facilities in India. "Why can't we do this ourselves?" Bangalore asked. Soon he and his team were laying the groundwork for the Indian operations.

"I stand amazed at how quickly the India initiative came together," says CFO Searfoss, who also admired PGS's immediate profitability. From the start, PGS looked beyond Year 2000 projects. It does fee-based systems work for a variety of clients and provides third-party training within India through a division called the Phoenix Academy, "the largest such center in Bangalore," Carl Chadburn reported upon his return from a site visit. "Due to the extraordinary efforts of Satish Bangalore and Ed Hourihan, PGS India is positioned very well."

In 1999, Carol Baldi, a former director of Phoenix, introduced the company to the management team from Bittencourt, a brokerage house in Brazil. This introduction culminated in an investment by Phoenix in Bittencourt, which enables the brokerage house to grow and gives Phoenix a window into Brazilian financial markets.

Phoenix extended its global reach farther by purchasing a minority interest in National Life Insurance Company of Oman in 1999, thus obtaining a foothold in that part of the world. Phoenix has since provided product development and actuarial expertise to broaden National Life of Oman's offerings, which will be marketed not just in Oman but to nearby countries, including the United Arab Emirates and Egypt.

Where in the world, geographically, is Phoenix headed next? Possibilities abound. Wherever appropriate opportunities may appear, one thing is certain: The company will continue to solidify its global expertise.

THE MOVE TOWARD DEMUTUALIZATION

On April 17, 2000, the board of directors took what may prove to be the most important step in Phoenix's history: it authorized management to develop a plan for Phoenix to convert from a mutual to a publicly traded stock company. The board was acting on management's recommendation that demutualization would enhance the company's ability to aggressively pursue new opportunities for growth within wealth management.

"It's prophetic and fitting to have taken this step in our 150th year in business," Bob Fiondella reflects, noting that Phoenix started its existence as a part-stock company and Home Life as a stock company. Both companies converted to full mutuality when business conditions made that change advisable, and even inevitable, for growth. In a sense, then, the company is coming full circle by yet again embracing change. "This is another step in the process of our drive to exist forever," Fiondella emphasizes.

The company first investigated demutualization in 1998. However, the taskforce concluded that Phoenix wasn't ready. "Being in a number of businesses then, we would have found it difficult to convince the investing public what Phoenix was about," Fiondella says. The chairman also admits that he personally wasn't ready, having been a staunch advocate of mutuality.

Why is the time right in 2001? "The environment in which we compete has changed immensely, so no company can stand still," Fiondella explains. "While the mutual structure served us well, it didn't give us the flexibility to deploy our existing capital and acquire additional capital in the most effective way. As a public company, Phoenix has access to the capital markets, providing the flexibility to grow on the right scale and at the right pace — all toward maximizing the opportunities in the high-net-worth market."

On a more personal level, Fiondella points to a lesson on timing that he learned from one of his key mentors, one that he has passed on to President Dona Young. "Our 11th president, Bob Jackson, always believed that there's never a 'right' time to do anything," Fiondella says. "You do what's right for the business. If a move makes strategic sense, do it and worry about external forces later."

From the merger with Home Life to the Confederation Life acquisition — also tackled during volatile financial times in the industry and in the financial markets — Phoenix has an impressive track record of undertaking huge projects and staying focused. "Soon after the demutualization plan announcement, a rating agency analyst told us he has absolutely no doubts about this company's ability to execute," Fiondella remarks. Unprompted, this analyst further offered a compliment that warmed the hearts of the chairman and president, both base-

"My grandfather would approve . . ."

Occasionally, at momentous times, a voice from the past seems to come forward to give its blessing. Such a thing happened in spring 2000 when this letter, postmarked from West Hartford, Connecticut, arrived in Dona Young's office:

Dear Mrs. Young,

Congratulations and best wishes on your appointment as President!

I am the grandson of your predecessor in that job from 100 years ago — John Marshall Holcombe — whose wife was one of the great leaders of her day....

The Courant *made one error, if my verbal history is correct, that is, in referring to [Phoenix's] 149-year heritage as a mutual insurer. I have always understood that my grandfather changed the company from stock to mutual perhaps 110 or 115 years ago....*

Things change and I believe my grandfather would see the differences and approve going back to a stock company. I look forward to owning a piece of it!

Sincerely,

Shepherd M. Holcombe, FSA

"I was touched that the grandson of a former president took the time to send a note of congratulations," says Young, who was named Phoenix's first woman president on February 28, 2000. "His words made me feel very connected to our history. I also felt encouraged that Mr. Holcombe affirmed our future. He saw that our step toward demutualization was very much in keeping with our roots."

Dona Young's appointment as president was a distinguished step in her 21-year career at Phoenix. Previously she served as general counsel and executive vice president of individual insurance.

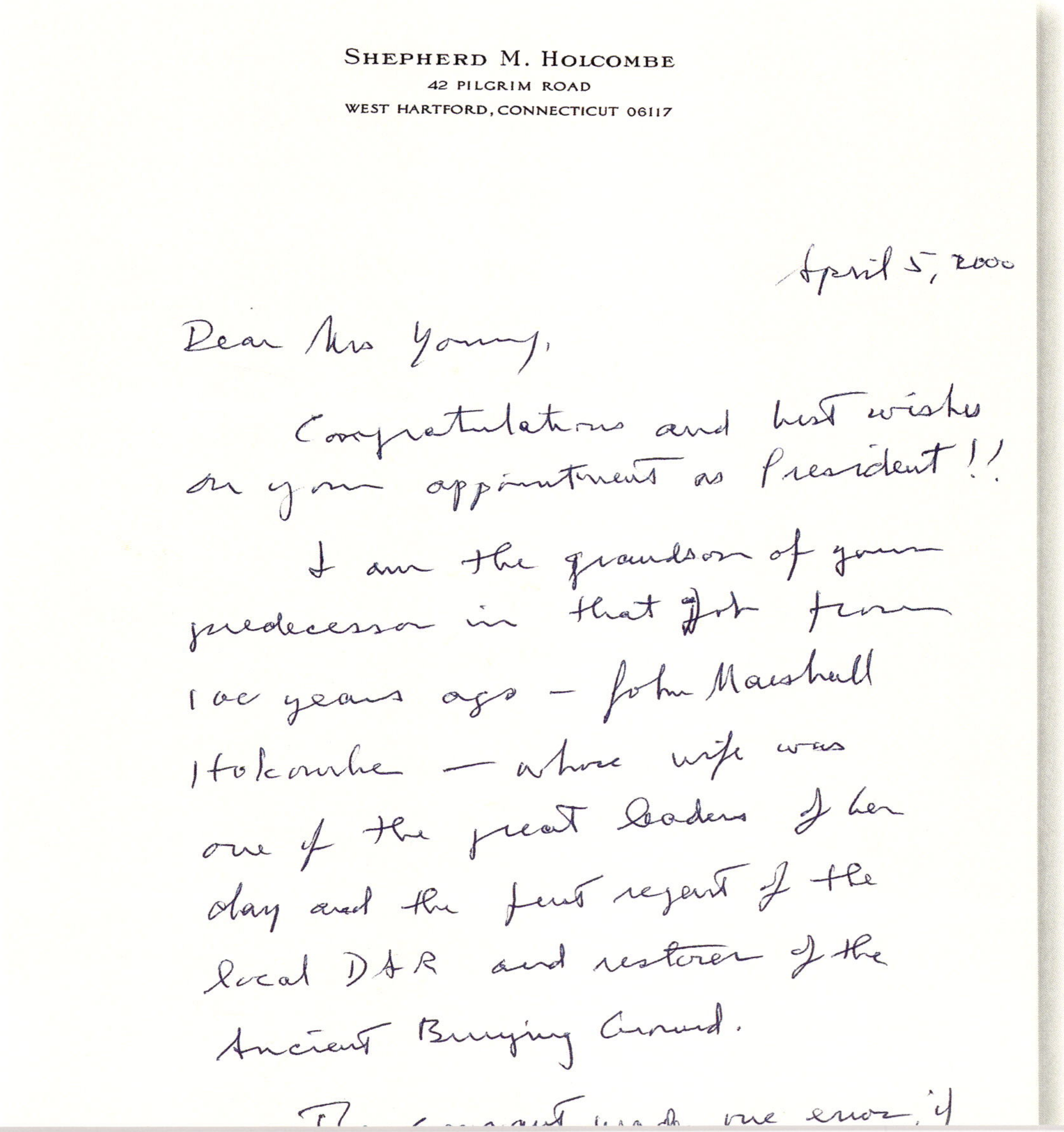

SHEPHERD M. HOLCOMBE
42 PILGRIM ROAD
WEST HARTFORD, CONNECTICUT 06117

April 5, 2000

Dear Mrs Young,

Congratulations and best wishes on your appointment as President!!

I am the grandson of your predecessor in that job from 100 years ago – John Marshall Holcombe – whose wife was one of the great leaders of her day and the first regent of the local DAR and restorer of the Ancient Burying Ground.

The Courant made one error, if

ball fans: "He said that if we were baseball players, we'd make Joe DiMaggio look like a chump."

Phoenix made it an early priority to communicate facts and news about demutualization to policyholders, supplying updates on the company's Web and intranet sites and through its toll-free client service lines.

The demutualization process usually takes 12 to 18 months, the time needed for review and approval by the company's board of directors, its policyholders and the New York State Insurance Department. Phoenix completed the process in just over a year.

In connection with the demutualization, Phoenix Home Life Mutual Insurance Company was renamed Phoenix Life Insurance Company and became a wholly owned subsidiary of a new publicly traded holding company, The Phoenix Companies, Inc. Eligible policyholders received compensation in exchange for their surrender of membership interests in Phoenix, paid in the form of common stock in the new holding company, cash or policy credits. Phoenix created a "closed block" to ensure that the reasonable dividend expectations of its policyholders would be met following the demutualization.

IT COMES DOWN TO THE PEOPLE

To change as fast as Phoenix is changing requires a very special kind of workforce.

"We have a lot of high-energy people here who don't like to plod along," says Donald Bertrand, pinpointing a vital ingredient in Phoenix's growth. "We do very well as a company when we have a challenge. Like a flag on the top of the hill, we go get it! As soon as Bob Fiondella and his executive team say 'there's the mountain,' we go for it." The focus on wealth management and the move toward demutualization — call them twin peaks — have energized the company in the same way that the merger did. In Bertrand's words: "We know we can do it, and we have fun doing it."

The company gives its employees new challenges and, just as important, the freedom to fail. This approach is organic; while no one uses the cliche "empowerment," one employee after another talks about how the company has trusted them with more responsibility than they ever thought they could handle — which is how they have learned and blossomed.

"Sure, we've had some misses, but most situations worked famously," McLoughlin says. "By giving people their head, so to speak, we've kept very good employees who otherwise would have left or lost their edge. And as a manager, it's so rewarding when you push someone in a direction where they've never been — maybe where you've never been, either — and all of a sudden there they are, shining like the sun."

Phoenix expects a lot and provides impressive support in return. Long before corporate America caught on to the need to balance work and family issues, the company offered medical and dental clinics (introduced in the 1960s), flextime and employee assistance programs (the 1970s), child care and fitness centers (the 1980s), generous benefits for part-time workers (the 1990s) and many other perks. Many of these family-friendly benefits were championed by Ann L. Cowen, now vice president of human resources.

Less tangible, but just as appreciated, is the daily culture. As companies grow or merge, many become less caring. Carl Chadburn says Phoenix retains its "friendly, small-college type of environment, even as we've gotten bigger." Wyrot Ward sums up the environment as one of "gracious informality, but never informal to a level of lack of respect. Our cafeterias, without executive dining areas, are examples of that common touch."

The lack of bureaucracy lets Phoenix stay nimble and adjust direction fairly quickly, an unusual trait in an industry where standard procedure usually involves written reports and multiple levels of approvals. Maura Melley, who was hired from another Hartford-based insurer, noticed the difference immediately. "To come here and find people writing ideas on Post-It notes and handing them to the chairman — it blew my mind! So did being able to resolve a lot of things verbally, without too much 'process.'"

As for salaries, "we never try to be the highest bidder; we want people to come here because they want to be here, because they like the culture," Ward explains. This is a Phoenix tradition. (Curiously, employees who are lured away by higher pay elsewhere often try to return — and Phoenix will welcome them back if the circumstances are right. Few other companies can duplicate that kind of chemistry.)

With about 1,700 employees and thousands of producers in its home offices and more than 81 locations, Phoenix is big enough to be successful but small enough to promote personal relationships and contributions. "One thing I talk about in recruiting is the visibility that all levels of employees enjoy," Ward says. "The person who does the work gets the recognition. You respect the chain of command, but the chain never takes credit for what you do."

As Phoenix celebrates its 150th anniversary and anticipates a momentous change in structure, its people will continue to do the hard work they love — and reap the emotional, intellectual and monetary rewards. "We test, we try, we experiment," Fiondella summarizes. "If it works, we do more. If not, we adjust. When mutuality became limiting, we created the option to demutualize. The one area we will clearly be in forever is wealth management. That is the growth business of the twenty-first century."

CHAPTER SEVEN

The Field

Phoenix's Extended Family

I could not sell cars. I could not sell you the suit you have on. Everybody says those are tangible and life insurance is intangible. No, life insurance is a very tangible product. I know the product and have confidence in it. I know how to talk about it. We sell life insurance through a notion — through love — through the need or desire to protect against loss of your family or your business.

— Ronald J. Bushwell, CLU, ChFC, award-winning Phoenix advisor since 1959

Robt. J. Crandall.
"Les" Merrell

If today's Phoenix advisors could meet their counterparts from 1851, they might discover a lot in common.

Training? Great salespeople have always studied, learned from the best and yet found their own path. Prospecting? Then as now, prestige recommendations worked best.

Writing high quality business? It's been a Phoenix tradition from temperance days to the new era of wealth management. Giving of themselves? Advisors still thrive on helping each other and contributing to their communities.

Fellow agents from 1851 and 2001 might even find they shared leisure activities. After all, golf in America dates back to colonial days, and Wall Street has had a stock exchange since George Washington was president.

Most of all, there has always been a powerful sense of family among producers. Look back on

On page 107, D. Gordon Hunter, an early Phoenix sales executive, presided over a 1921 class of agents. The agents at left attended a 1932 recognition conference in Hartford. The program is from a Home Life banquet for a similar purpose.

a 150-year roster and you'll find very few agents who weren't family-centered people first and foremost. You surely won't find one who didn't seek to solve problems for families and family-owned businesses — or who didn't take the time to ask about the family of a client or fellow agent. And you'll find plenty who have brought their own families into the business they've loved.

Successful advisors are relationship builders. The relationships that they build are what connects Phoenix to the world at large. They're the most visible members of the company's extended family. Paradoxically, they're out there alone in many respects, putting themselves on the line day in and day out.

No one can deny that the landscape has changed in the past few years, let alone the past 150 years. Products and services have become far more complex, evolving into customized solutions for far ranging needs. Professional credentials such as CFP (Certified Financial Planner) have taken their place beside the traditional CLU (Chartered Life Underwriter) and ChFC (Chartered Financial Consultant) designations. Distribution systems have expanded significantly in recent years to better serve Phoenix's focus on wealth management.

Yet the fundamentals endure. Award-winning advisor Robert B. Hardcastle, host of the nationally syndicated radio program *Money Talk*, puts it simply: "A lot of things have changed, but at the same time, the basic goals are usually the same for most people. They want to be able to make their money grow, to meet emergencies, to buy that dream home, to give their kids and grandkids a good education and to be able to retire in a style to which they've grown accustomed. If they own a business, they want to see it prosper. They want to leave a legacy for their families and their chosen charities. And my job throughout all those years has been to help people reach those goals."

Ray Ellis, seen here at his retirement dinner with Bill Wallace, represented Home Life for 81 years and was an eloquent speaker on insurance topics. John Packal described Ray as "very articulate, sophisticated, a gentleman. Ray and Chuck Murphy inspired me and a lot of people."

As times change, old-fashioned sales initiative also endures. "How far we shall go and how much we shall accomplish is a question to be answered by each individual and depends upon our own INTELLIGENCE and PUSH," wrote the late Raymond C. Ellis of Home Life. Ellis's message, complete with capital letters, is as relevant today as when he penned it in 1925. And Ellis lived his philosophy. As a producer and agency manager, he served his company and policyholders for a record-setting 81 years.

MULTIPLE DISTRIBUTION SYSTEMS, MULTIPLE STRENGTHS

Until the 1950s, all Phoenix and Home Life producers sold for their own company, which was the industry norm. Recruited and trained by their parent company, these "career agents" built lasting relationships with their clients, a tradition that continues today.

In a very recent development, career agents have now become advisors through WS Griffith Advisors Inc., a new distribution company that combines WS Griffith's traditional broker/dealer operations with a corporate general agency. Separate and distinct from its parent company, WS Griffith Advisors is a nationwide network of premier financial advisors who provide objectivity, advice and access to products from multiple sources.

Starting in 1954, Phoenix created a life brokerage department with a network of field offices and employees. Through this wholesaling organization, Phoenix encouraged producers of other companies to sell its products, a radical notion for its time. Phoenix cultivated the business so brilliantly that other insurers tried to emulate its success. Now called "life distribution,"

AT THE DESK OF

Maxine Niemeyer, CLU, ChFC, AEP

First job at Phoenix:
Secretary in field agency, 1961

Career growth:
Agent, 1966; one of five original field brokerage managers, 1967 to 1990, based in Detroit; member, Brokerage Hall of Fame.

Industry achievements:
Former national president of the American Society of Chartered Life Underwriters and Chartered Financial Consultants; former trustee of the American College and winner of its highest lifetime achievement award, the Huebner Gold Medal.

On insurance as a career:
"Every day you have to learn something new. It keeps me young and keeps me stimulated."

Phoenix's life wholesaling efforts are directed more broadly at a variety of distribution channels, including wirehouses and producer groups, as well as the original insurance advisor channel. In addition to life wholesaling, Phoenix has created wholesaling organizations to promote Phoenix's annuity products and mutual funds.

In the 1980s, Phoenix began focusing on what was then a third channel, independent producers known as PPGAs, or personal producing general agents. This channel began as a way to reach beyond the more urban areas served by career agents, but it continues today in a broader role.

From an advisor's point of view, multiple distribution systems make good sense. As John E. Farraj describes it, the company offers several ways "to find a comfortable nest and build it." Having spent almost 20 years as a career agent before becoming Phoenix's first PPGA, Farraj speaks from experience. "All distribution systems offer great comfort, great compensation and great psychological satisfaction according to how you want to set up your business," he observes.

From the company's point of view, multiple distribution systems are more essential than ever. Building on the life wholesaling strengths it has honed for almost 50 years, Phoenix now sells through an ever-widening range of professionals. "As a creator and marketer of life insurance products, we can't limit ourselves to traditional avenues of distribution," explains Robert E. Primmer, senior vice president, life distribution. "We take our lead from the high-net-worth individuals we serve. If their trusted advisor is a stockbroker, then stockbrokers are a channel for us. If they turn to their registered investment advisor or CPA for estate planning advice, then those advisors are channels for us. We've been selling through other companies' advisors for 50 years. These are simply new types of independent advisors."

Sidney Levine, CLU, AEP, a career agency manager and advisor with a substantial business clientele, appreciates the strategy. "The company needs to attract business from more than one distribution system," Levine affirms. "Margins have thinned over the years in all my clients' businesses. They have to work more efficiently today. Our industry is no different."

In short, Phoenix now relies on a vigorous and growing mix of affiliated advisors and nonaffiliated advisors. This approach keeps the company competitive and flexible. It also helps Phoenix consistently deliver performance and value to policyholders. (In the annual net cost performance surveys of A.M. Best Company, Inc., Phoenix has ranked no lower than fourth among 50 or more top life insurers since 1988. This ranking measures net cost value according to several mathematical variables, such as interest-adjusted value of premiums, net of dividends.) And, most important of all, as the company celebrates its 150th year, a diversified approach to distribution positions it strongly in the wealth management marketplace.

PATHWAYS TO SUCCESS

Successful advisors love the life insurance business for its sheer human diversity. "Our work involves more aspects of life and living and enterprise than any other business," raves Leon L. Levy, an advisor who has won every top honor and who has more in-force business than some entire life insurance companies. "It involves families, taxes, human resources, medicine, emotions, law, everything you can talk about."

What ties all those strands together? Trust is the word that keeps coming up when advisors talk about their relationships with their clients and colleagues within the Phoenix family. Above all, they emphasize that building trust takes *time*. It begins with the recruitment and training process.

A Living Legend: Leon L. Levy, CLU, RHU

Tucked amid the hundreds of awards and photos that fill Leon L. Levy's Philadelphia office is an illuminated sign that says "Gentlemen/Telephones." This humble item seems out of place — but, like Citizen Kane's Rosebud sled, it unlocks Levy's past and explains why Phoenix's record-setting sales leader never stops striving.

The sign hung in Philadelphia's now-defunct Warwick Hotel, where Levy's father, Haim, a Turkish immigrant, ran the men's room concession. "As a young man, I brought my books to the hotel to study and helped my father give out towels and so on," Levy recalls. Working for tips taught him a lot about human nature: "Converting a dime customer to a quarter customer is some of the toughest selling you'll ever do."

Forging a successful career in insurance, Levy emulated his hardworking parents but didn't talk about them much. "It took me years to admit that my father had such a humble job," he says. Levy's own hard-won security shattered when, at age 36, he left his previous employer over a matter of ethics. With three kids under seven and his wife, Fran, newly diagnosed with the chronic disease lupus, Levy made the move to Phoenix in 1971.

To say that Levy was driven to excel is an understatement. In his first three months, he sold more insurance than any Phoenix agent had sold that entire year. Indeed, his production was so astounding that it triggered an internal audit. Retired auditor Norman Blais remembers the incident well. "An audit seemed to make sense at the time," Blais says. "Leon was so far above the norm."

The company need not have worried. Levy has since led the company in sales a record 20 times and finished second seven times (as of year-end 1999). Hall of Fame member, Tiffany Award winner, sole 27-year qualifier for the Chairman's Council — there's no accolade he hasn't earned. Phoenix has even established the annual Leon L. Levy Award to perpetuate Leon's peerless commitment to industry, community and clients.

"What makes Leon perfect is that he's human and vulnerable," President Dona Young comments. "His humanity, coupled with his passion and inner drive, his values and his faith, makes him the person we all admire and respect."

Chairman Bob Fiondella loves to point out that some whole companies can't boast as much insurance in force as Levy has sold single-handedly. The figure is $1 billion and counting. Levy also raises huge sums for charity. Among his many Philadelphia-area causes are Gratz College, Historic Congregation Mikveh Israel (the Levys' temple, founded in 1740) and the humanitarian Golden Slipper Club & Charities. Also, Levy and his wife co-founded and are active in the American Lupus Foundation's Southern New Jersey chapter. Levy's touch reaches throughout the nation and across the globe with his support of the McDonald's House of Kids and Boys Town of Jerusalem.

How does Leon L. Levy manage to do so much — for Phoenix and for the world? "I make the time," he says. "That's another thing my father taught me. To help and contribute is what we're put on Earth to do."

Leon and Fran Levy attended the 1999 Career Honors Council in Bermuda. Leon's consistency, service and loyalty inspired the annual Leon L. Levy Award, which honors advisors who exemplify those qualities.

Group: A Distinguished History

For more than 40 years, Phoenix's group organization sold an extensive line of life, disability and health benefits through hundreds of outside brokers to thousands of employers nationwide. Founded in 1958 and developed by William Roth, group was admired throughout the company and industry for its professionalism and spirit.

Being much smaller than most competitors, the group organization had to be smarter. "I think group represented the very beginnings of entrepreneurship within the modern Phoenix," says retired vice president John Chmielewski, who interacted with group in numerous ways over the years. Despite cutthroat competition and a very price-sensitive marketplace, group grew through innovative products and creative business approaches. These included multiple employer trusts, which allowed small companies within the same industry to band together for better benefits, and specialized products that dovetailed with Blue Cross plans back when Blue Cross underwrote more than half of corporate America's medical coverage. Starting in 1988, group helped Phoenix take its first steps into the global marketplace through a remarkably successful and longstanding joint venture with Dai-ichi Mutual Life Insurance Company of Japan, the world's second largest life insurer.

"Group was so exciting," says retired regional group vice president Robert K. Griffin, CLU, a group beacon for 38 years. "I remember one typical day in my early years as a rep. In the morning, I presented a proposal to a managing partner of a Wall Street stock firm. That same afternoon, I enrolled a group of bricklayers at a construction site in New Jersey. In what other business could you find such diversity?"

"The people who headed the organization were always strong individuals with strong opinions about how their business should be run," Chmielewski adds. One such group head was Chuck Paydos, who retired in 1998 after 35 years of service that included four years on the board of directors. He was succeeded as top group executive by Senior Vice President Randall Giangiulio. Through the Dai-ichi venture and other avenues, Paydos and Giangiulio positioned group in the 1990s to compete in a dramatically changing and intensely competitive marketplace.

From the very beginnings of group, its employees built an operation that earned respect throughout the industry for its top-flight sales force, strong products, solid profitability (total revenues exceeded $500 million in 1998) and excellent customer service. The decision to sell group, therefore, was a difficult one. Given Phoenix's focus on wealth management and the need for capital in that business, however, the company could no longer make appropriate investments in group's growth.

Chairman Bob Fiondella told the 850 employees of the group business in his December 1999 announcement: "It was the strength and quality of our group operations that prompted several companies to approach us. After reviewing several alternatives, we decided to negotiate exclusively with GE Financial Assurance Holdings, Inc. (GEFA), because it made the commitment to maintain and expand the operations."

The sale was completed in 2000. "GEFA benefited from the addition of our high-quality employees and the fact that group was an established and growing business," Fiondella points out. "Equally importantly, our group customers have continued to receive the highest level of service."

Thanks to the work of professionals such as Bob Griffin, Phoenix set the standard for integrity and innovation in group insurance for more than 40 years.

Home Life agents had the advantage of the Planned Estates philosophy, which emphasized "problems to solve, not products to sell." Better yet, they were schooled and mentored by such masters as Training Director Charles A. "Chuck" Murphy Sr., whose legacy lives on through the annual "Rookie of the Year" award named for him. "We enjoyed tremendous training," proclaims Thomas R. Capehart, who in turn has mentored his share of beginners. "Chuck ingrained the ideas of service and studying and keeping things simple yet understandable."

At Phoenix, the secret weapon for career agents-in-training was CWP, or consecutive weekly production — a disciplined method of client-building. "Everybody who embraced that program became a success," says Ronald J. Bushwell, CLU, ChFC. "You had to get an application a week." Once Bushwell tried bringing in two applications on a Friday, one for that week and one for the next week. "No way! We ended up selling 100 to 150 life policies a year. Not posh sales, but we were taught to build a career." Robert J. Rudolf, CLU, ChFC, who also cut his teeth on CWP, says that sales quotas weren't the ultimate goal. "Agency managers made, and still make, a very concentrated effort to train and encourage beginners," he says.

Even with the best support, succeeding as an advisor is rarely an easy road. "I was ready to quit many times at the start, because I wasn't making it," recalls Marvin A. Address, who was recruited and developed by one of the all-time great agency managers at Home Life, Bill Wallace. "Bill kept telling me 'just do it one more time.'" Address, like many others quoted in this chapter, went on to win the Tiffany Award, the company's highest honor for career agents.

Particularly in the wealth management environment, today's advisor is more likely to be an experienced sales professional who is changing careers than a "green pea" fresh from college. "We look for extremely entrepreneurial and somewhat experienced people," says Lorraine M. Padilla, CLU, ChFC, manager of Phoenix's Uniondale, New York, agency and the company's first female career agency manager. "An advisor can't wing it. When you're working on highly complex areas like estate planning, for example, you have to understand the laws."

Phoenix's 26 Sales and Support Centers exist to help provide such expertise to all advisors, affiliated or nonaffiliated. "We help producers sell by supporting their business," Field Vice President C. Scott McIntire, CLU, ChFC, emphasizes. "We encourage them to come to us for expertise, even for on-site help if they want it. We can provide specialty illustrations for business owners, trust work or estate planning, helping them design sophisticated proposals for very sophisticated sales."

Most competitors don't offer such value-added services. They claim it's too expensive. McIntire, a Phoenix Hall of Fame life wholesaler who was instrumental in developing the Sales and Support Center system in the past few years, says the benefits outweigh the costs. "Phoenix has the infrastructure to deliver such services efficiently," he points out. "Our value-added services separate us from everyone else."

"The one thing that's very difficult for producers to put a price on is the service Phoenix offers," adds Jeffrey Levy, who came up through the brokerage system and manages the Philadelphia Sales and Support Center. "It's invaluable. We take service very, very seriously as a company."

FIELD AND HOME OFFICE: FAMILY DYNAMICS

"Advisors are among the most engaging, bright, creative, entrepreneurial, caring people ever," Dona Young says. "There is always something very real in the relationship you have with them."

Young puts her finger on the dynamic between home office and field. Like any good relationship, it embraces joy, frustration and every emotion in between. According to retired vice president David L. Howard, CLU, who for many years acted as "the bridge between the field organizations and the corporate environment," the common ground is mutual respect and trust.

"In the end it's relationships that build respect and trust between advisors and their clients, as well as between advisors and the home office," Howard says. "The relationships that are built over the years are, in many ways, like those built in a family."

Anyone who works with advisors quickly comes to appreciate their energy and warmth, expressed in a diversity of styles and approaches. "There are so many personalities out there, which makes working with the field one of my favorite things to do," Joe Kelleher says. He relishes the give-and-take: "Salespeople are fun. And they're smart."

"The field is why we're here," emphasizes Lisa Bassi, vice president, sales operations. Bassi worked directly with career agents for years and still takes the time to keep in contact with them. "Advisors are out there making our business happen every day," she adds.

Constant communication between the field and the home offices is a company tradition. Those who have worked elsewhere can vouch that Phoenix offers surprising accessibility. One person recalls how a previous employer — "a major company well regarded in the industry" — allowed calls to underwriting only on Tuesdays and Thursdays between 2 p.m. and 4 p.m. "And they'd take calls only from agency managers, not producers!" he notes. "By contrast, Phoenix has always welcomed and encouraged direct access."

The exchange of communication extends to company executives as well and works to the

All in the Families

Life insurance and wealth management are all about making lives better for families. So it's only natural that insurance and investments as a career virtually runs in the family throughout Phoenix's field organization. Indeed, Chairman Robert W. Fiondella's son is in the business. Robert J. Fiondella, CPA, CLU, represents Phoenix as a personal producing general agent based in Simsbury, Connecticut.

The Friedlers of New Orleans — Frank Sr., Frank Jr., CLU, ChFC, and Frank III, CLU, ChFC, JD, better known as Tripp — are the company record holders. Their affiliation began when Frank Sr. began selling for Home Life in 1927. They are the first agent family with three generations represented in the Phoenix Hall of Fame. They share their three-generation status with the Hollemans — the late Vernon W. Sr., the late Vernon W. Jr. and Vernon III — and the Murphys: the late Chuck Sr., Chuck Jr. and James.

Affinities often start young. Second-generation career agent Brian Bushwell, LUTCF, remembers the excitement of boyhood car trips from New Jersey to the home office in Hartford with his dad, Ron. "Once, Dad plunked me down to nap in an empty office and went off to another office," Brian recalls. "I woke up and went looking for him." The little boy discovered the unique layout of the Boat Building and the friendliness of its personnel. He grew up to join his father's business, as did his brother Greg. In 1998, Ron and Brian made Phoenix history as the first recorded father and son to qualify in the same year for the distinguished Career Chairman's Council. In 1999, they became the first father and son to earn honors on the same Top Ten Career Producer list in the same year.

While plenty of fathers bring their sons into the insurance business, combinations of fathers, mothers and daughters are scarce. The Joffe family has a unique legacy. Phoenix career agent Frederic Joffe trained his wife, Connie, to take over his business shortly before his untimely death. Inspired by her parents' example, Esther Joffe joined Phoenix directly from college and became an award-winning producer as well. Esther hopes that her own children will want to follow in the family footsteps.

The bond between Phoenix and the Friedlers of New Orleans began 74 years ago, when the late Frank Sr. (center) joined Home Life.

And it's not just parents and children who get in the act. "If you ever want to get into insurance, give me a call," Leon L. Levy would often say to his brother's kids. "I saw the emotional and financial rewards of Uncle Leon's work and I thought I'd try that road. More than 15 years later, I'm still with the same company and having a ball," says nephew Jeff Levy. This particular family duo doesn't work together, but insurance is one of their cherished links. (Leon, whose sons also work in his business, is a career agent in Philadelphia; Jeff is a Sales and Support Center manager in the same city.) "Leon has taught me success by the kind of role model he is," Jeff says.

Role modeling is the key. Most second- and third-generation agents are quick to say they never felt pushed into the business. Indeed, many (including Tripp Friedler and Vernon W. Holleman III) proved themselves in other professions first. They gravitated to insurance and financial services because they had seen the satisfactions of the career up close and personal. "To be in business for yourself yet affiliated with a strong company, to help people, to help your community, to have no limit on your potential income — all these things clicked," says David Rudolf, CLU, who was a U.S. Marine pilot and accountant before joining his dad, Robert Rudolf, CLU, ChFC, in the family's PPGA business. As recent conferences attest, there are plenty of young children waiting in the wings. Check in at the company's 175th anniversary and you may discover another generation of agents for whom Phoenix is a family affair.

Phoenix Advisors' Family Tree

Burkhard: Robert, Joe (son)
Bushwell: Ronald, Brian and Greg (sons)
Buxbaum: Robert, Michael (son)
Carvelli: Salvatore, Elaine (daughter)
Connelly: Peter, Fred (brothers)
Coyle: Michael, Terence (son)
Darragh: Robert E., Robert J. (grandson)
DeLeo: Frank Sr., Frank Jr. (son)
Dutzer: Robert, Brian (son)
Ford: William, Steven (son)
Friedler: Frank Sr., Frank Jr. (son), Frank III "Tripp" (grandson)
Grossman: Sidney, Jack (son)
Holleman: Vernon Sr., Vernon Jr. (son), Vernon III (grandson)
Hughes: Gerald, Alan (son)
Johnson: Harold, Carlton (son), Carolie (daughter-in-law)
Joffe: Frederic, Connie (wife) Esther (daughter)
Kalander: Bill, Bob (son)
Langdon: John, John H. (son)
Leader: George, Jack (son)
Lefebvre: Mark, Ken (brothers)
Levy: Leon L., Victor and David (sons), Jeffrey (nephew)
May: Edwin, Ted (grandson)
McCarthy: Jack Jr., Jack III (son)
Merber: Fillmore, Mitchell and Marc (sons)
Mevorah: Alan, Keith (son)
Meyers: Jack, Marv (son)
Moreno: Antonio Sr., Antonio Jr. (son)
Murphy: Chuck Sr., Chuck Jr. (son), James (grandson)
Otterbein: Kyle, Cort (son)
Plybon: Paul, Robert (son)
Samanchik: William, Paul (son)
Schick: Henry, Peter (son)
Siegfried: Norbert, Gary, Steve and Stan (sons)
Siracusa: Nino, John (son)
Tanquay: Leo, Lee (son)
Vitale: Brian, Kyle (son)
Wallace: Michael Sr., Michael Jr. (son)
Waters: Bernard, David (son)
Weldon: Win, Ray (son)
Wicksall: James "Mike," Russell (son)
Winkelman: Robert Jr., Robert III (son)

benefit of all. For example, veteran career agent H. Robert Weisman carved out a very early niche in sophisticated estate planning. Working with home office experts in advanced marketing and underwriting, Weisman raised the company's overall awareness of estate planning as an important sales direction. "We pushed Phoenix along a little faster, made them more aggressive," he says. As a result, the marketing department now includes 11 specialists in advanced marketing — attorneys and other professionals who understand the complexities of trusts and other estate-planning tools and who actively advise the field on critical cases. William F. Kelly, the retired New York brokerage manager renowned for his creativity, says that product ideas and refinements traditionally enjoy the same kind of warm reception. "Our actuaries have always been sales-oriented, willing to listen, think and act," Kelly explains. "Often when someone starts to innovate, he has enemies. But not at Phoenix."

"That's the kind of company we have," says Jeffrey Levy, more than a generation younger than Kelly. "You can pick up the phone and reach the chairman, and he'll talk with you. He may not take your advice, but that's why he's the chairman."

With policyholder satisfaction as the guiding force, the field and home offices rarely differ on objectives. As Levy humorously implies, however, they may not always agree on how to get there. Once again, candor and trust make the difference. Phoenix takes a team approach to improving its processes. When service issues arose in the 1980s, for instance, employees from Greenfield traveled to career agencies across the country to work face-to-face on new approaches. And as the company has grown, particularly in the post-merger years, the field advisory committees have been a strong voice for emerging technologies and other changes.

"It's frequently very time-consuming to include the field force in the development of solutions, and sometimes emotionally charged as well," says Kelly Carlson, CLU, a retired senior vice president who worked with the field in different capacities for over 20 years. "But if you want a successful outcome, as Phoenix does, you bring the field in early and make them part of the process. There's no other way."

FIERCELY LOYAL TIES

Phoenix producers are each other's biggest fans. They help each other to an extent that salespeople in other fields can only envy. The sharing of ideas and support is an industry tradition, but one that's particularly strong in this company. And many producers believe this tradition is what distinguishes them as trusted advisors in an increasingly crowded and contentious sphere of financial services.

Camaraderie? Fellowship? These words are too pale for the fiercely loyal ties that bind. "Family," Sid Levine firmly insists. "My closest friends still are people from the old Home Life. When my daughters got married, their weddings were like a convention — a family reunion."

"When we meet each other, we hug and kiss," Marvin A. Address unabashedly admits. "Hey, our families grew up together. I can go any place in this country and I have a buddy. I'm his guest. We share. If I have a problem, I can call any one of my friends and they'll say, 'Do you want me to come to you or do you want to come to me? Whatever you want me to do, I'll do it.'"

"Really, it's like family," John Farraj says. "You grow with your fellow agents. You sit down and meet at conventions; you eat and drink together. How could you help but be sensitive to them and their families?"

There's a special generosity of spirit from one generation of agents to the next. Ron Bushwell still remembers a lesson learned at one of his very first sales conferences in the 1950s. "My father had encouraged me to seek out the company leader at the time, Michael P. Coyle, CLU, and find out his secrets," he says. While Coyle wouldn't have hesitated to talk, Bushwell was "too afraid" even to approach him. The two men later became good friends. "I live my life just the opposite

Home Life conferences had their own anthem and agents their own "passport" for 1988 meetings in Marbella, Spain; Palm Desert, California; and Nashville, Tennessee.

today," Bushwell notes. "I seek out the newer producers so they don't have that fear."

To keep the family in touch, smaller groups of producers often have informal reunions each year. Some meet as study groups that combine learning and leisure. For others, the purpose is simply to celebrate old friendships. "We keep the torch going," says Ron Bushwell of the group called "Just Friends." In addition to Ron, the group includes legendary Phoenix career agents Albert J. Arruda, Joseph D. Gatti, CLU, ChFC, Bernard A. Hiller, LLB, Arnold H. Kaminer, CLU, ChFC, Leon L. Levy, George Miller, CLU, Irwin Tobin, Louis A. Spiazzi, Stanford B. Towerman, CLU, ChFC, MSFS, Bernard I. Waters, CLU, RHU, and H. Robert Weisman.

Reunions like this are also a Home Life tradition. For over 30 years, such award-winners as Thomas R. Capehart, Frank J. Friedler Jr., CLU, ChFC, Charles A. Murphy Jr., CLU, ChFC, John A. Packal, CLU, ChFC, and others have met to share their knowledge and friendship. (The late Vernon W. Holleman Jr., CLU, ChFC, a Home Life legend, was also active in this group.) "We don't have any secrets from each other," Capehart asserts.

The tradition continues among younger advisors and in different distribution systems. Jeff Levy explains: "In a home office environment, you have a peer group you can draw on, usually right down the hall. As a Sales and Support Center manager, my closest counterpart may be 200 miles away. So we seek out that camaraderie and bonding among ourselves." Levy is part of a group of eight that meets yearly for four days "to share ideas and marketing strategies, talk about what's going on in the company, and also determine whose golf game is better." And while study groups are independent, this group "writes a report from our meetings to relay information as we see fit to the appropriate regional and home office people." Several study group members have subsequently been tapped for advisory boards and committees formed by the home office. "A nice compliment," Levy adds.

CONFERENCES: WHERE THE PHOENIX FAMILY RECONNECTS

"There is more in conferences and conventions than the exchanging of ideas and formulating of plans. The greatest, most enduring value comes almost unconsciously.... Friendships are formed and renewed, mutual understandings are established, unity is secured, and thereafter each feels the joy of combined strength."

Phoenix was about halfway to its 150th anniversary when President Archibald A. Welch spoke those keynote words in Bretton Woods, New Hampshire, in 1925. There was only one annual conference then, for agency managers and agents who qualified for the "Quarter Million Club." Today's conferences include qualifying producers from all different distribution systems. Spouses have always been an integral part of the festivities (the inclusion of spouses in the early 1900s was another Phoenix innovation); now

Agents and spouses dine during awards night of the 1999 agents conference in Bermuda, top. Seated, left to right, are Liz and Dan Cotter of Cleveland, Sandy and Anthony Capobianco of Albany, Cindy and Hitomi Tsuyuki of Pasadena. Standing, left to right, are Jan and Dan Hazewski of Albany; Vicky and Mitch Merber of Long Island. Bullfighting was one of the more unusual conference activities when Home Life agents met in Marbella, Spain, in 1988.

children and grandchildren sometimes attend, too. And the locations have grown more exotic — ranging from Banff and the Bahamas to Barcelona, Spain — although good golfing remains a constant. The educational aspect is crucial: advisors spend their mornings discussing products, strategies and company direction.

What hasn't changed is the core of President Welch's message. The exchange of ideas and the joy of combined strength are still what conventions are all about. Or, as Steven E. McDermott, assistant vice president, corporate communications, puts it: "Our meetings have both the motivational as well as the family atmosphere. What we do makes people feel good about Phoenix."

To witness the pinnacle of accomplishment, one need look no farther than "Awards Night" at each conference. At the career agents' conference, for example, this gala evening has traditionally opened with the Hall of Fame procession. Members line up with their spouses and enter the hall couple by couple, according to year of induction. As each name is announced, the audience honors its colleagues with a standing ovation.

The respective Awards Nights salute the best and brightest — the top 10 sales leaders and new winners of the top awards in each distribution system. Younger advisors at their first or second conference often come up to veterans and say "I never thought it would be like this." They can't believe the camaraderie and they pledge never to miss a conference.

"While conferences are rewards and recognition events, they're also much more," Dona Young affirms. "They're a time for the Phoenix family to reconnect. It's the power of that connection, sharing and reaffirming our successes together, that makes them so special."

Winning a coveted award is the culmination of a career; certainly nothing can equal being recognized for outstanding achievement in the company of one's peers. But many advisors quietly confide that they're just as elated by the simpler rewards that life insurance and wealth management delivers in abundance. While all have their own success stories to tell, this one from John Packal will have to suffice.

"I got a call from a young man from Seattle. He thought I wouldn't remember his name, but I did," Packal says. "He told me that the insurance proceeds from his dad's death went toward his education. This young man had just graduated from medical school and was setting up a practice. He was ready to buy his own insurance from me."

The quintessential trusted advisor smiles. Any of his colleagues can finish the story — and have done so, over and over, in their illustrious and satisfying careers. "My biggest thrills are when things like this happen," Packal concludes. "That's what this business is all about."

For 65 years, the Phoenix Blue Vase Contest has symbolized the art of determination. This annual award is presented to producers who achieve outstanding sales performance, dedication and leadership. The Blue Vase traces its roots to a story first told in the 1920s about a supremely persistent salesman named Bill Peck. The award honors those who share Peck's resourcefulness and his ability to overcome all obstacles. Each year fewer than 10 percent of career agents earn a Blue Vase, making it Phoenix's most coveted sales prize.

Spouses Speak

It's no surprise when a young couple takes a drive or goes to the movies. Tom and Karen Capehart did those things as newlyweds. They'd drive to Tom's sales appointments, and then Karen would catch a movie while Tom met with prospective clients. On the way home, they'd talk eagerly about their evening and the future they were building together. These unusual dates, Karen says, became the foundation of a marriage that has lasted 44 years.

Newlyweds often look forward to starting a family as soon as possible. Bob and Bee Weisman did too, but they waited. Bee remained at her job — supervisor at a shoe factory — because she earned more money than Bob during his first years as a career agent. Now the Weismans are grandparents, and turnabout is fair play. "Bob will never retire," Bee says.

Spouses of agents deserve a special place in Phoenix history. Abundantly supportive, remarkably adaptable, they tend to deflect praise back onto their "better halves." But they have earned their own time in the spotlight.

"My wife, Ann, was really the one who raised our six kids," says Bob Rudolf. "I'd have to agree with that," says Ann. Curiously, their children feel that both parents did an equal job, even when Bob was working nights and Saturdays.

Tiffany Award winner Tom Capehart stands with his wife, Karen.

Sallie Wallace was always proud of what her husband, Bill, did — even before he began winning every award the life insurance industry has to offer. "I understood what life insurance is about, because I understood what it meant not to have it," Sallie says. A few years before marrying Bill, she had been suddenly widowed with two children under age three. She and the Wallace family made many moves during Bill's career. "Now, after more than 40 years, we do what Sallie wants," Bill says.

Husbands of insurance professionals have their own special memories. "Make sure you remind everyone of the early sales conferences where I was just about the only male spouse," Sam Padilla told his wife, Lorraine, who made company history in 1992 when she became Phoenix's first female career agency manager. (Lorraine joined the company in 1975.) The quintessential good sport, Sam took part in every spousal program offered. One year, he cheerfully attended a fashion show. "Everyone in the audience was given pearls at the end," Lorraine laughs. "Of course, Sam came out wearing his. Considering that he owns and runs a construction company, I'd say his ego is pretty secure. Now there are other male spouses, one of them being Dona Young's husband, Roland. But Sam was unusual at the start. The fact that he has always taken time from his business to join our three kids and me at conferences is so important. I would have gone by myself, but it's just not the same."

The wonderful thing about such strong partnerships is that they grow stronger. "Sure, there are ups and downs, but this field has given us such wonderful friends and a beautiful life," says Brenda Levine. Her husband, Sidney, speaks for many advisors and agency managers when he says he couldn't have succeeded without a supportive spouse. He smiles: "Even today, when I left for the office this morning, she wished me good luck."

CHAPTER EIGHT

Service

Corporate Citizenship

If you do well, you should do good. To have that philosophy as part of a corporate culture is pretty remarkable.

— Maura Melley, senior vice president, public affairs

RED FEATHER
SPECIAL
ANOTHER TEAM
OVER THE TOP

Phoenix has long been committed to its numerous sponsorships and community programs. In each city and town where it has corporate offices, the company gets involved and gives back. Field offices nationwide share the same ethic. As Bob Fiondella often says: "We believe profit and social responsibility are compatible."

Phoenix's founders believed the same. Consider the company's very first recorded act of corporate giving. In 1871, Phoenix Mutual contributed $5,000 to a fund for survivors of the fire that destroyed most of Chicago. The company had no established sales presence there; donating toward "the relief of sufferers" in another major American city was simply the right thing to do. And the gift was generous. It equaled President Edson Fessenden's annual salary.

CHARITY BEGAN AT HOME

For almost 100 years at Phoenix and Home Life, however, charity mainly began at home. The contribution of Arthur Collens is a good example. In 1924, 11 years before becoming president of Phoenix, Vice President Collens was instrumental in establishing the Hartford Community Chest. It was one of many ways Collens supported the city he loved. This organization developed into the local chapter of the United Way, which Phoenix still supports.

While the companies historically supported major causes, their own employees received the lion's share in lieu of defined employee benefits, until the latter were the norm. Until World War II, workers would pay a small amount — typically 1 percent of salary — toward modest pensions, major medical fees and disability coverage. The companies made up the difference, contributing (as Phoenix did) "whatever amount it knows will be necessary to make the fund sufficient to pay all benefits." Employees raised extra funds for these purposes as well. For example, in the cafeteria at 79 Elm Street when coffee cost a dime, five cents per cup went into the workers' hospital fund. The nickels added up and helped cushion employee medical expenses to the tune of thousands of dollars each year.

VOLUNTEERISM: THE TRUE BOTTOM LINE

Today, corporate giving still begins at home — but extends far beyond. Phoenix, its employees and its agents support hundreds of nonprofit, civic and educational organizations in their communities. Indeed, company policy actively encourages volunteerism. Workers can devote up to 40 hours of company time per year to volunteer

Painting Norm Morey's House

Norm Morey was chief shipping clerk at Phoenix's old headquarters at 79 Elm Street. He joined Phoenix out of high school and was the kind of employee everyone knew and liked. In 1956, at age 38, a heart attack took his life. It happened while Morey was on vacation at home in Manchester, Connecticut, getting ready to paint his house.

"We know he is gone, but we can't comprehend it," said the anonymous writer of the obituary in the company newsletter. To assuage their shock and grief, a crew of employees went to work, after work, painting Morey's house. The men wielded the brushes; the women handled the cookout. Others provided the paint and the food.

Retiree Ed Richardson recalls helping to organize the operation. "We had all been active with Norm in the Phoenix Mutual Club and the Phoenix Players," he says. "It was natural to pitch in at a time of crisis, in this case to help Norm's family, and I think that tradition continues today."

Altruism is woven into the company's history. These Phoenix employees, on page 121, raised funds for the Hartford Community Chest, which later became the United Way, in the early 1940s.

A Home Life Legacy

Another vital connection is the one between Phoenix and the Christopher Reeve Paralysis Foundation. Formerly known as the American Paralysis Association, this was a cherished charity for Home Life. Its president from 1978 to 1988, Kenneth C. Nichols Sr., CLU, championed the cause, as did his successor, Bill Wallace. At his retirement, Wallace specifically asked Bob Fiondella to continue to support the organization, whose mission is to encourage research and find a cure for paralysis caused by spinal cord injury and other central nervous system disorders.

Fiondella and Phoenix have kept the promise spectacularly. In 1998, the company co-chaired "Rise to the Occasion," a gala benefit in Hartford that raised $700,000 for spinal cord research. Actor Christopher Reeve, who was paralyzed in a horseback riding accident, and his wife, Dana, were honored guests. But the spotlight was on Dr. Alexia Bouckoms, a Connecticut dentist whose story galvanized people across the country.

In a freak accident, Bouckoms lost her husband and one of their three young children when gale-force winds blew a tree onto their car as the family was driving. Her own spinal cord was crushed, causing traumatic brain injury and paralysis of her legs. But Bouckoms's spirit emerged whole. "A tragedy remains a tragedy unless you make something good come from it," she told the audience that night. "I'm trying to do just that by pushing scientists to 'bridge the gap' so I can start training to run the Boston Marathon."

The funds raised by the gala benefit and other "Rise to the Occasion" initiatives have gone directly into substantial grants for spinal-cord researchers at Yale, the Albert Einstein College of Medicine and other prestigious organizations. Their goal is to find treatments and cures for spinal cord injuries — and their research may hasten progress against other neurological disorders such as Parkinson's and Alzheimer's disease as well.

"The progress of the last five, six, seven years has been truly breathtaking," according to Susan Howley, the foundation's director of research. "My expectation is that within the next few years, we're going to begin to see innovations move off the research bench and into clinical trials."

activities, provided it is matched by the same amount of personal time.

For those with an eye on the bottom line, Fiondella points out the tangible values of social involvement and sponsorships. They boost the company's name recognition, a critical goal in a crowded marketplace, and strengthen business and marketing relationships. By directing assistance toward areas of critical need, Phoenix is a catalyst for broader economic growth in its communities.

But there are even more important reasons. "It is in our policyholders' best interests that we do good things, because employees feel good about themselves and give so much of themselves," Fiondella notes.

"Employees who volunteer attack their jobs here with a lot more vigor and passion," the chairman emphasizes. "I haven't seen one person who hasn't given more than we have a right to expect — because they're able to be total people, whole persons. We take on major transactions and execute them incredibly well. Because people can express themselves fully, that makes them willing to do whatever is required to get the job done."

THE PHOENIX FOUNDATION

In deciding where and how much to contribute, Phoenix takes an admirably businesslike approach. In 1996, it created the Phoenix Foundation as a vehicle to direct charitable giving in its home office communities. A board of directors decides on recipients after weighing a number of factors. "We give more to organizations where Phoenix people are involved as volunteers," says Maura Melley, senior vice president, public affairs.

"We reject, in writing, five requests for each one we approve," Melley adds. "We look at the

Phoenix Loves Kids

Tricia Ethier, vice president and general manager of the Albany Operations Center, will never forget a recent holiday party. The guests were young children from the local Head Start childcare program, which Phoenix supports through the Rensselaer County Council for Economic Opportunity.

"Every kid got a toy and every kid got a coat," Ethier says. Employees chipped in for the toys, while Ethier provided the coats out of Albany's contribution budget. "One four-year-old boy was so excited when he opened his package and found his own new coat," she recalls. "He ran to show it to his mother. We were all in tears. He didn't care about his toy. It was incredible because you forget there are kids out there like that. The next year, hats and mittens were on the gift list."

Kids have always had a special place in the collective heart of Phoenix. Through charitable grants and employee volunteerism, the company focuses on youth development from pre-school to college age. Among the most notable programs:

Community Programs in Franklin County, Massachusetts

In the family-oriented city of Greenfield, the Community YMCA plays an important role. When space got tight there, Phoenix helped the YMCA enlarge the building. "We are good neighbors," says G. Jeffrey Bohne, vice president and general manager of Greenfield operations. "There are also playgrounds that exist throughout Franklin County because Phoenix is here. There are schools that have computers, that might not have had them, because Phoenix is here." Most of all, there are local organizations that have volunteers because Phoenix's Greenfield employees give generously of their time and talents.

Students from the Fred D. Wish School thanked Phoenix with a handmade quilt, left.

Trinity College Boys and Girls Club

Phoenix contributed $75,000 to establish the Trinity College Boys and Girls Club, a unit of Hartford's Boys and Girls Club. As part of Trinity College's Learning Corridor concept, it breaks down the barriers between "town and gown," providing educational, cultural, health and sports programs for neighborhood children and teenagers. It's the first such club to be opened at a college or university. "The idea is to welcome the community, to reach out — a very healthy development," says Donald Bertrand, vice president and insurance and investment products counsel, who has worked in Model Cities programs.

Hartford's Fred D. Wish School

Since 1986, numerous Phoenix employees have taken an hour from their weekly work schedule to tutor Wish School students in grades three through six. The company transports the kids to the Hartford office throughout the school year and helps to fund after-school programs, field trips, school supplies and teacher training. Volunteers arrange enrichment

activities and year-end parties for the kids, too. Students thrive on the individual attention, and school administrators report improved attendance and significantly higher scores on state mastery tests. For Diana Allen, a longtime volunteer tutor, the Wish School connection opened new worlds. Upon retiring from Phoenix after 31 years, she went back to school for a graduate degree in elementary education so she can teach in the inner city. "I could have found another job in insurance, but this is my passion," Allen says. "These kids are our future."

Much of Phoenix's contribution to its community involves employees volunteering their time. Above, Phoenix employee Judy Longhi (right) tutors Fred D. Wish student Chastity Hyman.

history of an organization. We do a real audit, checking 501(c)3 nonprofit status and looking at the financials." The foundation looks beyond the numbers, too, at whether the organization is considered effective and why it is seeking a donation.

As a result, Phoenix is helping an impressive range of organizations that make a difference in our quality of life — from Special Olympics and Amistad America, to youth groups and soup kitchens in Hartford, Albany, Greenfield and Enfield. It would take a separate book to profile them all, but here are a few examples.

SPECIAL OLYMPICS, SPECIAL COMMITMENT

When Phoenix organized the Special Olympics World Games softball competition in 1995, the event represented a defining moment in the history of the company. The Games brought together more than 2,500 employees, family members and friends from the Connecticut, Massachusetts and New York home offices. They gave 40,000 hours of their time and 100 percent of their hearts to planning and running the softball venue. Field offices pitched in, too, raising more than $125,000 to help local Special Olympics organizations in their communities send athletes to the games. "The event really clinched the merger. We came together as one company," says Bob Fiondella.

Employees were so moved by the Special Olympics experience that they asked Phoenix to continue its support. The company embraced the cause by becoming "partner sponsor" of the Connecticut Special Olympics, then title sponsor of the statewide Unified Sports Championships, which pairs Special Olympic athletes with non-disabled partner athletes.

Many volunteers continue their involvement locally. "For instance, in Greenfield, we have 60 people a year who go to Natatuck Park for the Western Massachusetts softball tournament," Jeff Bohne says. "People look forward to it. It's not

As Special Olympics athletes take pride in their accomplishments, Phoenix takes pride in being the organization's first Official Worldwide Partner.

on the scale of the New Haven World Games — we drive in our own cars and eat on our own — but that doesn't matter. Phoenix's initial involvement has carried and multiplied."

In every venue, volunteer assistance takes many forms. Employees might escort players, coach, umpire or keep score. Some people work behind the scenes, helping local organizations to run more smoothly. Bohne notes: "One of our employees has been treasurer for the local chapter for years. He provides an important service and a stabilizing influence."

The natural next step for Phoenix was sponsorship of the biennial World Games through the year 2004, making the company the first Official Worldwide Partner of the Special Olympics. And Phoenix's efforts extend beyond the playing field. Educational materials and seminars help families with special needs plan for their financial futures.

SPORTS SPONSORSHIPS: IN A LEAGUE OF THEIR OWN

Corporate sports sponsorships make good business sense, because they boost the local economy, strengthen relationships and complement the other aspects of Phoenix's social involvement program. Sports initiatives for high school and college students also tangibly extend Phoenix's commitment to youth.

"There's a real economic development and educational impact wherever Phoenix's sports activities take place," emphasizes Carl Chadburn, executive vice president. "And sponsorships were a more cost-effective method than advertising to build initial name recognition for Phoenix. As we are growing, we now combine sponsorships, public relations, event-based marketing and advertising to get our name and wealth management message out there."

The Phoenix ATP Tour World Doubles Championship elevated Phoenix's name in the eyes of tennis fans and others nationwide. Sponsored by Phoenix in conjunction with the U.S. Tennis Association and the Association of Tennis Professionals, the Tour brought the best in men's doubles tennis to Hartford every November from 1995 to 1999, when the ATP decided to base future matches in Europe. The 1998 ATP championship was notable as the official 25th anniversary celebration of Billie Jean King's victory over Bobby Riggs in the historic 1973 "Battle of the Sexes" match. Eight legendary women players commemorated the event by competing in a unique format — Chris Evert's team vs. Martina Navratilova's team — to the delight of television audiences across the world. King chose the Hartford venue as the exclusive site of the celebration in part because of Phoenix's commitment to women.

Phoenix's name also stands proudly in the big-league roster of 18 companies that have joined forces in support of the National Collegiate Athletic Association. Fellow NCAA corporate partners include such illustrious brands as General Motors, Gillette, Marriott, Nabisco, Pepsi and Sears. The Phoenix logo is prominently displayed at the men's and women's Final Four basketball championships, as well as 79 other championship events in 22 sports at more than 500 sites nationwide. Formidable publicity surrounds these NCAA events, including television and radio spots, print ads, consumer promotions, cross-licensing with NCAA member institutions, and grass-roots events like "Take a Kid to the Game."

"Being an NCAA corporate partner is an exceptional opportunity to broaden our marketing efforts," Fiondella emphasizes. In fact, the NCAA connection puts the Phoenix name before millions of potential customers — 110 million college sports fans and alumni, 15 million students and 1,152 institutions with five million employees, to be precise.

On a smaller scale, Phoenix is the title sponsor of the Phoenix WBCA High School All-America Game, televised live each April by ESPN, which showcases the top 20 female high school basketball players in the United States. On the East Coast, the Phoenix Classic is the tournament to catch every December. It features four NCAA Division I men's basketball teams — contenders have included Yale, Fairfield University, Central Connecticut State University and the University of Hartford — facing off in spirited competition.

Because many of Phoenix's sports sponsorships are Hartford-based, the events draw volunteers from the Connecticut and Massachusetts home offices. Sports fans, especially, enjoy the opportunity to apply their energy and creativity to a greater cause. Sally Roberts, an employee for more than 20 years who directed group policyholder services in Greenfield, has coordinated pre-tournament clinics and run guest services at the World Doubles Championship. A tennis player herself, Roberts was thrilled to meet celebrities like Billie Jean King. However, the chance to work with Phoenix people from Hartford and Enfield has meant more to her: "I've gotten to know so many fantastic people I otherwise wouldn't have met."

WOMEN'S BASKETBALL

Of all of Phoenix's sports sponsorships, the sentimental favorite may be the connection with women's basketball at the University of Connecticut. In 1994, before the UConn women's team continuously knocked off major competitors and won its first national championship, Phoenix began underwriting their games on Connecticut Public Television. As fast as you can say national champions, the telecasts soared to the top of CPTV's most-watched list. The women Huskies are perennially ranked among the top teams in the country, and the individual players are role models on and off the court. Their phenomenal success has generated enormously positive publicity, not just for the university but for the state — and that can't help but boost employee recruitment and name recognition for Phoenix.

In fact, very few corporations are as devoted to women's sports as Phoenix is. That commitment does not waver despite the unfortunate demise in 1998 of the American Basketball League, a women's professional league of which Phoenix was a charter sponsor and part-owner. Phoenix also sponsored the New England Blizzard team, a league member. Although it attracted fervent crowds in Hartford, the ABL

Tennis legend Billie Jean King celebrated the 25th anniversary of her victory over Bobby Riggs with a special event at the Phoenix ATP World Tour Doubles Championship in Hartford.

Supporting Young Women in Sports

Teenage women who play sports regularly are less likely than nonathletes to drink, use drugs or break the law. They also have significantly lower rates of teenage pregnancy.

— From a 1999 survey of 12,000 adolescents by the Women's Sports Foundation, as reported in *USA Today*

Female college basketball players graduate at a higher rate than student bodies as a whole: 66 percent versus the national average of 56 percent.

— National Collegiate Athletic Association 1999 statistics

Televised live each April on ESPN2, the Women's Basketball Coaches Association High School All-America Game showcases the nation's best female high school basketball seniors. As the title sponsor, Phoenix is proud to partner with the WBCA and Nike, the presenting sponsor, to showcase the future of women's basketball.

(like fledgling women's pro leagues in other sports such as soccer and hockey) had difficulty winning the necessary television coverage. When the league folded, two top television sports executives told *Business Week* that there was little room for women's teams on national networks. Their attitude speaks volumes about the uphill battles faced by pioneers like the ABL.

Fortunately, Phoenix believes otherwise. The work of the ABL laid important groundwork for other women's professional leagues. "We believe women deserve the right to fulfill their dreams, including participating in professional sports," Dona Young says. "We remain committed to our long-standing support of women's athletics because it is the right thing to do and because it is linked to our business strategy. Women are an increasingly important market for us."

In the case of the ABL, doing the right thing included hiring staff members of the New England Blizzard for a two-month transition period upon the league's demise. Given that the staff had suddenly lost their jobs two days before Christmas, it was an especially kind gesture. "We had previously run a 10-week sales internship and career development program for ABL and Blizzard women, as part of our larger commitment to the league," says Wyrot Ward. "The Monday after that Christmas, the Blizzard staff came to us and human resources was ready with an orientation. Bob Fiondella himself came to greet them that morning." Not your usual corporate stance, but quintessentially Phoenix.

AMISTAD AMERICA

"Give us free! Give us free!"

These words rang through a Hartford courtroom in 1839, when 53 illegally enslaved Africans were tried for rebelling and seizing the ship *Amistad* off the coast of Connecticut. They had been kidnapped and shipped to Cuba, where

Teaching the history of the Amistad incident of 1839, the *Amistad* encourages dialogue on racial tolerance. Phoenix acted as the project's founding sponsor, and many employees became involved on a personal level as volunteers.

they were forced aboard the *Amistad*. Their cry echoed almost 160 years later — this time in celebration of the captives' eventual freedom — when the keel was laid at Mystic Seaport for a reproduction of the historic vessel.

Considering that Francis Gillette, one of Phoenix's founders in 1851, was also a prominent opponent of slavery, the reproduction schooner *Amistad* was a project the company couldn't miss out on. Phoenix was instrumental in funding the project and, with Amistad America, Inc., in increasing awareness of its historical significance.

"We believe in the value of Amistad America as an educational tool and as a tribute to Connecticut's role in our nation's history," Bob Fiondella explains. The vessel, launched officially on March 25, 2000, is a floating classroom. It sails to American and international ports to bring the *Amistad*'s lessons of history, cooperation and leadership to people of all ages, interests and cultural backgrounds. Phoenix also sponsored three hours of Connecticut Public Television programming, later made available to stations across the country, that was dedicated to the Amistad saga.

"The *Amistad* incident was the first time in our nation's history that whites and blacks worked together to secure justice," says Christopher Cloud, executive director of Amistad America, Inc., the nonprofit organization that raises funds and operates the vessel. "The principles and values that were so important to the outcome of the incident are still meaningful today, and we hope to convey their importance for generations to come."

The project moved from dream to reality when Phoenix, as the founding sponsor, donated a leadership grant of $100,000 and guaranteed that a total of $300,000 would be raised through the private sector. That, in turn, triggered the release of a $2.5 million Connecticut state bond that permitted construction to begin. The company furthered the cause by funding the creation of a fundraising video documentary that Amistad America still uses to interest potential sponsors. As in all of Phoenix's charitable efforts, however, money tells only a small part of the story. Volunteer and in-kind efforts multiplied the value of every dollar.

The idea of sponsoring the *Amistad* project was brought to the company by Fredrica Gray, director of individual marketing development. Gray also serves as a volunteer vice chairperson on the board of directors of Amistad America. Phoenix employees helped raise the *Amistad*'s sails by developing and printing informational materials, supplying administrative support and providing executive director Cloud's office space in Hartford. And in a very real sense, Phoenix's fingerprints are all over the project: employee Dan Hendricksen, who works in facility systems in

Hartford, volunteered his carpentry skills to help build the schooner.

An experienced cabinetmaker, Hendricksen traveled monthly to Mystic Seaport to plane logs, tighten bolts and do precision "finish work" on the 80-foot, hand-hewn vessel. "This was a totally different facet of carpentry than I've ever tried before," he says. "I'd never taken an actual tree and turned it into a finished product." Quentin Snediker, the veteran boat builder in charge of the construction, praised Hendricksen's "tremendous skill."

The *Amistad* saga has local significance in other ways. After being arrested by the U.S. Navy, the ship's 53 captives faced two years of court trials in Connecticut. Many were held in the Old State House in Hartford, just across the street from Phoenix's boat building. In fact, Phoenix helped to restore the Old State House — right down to the very room where the *Amistad* trials took place and where they are reenacted for visitors today.

COMMUNITY CONNECTIONS

Helping to restore the Old State House is a fine example of Phoenix's broad-ranging commitment to the communities in which it does business. In the 1980s, Chairman John Gummere chaired the board of directors of the historic 1796 building, which is the nation's oldest state house. (It is also considered Connecticut's most important building, as it stands on the site where the state was founded in 1636.) The board set in motion the $12 million, four-year renovation that stabilized the foundation and restored the building to its full Colonial splendor for its 200th anniversary.

Along with Phoenix's $100,000 contribution to the Old State House, heartfelt, hands-on support came from its people. Ed Richardson, who kept the boat building running so smoothly for years, shifted his attentions to the Old State

A Great Debate

When President Bill Clinton and Bob Dole faced off before the world in Hartford on October 6, 1996, Phoenix was everywhere behind the scenes.

The company was a founding sponsor of the event, which was the first national presidential debate held in New England. Almost 100 employees pitched in for weeks preceding to make the evening shine. Their main responsibility was to direct the efforts of more than 500 debate volunteers, a big job that grew more hectic by the day. For example, when outside coordinators realized two nights before the event that no one had produced a transportation schedule for the press, the Phoenix Print Center swung into action to produce 5,000 copies within hours.

While the spotlight was on the candidates, the debate showcased Hartford and its renaissance as well. Maura Melley, senior vice president, public affairs, says that the sponsorship met two of Phoenix's key goals: "Supporting the community and giving employees the opportunity to be active in the democratic process."

The Clinton-Dole face-off in Hartford ran like clockwork, aided by tireless volunteer support from Phoenix employees. Senator Christopher Dodd of Connecticut signed this commemorative poster for Bob Fiondella, thanking the company for its support as a founding sponsor.

Phoenix's Print Center: Donations in Kind

Money isn't the only way that Phoenix makes corporate donations. Organizations always need printed promotional materials, which Phoenix can provide free or at low cost through its own presses in Enfield.

"We take great pride in our print center," says Director James W. Callahan. His staff of 25 works two shifts, printing more than half of Phoenix's publications and forms. The in-house facility achieves significant savings for the company and makes it possible to offer a valuable charitable service at the same time.

The centerpiece of the print center is a state-of-the-art Heidelberg Speedmaster, capable of printing five colors in one pass. This 36-ton behemoth has produced magazines for the Special Olympics; programs for the Phoenix ATP Tour World Doubles Championship; posters for the Greater Hartford Arts Council and Enfield Loaves & Fishes, a local food bank; and thousands of other eye-catching projects. Smaller presses handle less glamorous but equally useful pieces, such as letterhead.

Callahan admits to a special fondness for Special Olympics work. "Volunteering at the World Games in 1995 was one of the best experiences of my life," he says. He and many other print center employees keep up the spirit by volunteering each year for the Special Olympics Unified Volleyball and Softball competitions in Connecticut and Massachusetts.

House immediately upon his retirement. Richardson helped develop the long-range renovation plans, while other retirees and employees lent their expertise in areas ranging from heating systems to computer systems. Ralph Acanto, then building superintendent at One American Row, was Richardson's strong right arm during the project and continues on the Old State House building committee during his retirement. No doubt Phoenix's founders would have approved, because they knew the building well. It served as the State Capitol until 1878, and was the grandest sight visible from the company's first offices on Pearl and Main Streets.

Like the Old State House, civic and cultural institutions create a strong foundation for economic and educational activity in communities. This is why Phoenix maintains ongoing partnerships with local organizations such as the Mark Twain House in Hartford and the Albany Institute of History and Art. Employees also contribute to numerous campaigns for the arts, such as the Greater Hartford Arts Council and Business Fund for the Arts in Franklin County, whose funding makes a crucial difference to hundreds of smaller arts and entertainment ventures.

Phoenix has a rich history of supporting local artists. For many years following the opening of the boat building in 1963, the west end of the lobby served as an exhibit space. A rejuvenated art program began in the mid-1990s. As Carl Chadburn explains, this latest idea was reprised when the time came to decorate the Albany home office upon completion of the new building in 1997. "Our goal was to showcase a combination of Albany-area established and emerging artists whose work is museum-quality."

Barbara A. Hudson, an independent curator of American art and former curator of the Wadsworth Atheneum in Hartford, selected and installed the art after consulting the best museums and galleries in the area, contacting some 60 professionals and evaluating their work. The artists selected represent 18 area towns and a variety of cultures from Native American to Vietnamese.

"It's unique for a company to purchase artwork in this manner," Hudson said of the process. "Because the Albany facility is an operations center, there aren't the number of visitors you might receive in a business or corporate office. So the art collection is primarily for employees to enjoy. That says a lot about Phoenix." The company has expanded the program to Enfield, giving dozens more area artists an appreciative audience for their work.

By helping health and human services organizations, the company helps build healthier communities. A jewel in this crown is the Phoenix Community Cancer Center in Enfield, built in partnership with the Johnson Memorial Corporation. Through a unique nonprofit partnership called Community CancerCare — which includes Johnson Memorial Hospital, Hartford Hospital, Manchester Memorial Hospital and Rockville General Hospital — the center provides radiation therapy, as well as medical oncology, a community resource library and other services. Phoenix employees annually help organize fund-raising efforts to support the Cancer Center.

Employees at all four home offices also spend a portion of each August and September raising funds for United Way — and have a carnival's worth of fun doing it. In Albany, for example, fund-raising events have ranged from midday barbecues to car washes and sports competitions. Enthusiastic Hartford staffers organized a "jail and bail" day, in which employees dressed as keystone cops "arrested" coworkers who remained in jail until their colleagues bailed them out with donations. In Greenfield and Enfield, employees contributed $1 per vote to "elect" officers to kiss a pig. Where the United Way is concerned, indeed, participation pours forth from every level: Bob Fiondella has faced off on the basketball court against former *Hartford Courant* publisher Michael Waller, with Hartford mayor Mike Peters acting as referee.

"It doesn't just come around to who wins the game," Fiondella summarizes, referring to all of Phoenix's charitable undertakings. "It comes down to how you live.

"We are a company devoted to helping people fulfill their financial dreams, so it is natural and right for us to give back to the communities where we live and work."

Adriaen's Landing

"My view is simple. We have a responsibility to be constructive and to help Hartford solve its problems," said Bob Fiondella a few years ago as he looked out of his office window onto the riverfront parking lots that will be transformed into Adriaen's Landing.

Phoenix has been an active leader in the community's effort to reconnect the City of Hartford with the Connecticut River. In the 1990s, Riverfront Recapture, Inc., constructed a promenade to give the public access to the riverfront from Phoenix's own American Row headquarters.

Fiondella assembled a group of experts and community members to brainstorm about the best usage of the company's landholdings on the Connecticut River. Phoenix committed a substantial financial contribution to develop Hartford's waterfront and helped secure government funding.

The project was named for the Dutch explorer Adriaen Block, who sailed up the Connecticut River into Hartford in 1614. Almost 400 years later, his landing spot may prove to be the center of the city's resurgence. Now being developed by the State of Connecticut working with a private developer, Adriaen's Landing is expected to create more than 4,500 construction and permanent jobs. Plans include a convention center, a retail-entertainment complex, a hotel, upscale housing and a major family attraction.

Its completion will be a tribute to public/private partnerships — and to Bob Fiondella's persistence.

Epilogue

Phoenix is at a point of passage in its life. The past few years have been packed with momentous decisions. If Bob Jackson were here, he'd ask me (just as he always asked himself) whether our choices were benefiting our managers, our advisors or our policyholders.

With policyholder and shareholder value as our constant guide, we're confident we have made the right choices.

I sometimes feel as if this company, at the age of 150, is graduating. As happens at any graduation, we're indulging in a bit of nostalgia about our past. At the same time, we're fully engaged in the business of the present and the excitement of the future.

Over the past 20 years, Phoenix has evolved from a mutual insurance company with investment capabilities to a sophisticated, focused wealth management enterprise. We're still headquartered a stone's throw from where we started in 1851. But our web of relations now stretches across the world.

We've weathered wars and depressions. We've confronted major economic and regulatory challenges. We've executed huge changes, such as the merger, which popular wisdom said couldn't be done. We've forged strong alliances.

In short, Phoenix has lived up to the symbolism of its name. We stay the course as the course changes. Going public is the latest step in our drive to provide value to our policyholders and to thrive in this new century.

Anyone who has been involved in any way with our growth has cause for tremendous pride. Your hard work is the reason we're celebrating 150 years. On behalf of all of our senior executives, I want to thank:

- our employees, for their energy and dedication;
- our extended family in the field — our advisors — for their passion;
- our boards of directors, for their steady guidance;
- enlightened regulators and legislators, for their responsiveness, and outside attorneys, lobbyists and other counsel who advised us at critical junctures.

There is no final chapter in our story. This is simply the latest chapter.

Robert W. Fiondella

Robert W. Fiondella
Chairman and CEO

Acknowledgments

The author John Updike once quipped about the 1950s: "I entered them as a virgin and left them as the father of four." That comment resonated for me a few times during this project, which represents my fifth book and my first corporate history. I entered it as a writer and left it as a corporate historian, or at least as an author who attempted to chronicle a company with a rich past and an intriguing future.

Just as it has done with generations of employees, Phoenix gave me more responsibility than I initially thought I could handle — then let me do the job. The experience was a pleasure, thanks to the generosity of everyone at the company. They were unfailingly responsive and kind, even amid Phoenix's ever-accelerating changes.

Above all I must thank Melissa Regini for two and a half years of expert quarterbacking and warm support. Special gratitude goes to Fred Sawyer for championing Phoenix's history and masterfully researching the Goodman controversy. Brian Hartnett, Jo-Anne Leventhal, Ed Richardson and Pete O'Connell also lent their sharp eyes and sympathetic ears.

Senior executives could not have been more gracious. It has been a privilege to get to know Bob Fiondella and Dona Young as they guide their beloved company into the twenty-first century.

John Gummere, Bill Wallace and Dennis Hardcastle were also forthcoming and patient with my rounds of follow-up questions; fortunate is the historian with access to sources of this caliber.

I conducted some 60 oral history interviews with present and past Phoenix and Home Life employees and agents for this book. Simultaneously, I wrote a monthly "Here for Good" series of employee profiles for the company newsletter and Web site, thus interviewing many others who added to my understanding of this unique company. I also enjoyed access to Corporate Communications/Media Services' 150th anniversary video project, which captured the voices of dozens of eloquent retirees, and to artifacts and written memories that people shared. Hoping that I have not omitted anyone who contributed to this book, and including those named above, I thank all of you:

Marvin Address, Diana Allen, Satish Bangalore, Lisa Bassi, Mary and Russell Berry, Donald Bertrand, Doriza Bisaillon, Norm Blais, Jeff Bohne, Dick Booth, Ian Bowers, Sharon Bray, Debbie Brown, Ron and Brian Bushwell, Blanche Campbell, Tom Capehart, Kelly Carlson, Virginia Carman, Carl Chadburn, Bob Chipkin, John Chmielewski, Dan Cotter, Jane Driscoll, Alice Ericson, Tricia Ethier, Michele Farley, John Farraj, Barbara Fernandez, Larry Fleming, Pat Fontana, Marty Gavin, Randy Giangiulio, Fredrica Gray, Bob Griffin, Bill Hampton, Ann Harris, Glen Harris, John Herndon, Vernon Holleman III, Eileen Hollingsworth, Ed Hourihan, Dave Howard, Esther and Connie Joffe, Jack Judge, Joe Kelleher, Bill Kelly, Naomi Kleinman, Bob Lautensack, Terry Lerud, Sid and Brenda Levine, Leon Levy, Jeff Levy, William MacLachlan, Patricia Madott, Shalaka Madkekar, Veronica Maldonado, Dave Martin, Richard Martin, Carole Masters, Linda McGinley, Scott McIntire, Phil McLoughlin, Maura Melley, Jo Melusky, Bob Merritt, Margaret Murphy, Maxine Niemeyer, Russ Noyes, Beverly O'Leary, Cheryl O'Sullivan, John Packal, Lorraine Padilla, Pam Palmer, Bob Primmer, Anita and Perley Putnam, Phyllis Ripley, Sally Roberts, Gerard Rocchi, Paula Ross, Bob and Ann Rudolf, David Rudolf, Gerald Rugger, Dave Searfoss, Olivia Shaw, Lew Singer, Richard Smith, Holly Sweeney, Simon Tan, Marybeth Twitchell, Wyrot Ward, Bob Weisman, Richard Wirth and Walt Zultowski.

Marian Calabro

Timeline

1851
Phoenix's predecessor, the American Temperance Life Insurance Company, is established in Hartford, Connecticut. It is a part-mutual, part-stock company that insures only those who abstain from alcohol. Headquarters is a rented office at the corner of Main and Pearl Streets.

Barzillai Hudson is elected as the first president of American Temperance.

1852
Benjamin E. Hall succeeds Hudson as the second president of American Temperance.

1853
Edson Fessenden succeeds Hall as the third president of American Temperance.

1860
Home Life is established in Brooklyn, New York, with offices at the corner of Court and Joralemon Streets in Brooklyn and 16 Wall Street in Manhattan. A stock company, it is the first life insurer authorized by the New York Insurance Department to do business in the state. Walter S. Griffith is elected its first president.

1861
Directors of the American Temperance Life Insurance Company rewrite the charter to allow sales to non-teetotalers. It becomes the Phoenix Mutual Life Insurance Company and builds its agency presence to 28 states and Canada. It adopts the popular half-note system of accepting IOUs as partial payment for premiums.

Home Life sets up field offices in Eastern cities, as well as St. Louis, Chicago and Cincinnati, and sells $1 million of life insurance. The company resists the half-note system.

The American Civil War begins. Home Life holds the jobs and pays the salaries of employees who join the military over the next four years until the conclusion of the war in 1865. Phoenix insures President Abraham Lincoln.

1866
Home Life becomes the first insurer to remove all travel restrictions from its policies and to abolish extra premiums on female policyholders.

1868
Home Life moves from Brooklyn to a four-story office in Manhattan on Broadway, opposite City Hall.

1871
Phoenix expands to the entire building at Main and Pearl Streets in Hartford. The company contributes $5,000 to a fund for survivors of the Chicago fire, the first recorded major act of corporate giving.

1872
George C. Ripley succeeds Griffith as the second president of Home Life.

1873
The United States experiences an economic panic that triggers seven years of severe financial depression.

Phoenix achieves $75 million of life insurance in force.

1874
Outsiders threaten an unfriendly takeover of Home Life; the board encourages stockholders not to sell by paying their dividends in gold.

1875
Aaron C. Goodman succeeds Fessenden as the fourth president of Phoenix.

1876
Phoenix moves across Pearl Street to larger rented quarters.

1882
Goodman becomes majority shareholder of Phoenix.

1889
Goodman attempts to sell Phoenix to a buyer from Philadelphia. With the support of the Connecticut insurance department and state legislature, company directors form a temporary trust to buy Goodman's stock and turn it over to policyholders. The policyholders retire the stock and vote to make Phoenix a wholly mutual company.

Jonathan B. Bunce succeeds Goodman as the fifth president of Phoenix.

1890
Phoenix hires the nationally renowned Archibald A. Welch, FSA, as chief actuary and begins to rebuild its agency organization, which had eroded during Goodman's tenure.

Home Life achieves $25 million of insurance in force.

Charles A. Townsend succeeds George C. Ripley as the third president of Home Life.

1892
George H. Ripley succeeds Townsend as the fourth president of Home Life.

1893
Fully mutual in practice since 1889, Phoenix legally achieves mutuality when it acquires the 10 remaining shares of stock transferred to Goodman from his nephew four years earlier.

1894
George E. Ide succeeds George H. Ripley as the fifth president of Home Life. The company builds and moves into its headquarters at 256 Broadway, New York City. The 16-story building encompasses the company's previous four-story quarters. It is the world's first steel-framed skyscraper and, for a short time, the world's tallest building.

1895
Home Life's steel-framed headquarters withstands a major fire.

1896
Guided by Head Actuary Welch, Phoenix introduces the industry's first policies with cash values. It sets new guidelines that become industry standards: face value of policies can exceed $15,000; restrictions are dropped after two years (except for military service in war); claims are paid immediately; surrender charges are reduced.

1897
Phoenix moves into its headquarters, built at 49 Pearl Street, Hartford.

1900
Home Life achieves $50 million of life insurance in force.

1901
Phoenix publishes the first issue of the *Field*, believed to be the first regular industry publication for agents.

1904
Phoenix holds its first regional field conferences. Agents also form their own group, the General Agents Association.

John M. Holcombe succeeds Bunce as the sixth president of Phoenix.

1905
Investigative journalism sparks the Armstrong Investigation, which examines all life insurance companies doing business in New York State. Many companies are charged with misconduct, but Home Life and Phoenix are praised for their blameless records. Phoenix's Archibald A. Welch helps to draft 1907 regulations that become a model for states nationwide.

1906
Phoenix introduces the first correspondence training course for agents ever used by a life insurance company, "A Prospectus and Ten Lessons," written by San Francisco agent Jay Dwiggins.

1907
Following its excellent showing in the Armstrong Investigation, Home Life achieves an annual sales record of $14.6 million.

1912
Phoenix is the first life insurer to use direct mail advertising.

1914
Phoenix discontinues most brokerage business and becomes the first life insurer to eliminate part-time agents.

1916
The U.S. enters World War I. Home Life buys back its stock out of surplus funds and becomes a mutual. It becomes the first life insurer to pay its dividends from surplus.

The Home Life Employees Club, a social and athletic organization, is established.

1919
Phoenix achieves $250 million of life insurance in force and establishes the first home office training school for agents. Merging earlier, separate clubs for men and women, Phoenix employees create the Phoenix Mutual Club. The volunteer-run club sponsors social, athletic, educational and charitable activities until 1992, when it is replaced by the Phoenix Employees Club.

William A. Marshall succeeds Ide as the sixth president of Home Life.

1920
Phoenix builds and moves into its headquarters at 79 Elm Street, Hartford.

1923
Phoenix creates the first advertisement that promotes the value of life insurance; the ad runs in *Literary Digest*.

1924
Phoenix is one of two U.S. insurance companies to provide benefits to its career sales force.

Archibald A. Welch, FSA, succeeds Holcombe as the seventh president of Phoenix.

Home Life reorganizes its agency system to eliminate part-timers.

Ethelbert I. Low succeeds Marshall as the seventh president of Home Life.

1925
Phoenix is among the first life insurers to offer a "selective risk and non-medical plan," which waives medical examinations for selected applicants.

1926
Phoenix first advertises its retirement income plan in national magazines.

1927
Home Life introduces preferred risk underwriting.

1929
Phoenix's famous "Fisherman" ad is launched. This campaign lasts almost four decades and sells more than $500 million of insurance.

James A. Fulton succeeds Low as the eighth president of Home Life.

Reflecting a decade of prosperity, life insurance in force at all U.S. companies reaches a new high of $100 billion. The stock market crashes in October, causing financial panic and the onset of the Great Depression.

1933
Under James A. Fulton and William P. Worthington, Home Life introduces "Planned Estates," a career-based approach to life insurance sales that emphasizes "problems to solve, not prospects to sell." Despite the Great Depression, Home Life's business grows 60 percent from 1933 to 1939.

1935
Arthur M. Collens succeeds Welch as the eighth president of Phoenix.

1937
Phoenix establishes an internal sales record when agents write more than $1 million of life insurance each day for five consecutive days.

1939
World War II begins, leading to government-instituted wage controls and government-sponsored life insurance for soldiers.

1944
Home Life wins an exemption from government wage controls for its field underwriters.

1947
Home Life purchases an adjoining building, 253 Broadway, and expands its headquarters. It begins conferences for qualified field underwriters.

1948
Benjamin L. Holland succeeds Collens as the ninth president of Phoenix. The company achieves $1 billion of life insurance in force.

Home Life achieves the highest average policy sale ($14,139) of all New York-based insurers.

1949
Home Life establishes a group department and sells its first group policy in 1950.

1950
William J. Cameron succeeds Fulton as the ninth president of Home Life.

1951
Phoenix celebrates its 100th anniversary.

1952
Home Life achieves $1 billion of life and group insurance in force.

1953
William P. Worthington succeeds Cameron as the 10th president of Home Life.

1954
After a 40-year hiatus, Phoenix reenters the brokerage field.

1955
Phoenix pioneers lower premiums for women, which become an industry standard. Phoenix and Home Life begin introducing a series of innovative products, including Phoenix's first major medical expense policy and Family Protection Plan, a product that covers parents and children on a single policy. They further expand their offerings with such products as "College Paid For" plans, home mortgage protection and pension trust contracts.

1957
Phoenix establishes a group department and sells its first group policy in 1958.

1960
Home Life achieves $2 billion of life and group insurance in force and celebrates its 100th anniversary.

Phoenix announces it will build a new headquarters on Constitution Plaza in Hartford.

1961
Lyndes B. Stone succeeds Holland as the 10th president of Phoenix. The company breaks ground for its new headquarters.

1962
J. Harry Wood succeeds Worthington as the 11th president of Home Life.

1963
Phoenix moves into its headquarters on Constitution Plaza at One American Row, Hartford. The edifice, designed by the architectural firm of Harrison and Abramowitz and popularly known as the Boat Building, is the world's first two-sided building.

Phoenix's group department refines and markets Multiple Employer Trusts, an innovation by which small companies can band together for lower rates.

Phoenix achieves $3 billion of life and group insurance in force; assets exceed $1 billion for the first time.

1965
Phoenix enters the field of reinsurance and installs ServiData, the first computerized policyholder service system to be used in a major life insurance company.

1967
Phoenix is the first life insurer to offer lower rates to nonsmokers across all policy lines, which becomes an industry standard.

1968
Phoenix separates brokerage from career agencies; becomes the first insurance company to introduce video training for agents; and establishes a subsidiary to sell mutual funds, Phoenix Equity Planning Corporation (PEPCO).

1969
Home Life achieves $5 billion of life and group insurance in force.

Gerald K. Rugger succeeds Wood as the 12th president of Home Life.

1970
Phoenix achieves a record $1.4 billion in annual sales, reaching more than $7 billion of life and group insurance in force.

1971
Phoenix builds and opens a second home office, in Greenfield, Massachusetts. It becomes the first insurance company to offer policyholder services through a centralized, toll-free call center.

Robert T. Jackson, FSA, CLU, succeeds Stone as the 11th president of Phoenix.

1973
Phoenix adopts its management operation policy and establishes a stock subsidiary, Phoenix American Life Insurance Company, for the development and marketing of specialized insurance products.

1976
Phoenix enters the property/casualty field by establishing Phoenix General Insurance Company, later renamed American Phoenix.

1977
Home Life achieves $10 billion of life and group insurance in force.

1978
Dennis F. Hardcastle, CLU, succeeds Jackson as the 12th president of Phoenix. Phoenix introduces consciousness-raising workshops on gender and race.

Kenneth C. Nichols Sr., CLU, succeeds Rugger as the 13th president of Home Life.

1981
John Gummere, FSA, succeeds Hardcastle as the 13th president of Phoenix.

American Phoenix, a property/casualty subsidiary of Phoenix, is created.

Phoenix builds and opens a third home office in Enfield, Connecticut. Throughout the 1980s, this facility will expand to three buildings and a child care center for employees' children.

1982
Phoenix offers survivorship life insurance (also known as second-to-die insurance), which becomes a premier product. Under its American Phoenix subsidiary, Phoenix establishes Phoenix Re, a property/casualty reinsurance management company.

As part of a sweeping expansion plan, Home Life introduces its first money market fund. It purchases Orange State Life of Largo, Florida, a stock life insurance company, and changes the name to Home Life Financial Assurance Corporation.

1983
Phoenix implements a major expense reduction program, which includes its first early retirement program.

1984
Phoenix leads the industry in defeating unisex pricing practices.

1987
Phoenix sells 70 percent of its interest in Phoenix Re in a public offering.

Robert W. Fiondella succeeds Gummere as the 14th president of Phoenix.

1987-1988
Home Life sells 253-256 Broadway, moves its executive offices to 75 Wall Street and opens a new operations facility in Piscataway, New Jersey.

1988
Phoenix forms an alliance with Dai-ichi Mutual Life Insurance Company to provide employee benefits to Japanese companies doing business in the U.S.

William B. Wallace, CLU, ChFC, MSFS, succeeds Nichols as the 14th president of Home Life.

1991
Phoenix and Home Life agree to merge.

Richard Goldman succeeds Wallace as the 15th president of Home Life.

1992
The legal merger of Phoenix and Home Life takes place on July 1; the name of the merged company becomes Phoenix Home Life Mutual Insurance Company, and the legal domicile is East Greenbush, New York. John Gummere becomes chairman and chief executive officer and William B. Wallace becomes vice chairman and chief operating officer. Robert W. Fiondella continues as president and adds the title of principal operating officer.

1994
Robert W. Fiondella succeeds Gummere as chairman and chief executive officer, retaining the title of president. Initial sponsorship begins of University of Connecticut women's basketball televised on Connecticut Public Television.

1995
PEPCO becomes a publicly held company known as Phoenix Duff & Phelps Corporation.

More than 2,500 employees, family members and friends volunteer at the Special Olympics World Games in New Haven, Connecticut. Phoenix goes on to become the first Official Worldwide Partner of the Special Olympics and sponsors the biannual World Games through 2004.

1996
The company enters the trust market with the creation of Phoenix Charter Oak Trust Company.

An alliance is established with Aberdeen Asset Management, PLC, a Scottish fund manager founded in 1897.

Phoenix establishes Phoenix Global Solutions (India) Pvt. Ltd., an information systems subsidiary in Bangalore, India.

The Phoenix Foundation for corporate philanthropy is created.

The company co-sponsors the Clinton/Dole debate in Hartford, the first national presidential debate held in New England.

The 200th anniversary of Connecticut's Old State House in Hartford is commemorated with a renovation funded in part with company donations and volunteer work by employees.

1997
The company constructs and opens the Albany Operations Center in East Greenbush, New York.

Phoenix invests in Emprendimiento Compartido, S.A. (EMCO), a pension manager and life insurer based in Buenos Aires, Argentina.

A successful bid for a large corporate-owned life insurance (COLI) case generates $29 million in annual premium, the largest piece of business in Phoenix's history.

A successful bid for $166 million of in-force U.S. premium from the liquidated Confederation Life Insurance Company of Canada marks Phoenix's largest acquisition ever.

Phoenix begins a two-year charter sponsorship of the American Basketball League, the first woman's professional league of the modern era of women's basketball.

1998
Phoenix opens a new building for Phoenix Global Solutions (India) Pvt. Ltd.

The majority of real estate holdings are sold to a real estate fund managed by Donaldson, Lufkin & Jenrette, Inc.

Phoenix Realty Securities and Phoenix Realty Advisors are sold.

Phoenix Duff & Phelps Corporation changes its name to Phoenix Investment Partners, Ltd. (NYSE ticker symbol PXP). PXP begins providing distribution services for eight investment partners: Aberdeen Fund Managers, Inc.; Duff & Phelps Investment Management Co.; Phoenix Investment Counsel, Inc., advisor to the Phoenix-Goodwin, Phoenix-Hollister and Phoenix-Oakhurst funds; Roger Engemann & Associates, Inc.; Seneca Capital Management LLC; and Zweig/Glaser Advisers LLC.

PXP begins managing the U.S. assets of Aberdeen Asset Management; Aberdeen begins managing the non-U.S. assets of Phoenix.

1999
Phoenix focuses on a global wealth management strategy, targeting affluent and high-net-worth individuals and business owners.

The following businesses are sold: American Phoenix (to Hilb, Rogal & Hamilton Company); Financial Administrative Services, Inc. (to Policy Management Systems Corporation); the reinsurance business (to ERC Life, a subsidiary of GE Capital's Employers Reinsurance Corporation); and the group business (to GE Financial Assurance Holdings, Inc.).

The following businesses are acquired: the private placement variable life and annuity business of The Guarantee Life Companies Inc.; and minority interests in National Life Insurance Company of Oman, Lombard International Assurance of Luxembourg, and Bittencourt, a Brazilian brokerage house.

A major advertising and public relations campaign begins, emphasizing Phoenix's expertise in wealth management.

2000
Dona D. Young succeeds Fiondella as the 15th president of Phoenix. Fiondella remains chairman and chief executive officer.

The board of directors adopts a plan to convert from a mutual insurance company to a stock insurance company through a process called demutualization.

Phoenix establishes Phoenix Global Investments, K.K., an institutional money manager based in Tokyo.

2001
Phoenix Investment Partners, Ltd., a public company since 1995, once again becomes a private, wholly owned subsidiary when Phoenix purchases the outstanding shares.

Dona D. Young is elected chief operating officer.

Phoenix policyholders approve Phoenix's demutualization plan. In connection with the demutualization, Phoenix Home Life Mutual Insurance Company is renamed Phoenix Life Insurance Company and becomes a wholly owned subsidiary of a new publicly traded holding company, The Phoenix Companies, Inc.

Awards

RECENT TIFFANY AWARD WINNERS

The Tiffany Award is presented to exceptional career agents who have made outstanding contributions to the company, industry and community. This cherished award, which originated at Home Life, is the ultimate honor the company can bestow upon an individual and is reserved for only a few who embody the highest ideas of dedication and professionalism throughout their lifetime.

1984 John A. Packal, CLU, ChFC
1985 Vernon W. Holleman Jr., CLU, ChFC
1986 Charles A. Murphy Jr., CLU, ChFC
1987 Michael T. Wallace Sr.
1988 Fred Stone, CLU, ChFC
1989 Joseph G. Mathews, CLU, ChFC
1990 Marvin A. Address
1991 Thomas K. Leach, CLU, ChFC
1992 Sidney Levine, CLU, AEP
1993 Ronald J. Bushwell, CLU, ChFC
1994 Frank Friedler Jr., CLU, ChFC
1995 Leon L. Levy, CLU, RHU
1996 Stanford B. Towerman, CLU, ChFC
1997 Robert B. Plybon, CLU, ChFC
1998 H. Robert Weisman
1999 Thomas R. Capehart
2000 Bernard A. Hiller, LLB

GRANITE AWARD WINNERS

Granite has long been valued for its qualities of strength and permanence. Similarly, the Granite Award symbolizes the strength, endurance and persistence that are required to provide the highest level of service to clients. Awarded periodically to an outstanding career agent, it reflects highly polished professionalism and deep-rooted dedication to industry standards.

1993 John A. Packal, CLU, ChFC
1994 Stanford B. Towerman, CLU, ChFC
1995 H. Robert Weisman
1996 Michael T. Wallace Jr., CLU, ChFC, CFP, LUTCF
1997 Albert J. Arruda
1998 Jerome Krantz, CLU, ChFC
1999 Brian Vitale
2000 David G. Schilling, CLU, ChFC

PPGA AND BROKERAGE HALLS OF FAME

These Halls of Fame pay tribute to outstanding members of the field force whose Phoenix careers epitomize consistent and continuous quality sales and service.

PPGA Hall of Fame

Marvin A. Address
B. Carroll Berry, CLU, ChFC
John E. Farraj
Michael A. Harrington, CLU, ChFC
Vernon W. Holleman Jr., CLU, ChFC
Charles E. Lewis Jr., CLU
Robert O. Lenoir, CLU, ChFC, LUTCF
Robert J. Rudolf, CLU, ChFC
Jerry N. Ward, CLU, ChFC

Sales and Support (formerly Brokerage) Hall of Fame

William F. Kelly
C. Scott McIntire, CLU, ChFC
Maxine Niemeyer, CLU, ChFC, AEP

AGENCY MANAGEMENT HALL OF FAME

The Management Hall of Fame recognizes consistent and outstanding performance by career agency managers based on recruitment, selection, training, supervision, development and retention of productive agents.

Julius A. Averna, CLU
Steven D. Berger, CLU
Joseph V. Casale Sr., CLU, ChFC
Elmer DeMarest, CLU
James S. Dudley Jr., CLU
Raphael W. Edwards, CLU, ChFC
William E. Ford, CLU
Frank Friedler Sr.
John S. Kerr, CLU, ChFC
William J. Lynch Jr., CLU
Charles A. Murphy Sr.
Clarence Oshin, CLU
Louis A. Russo, CLU, ChFC, MSFS
Paul F. Saint, CLU, ChFC
Norbert A. Siegfried, CLU
Nino Siracusa, CLU
William B. Wallace, CLU, ChFC

PORTRAIT HALL OF FAME

Inducted in:

1971
Thomas R. Capehart
Frank J. Friedler Jr., CLU, ChFC
Robert M. Hemphill
James J. McCann, CLU
John A. Packal, CLU, ChFC
William Rafkind
Clune J. Walsh Jr., CLU, ChFC
Bernard I. Waters, CLU, RHU
H. Robert Weisman

1972
Ronald J. Bushwell, CLU, ChFC
T. Dale Forshag
Bernard A. Hiller
Stephen G. Reich, CLU, ChFC
Stanford B. Towerman, CLU, ChFC, MSFS

1973
Peter R. Butler, CLU, ChFC, AEP
Richard W. Hynson, CLU
Arthur R. Jacobs
Milton A. Laitman, CLU
John A. McKnight
Charles A. Murphy Jr., CLU, AEP
Harold F. Reichenthal, CLU

1974
William R. Kalander Sr., CLU
Norman Robinson, CLU
Frank P. Sheldon, CLU

1975
Albert J. Arruda
William R. Delashmutt
Sidney Grossman
Henry W. Schick

1976
David C. Chotin, CLU, ChFC
Raymond Lonowski
George Miller, CLU

1977
Joseph G. Mathews, CLU, ChFC, MSFS
Gerald N. Van Atta, CLU

1978
Joseph D. Gatti, CLU
Sidney Levine, CLU, AEP
Fillmore A. Merber

1979
L. William Moll
Anthony P. Termotto, CLU, ChFC

1980
Seymour Fisher, CLU, ChFC
Thomas K. Leach, CLU, ChFC
Paul Rothkrug, CLU
Louis Spiazzi

1981
J. Richard Arellano, CLU, ChFC
Leon L. Levy, CLU, RHU
Robert L. Levy
Sam L. Rosenfield, CLU, ChFC
Elia J. Shulam, CLU, ChFC
Joseph I. Siegal, CLU, ChFC

1982
Jack S. Grossman, CLU, ChFC
Robert H. Harmon, CLU, ChFC
Arnold H. Kaminer, CLU, ChFC
John J. McCarthy Jr., CLU, ChFC
Edward F. Meier, CLU, ChFC
James E. Perry
Philip S. Richards
George H. Seifert
Jon David Smith, CLU

1983
Hugh Cole, CLU, ChFC
Walter G. Schnee III

1984
Stanley L. Sharp
E. Francis Way, CLU

1985
Bardell T. Bailey
Neil J. Barsky
Robert J. Burkhard
Frederick DeMyer, CLU, ChFC
James T. Farrell III
Harry E. Jacobs, CLU, ChFC
John A. Patricco
Louis A. Russo, CLU, ChFC, MSFS

1986
David J. Farr, CLU
Bela Gajary
Keith D. Gallagher, CLU, ChFC
Dennis R. Greensage, CLU, ChFC
Herman D. Schachtel, CLU, ChFC
Brian Vitale
Thomas E. Weinshenker

1987
Daniel P. Barbiero, CLU, ChFC
Alan L. Bernstein, CLU, ChFC
Harry S. Brown
Leonard Burke
Robert L. Bush, CLU, ChFC
Harold C. Johnson Jr., CLU, ChFC
Jerome Krantz, CLU, ChFC
Robert B. Plybon, CLU, ChFC
David G. Schilling, CLU, ChFC

1988
Donald E. Chambers
Robert S. Israel, CLU
Everette W. McFadden Jr., CLU, ChFC, MSFS
John R. Scola

1989
Robert D. Buxbaum, CLU, ChFC, AEP
A. Dennis Muia
David A. Patton, CLU, ChFC

1990
Robert C. Canapary, CLU, ChFC
David E. Hughes
Frederick G. Levin
W. Thomas Wilson II, CLU

1991
Gordon Clarke, CLU, ChFC
Peter C. DeRosa, CFP

1992
Richard L. Greene, CLU, CFP
Michael T. Wallace Jr., CLU, ChFC, CFP

1993
Peter L. Pace

1994
William H. Bestgen Jr., CLU, ChFC, AEP
Robert B. Hardcastle
John C. Moshides, CLU

1996
Anthony J. Capobianco Sr., CLU, ChFC
Richard J. Chaffee Jr., CLU, ChFC
Rhoda H. Goldstein
Michael J. Hannigan, CFP
Mitchell I. Merber, CLU, ChFC, RHU
James T. Niemeyer
Richard G. Piccinini
Paul P. Samanchik
Curtis M. Seale, ChFC, LUTCF

1997
Salvatore J. Ferranto, CLU, ChFC
Tripp Friedler, J.D., CLU, ChFC
Joseph F. Metzger
Thomas N. Tessier
Leonard F. Valletta, CFP, MS

1998
Harry Bonn, CLU, ChFC
Ted N. Shapses, CFP
Stuart J. Spivak, LUTCF
J. Hans Stumm, CLU, ChFC, CFP

1999
Nabil S. Abdelhamid, CLU, ChFC
Jim Tom Blair, CFP
Daniel B. Cotter
Alfred J. Opas Jr., CLU, LUTCF
Peter S. Rosengard, CLU, RHU
Hitomi Tsuyuki

2000
John F. Black Jr., CLU, ChFC, AEP
James A. Nelson
W. Luther Pierce IV, CLU
Alfred S. Russo, CFP, CPA
David S. Waters, CFP, RHU

CAREER HALL OF FAME

Inducted in:

1970
Ellison F. Beckwith, CLU
C. Nelson Black
Larry W. Day, CLU
Arthur Felker
Vincent W. Koehler, CLU
P. Eric Kuusinen, CLU
George Leader
Jack Meyers, CLU, ChFC
Edward J. Saillant, CLU
Richard C. Sanford
Gerard E. Seufert
Edward C. Wilkins, CLU

1974
Bayne B. Isaacson, CLU, ChFC
Roger O. Nelson
Anthony M. Parise, CLU

1975
Louis F. D'Elena
Harry Lowenberg
Stuart M. Nachtman
Stanley N. Notkin
Philo M. Simpson, CLU
Marcel B. Vahlkamp, CLU
Bert A. Weinshenker, CLU
Robert B. Winkleman Jr.

1976
Gilbert S. Budnick, CLU
Frederick J. Hausenstein, CLU
Keith B. Shaver

1977
Michael E. Fitzgerald, CLU
Stanley A. Wilson
George V. Worth, CLU

1978
David R. Bamberger III, CLU
William Palmer
David R. Tingley

1979
Robert E. Darragh
John F. Hochgraefe
Wendell L. Hunsucker
Irwin Tobin

1980
David R. Wilkinson, CLU

1982
Jeffrey W. Szekely

1983
Anthony W. Bucci Sr., CLU
Abraham Cabasso, CLU, ChFC
Salvatore G. Carvelli, CLU, ChFC
David S. Joyce
R. Wallace Littell, CLU, ChFC

1984
Michael J. Bellisano
Bennett A. Schreiber, CLU, ChFC

1985
Frank J. DeLeo Sr.
John W. Miller
Milton B. Tessel, RHU

1986
Donald M. Goldberg, CLU, ChFC

1987
William Bergsohn
Leslie J. Levine, CLU
Edwin H. May III, CLU, ChFC
Peter B. O'Brien

1989
William J. McLaughlin Jr., RHU

1990
Steven Leshner, CLU, ChFC, AEP
Leonard P. Parness, CLU
Michael A. Radler
Robert D. Schlossberg

IN MEMORIAM HALL OF FAME

Frank E. Baird
Gerald E. Bassler, CLU
Edward Brancati, CLU
Iram H. Brewster
Jon M. Brown
David L. Burkley
Richard S. Carpenter, CLU
Arthur H. Christ, CLU
Albert J. Corderre
Michael P. Coyle, CLU
Robert P. Cranston
Arthur H. Dauman, CLU
James A. Delaney
Robert Duval, CLU
Richard L. Emerson, CLU
Marvin H. Fine
Milton Fischer
D. Allen Fisher, CLU
William T. Fleming
Wes L. Fodero
Frank P. Fonvielle Sr.
Sheldon R. Fruchter
Donald J. Gilson
Leonard H. Gottlieb
Frank L. Gulino, CLU
Robert S. Hardin, CLU, ChFC
Ellwood N. Hennessy, CLU
Frederic Joffe
John H. Kull
Kenneth E. Lake
Jon F. Leyens, CLU
Edward V. Lollis
Ken Martin, CLU
Albin G. Matson
Paul S. Mechling
Louis M. Merwick
J. Renwick Montgomery
L.M.B. Morrissey Jr.
James Movitch
Mark C. Muller, CLU
Clarence B. Naramore Jr.
Charles K. Oaks, CLU
Paul C. Plybon
A. William Rose
Julius S. Rothchild
Herman Schaar, CLU, ChFC
Gerald R. Schroeder, CLU
George G. Scott Jr.
George J. Sieburg Jr.
Ralph J. Stich
Fred Stone, CLU, ChFC
Howard Sultan
Thurman L. Tucker
George S. Vrionis
Michael T. Wallace Sr.
Irving Wasserman
Lowell A. Weaver
Herbert L. Weiner, CLU
Emanual M. Weinstock
R. Edwin Wood, CLU

Index

Page numbers appear in boldface for illustrations.